Pitts
477
Pitts

D0113704

PITTSBURGH FILMMAKERS LIBRARY

10000858

Cecil B. DeMille
Charles Higham
Category: Film
Subcategory: Directors, Filmmakers

DATE		ISSUED TO

Cecil B. DeMille
Charles Higham
Category: Film
Subcategory: Directors, Filmmakers

PN
1998 A3 D39

DeMille, Cecil B.

DEMCO

Cecil B. DeMille

Pittsburgh Filmmakers
477 Melwood Avenue
Pittsburgh, PA 15213

Other Books by Charles Higham

ZIEGFELD (1972)

THE FILMS OF ORSON WELLES (1970)

HOLLYWOOD CAMERAMEN (1970)

THE CELLULOID MUSE: HOLLYWOOD DIRECTORS SPEAK (1970)

HOLLYWOOD IN THE FORTIES (1968)

Cecil B. DeMille

Charles Higham

Charles Scribner's Sons

New York

Copyright © 1973 Charles Higham

Library of Congress Cataloging in Publication Data
Higham, Charles, 1931–
Cecil B. DeMille.

Bibliography: p.
1. De Mille, Cecil Blount, 1881–1959.
PN1998.A3D39   791.43′0233′0924 [B]   73-1119
ISBN 0-684-13379-2

This book published simultaneously in the
United States of America and in Canada—
Copyright under the Berne Convention

All rights reserved. No part of this book
may be reproduced in any form without the
permission of Charles Scribner's Sons.

1 3 5 7 9 11 13 15 17 19 C/C 20 18 16 14 12 10 8 6 4 2

Printed in the United States of America

For James Card
of George Eastman House—
Keeper of the Flame.

CONTENTS

AUTHOR'S NOTE

AND ACKNOWLEDGMENTS

I had planned a biography of Cecil B. DeMille for many years without embarking on it; I had been put off by several of his films, and by a widespread belief that he was a cynic, exploiting the masses for his own gain. Then a chance meeting with Adolph Zukor at the Paramount commissary in 1969 illustrated something I had never considered: that so far from being consistently and ruthlessly successful, DeMille had, for the first twenty years of his career, endured a constant struggle against adversity, and had suffered at least as many financial failures as he had enjoyed successes. A conversation with Bessie Lasky, the widow of Jesse L. Lasky, who, together with Zukor, had run Paramount during DeMille's formative years as a film maker, convinced me that DeMille, so far from being a cynic, was a devout believer in the Bible who saw himself in a missionary role, making the Scriptures attractive and fascinating to the masses in an age of increasing materialism and heathenism. A deeply committed Episcopalian, he literally accepted every word of the Bible without question, and went on record as saying that every word of it with the exception of the Book of Numbers could be filmed exactly as it stood.

My interest quickened as soon as I discovered this key to his character, and I reran some of his films on pagan subjects, or on subjects of simple adventure. At once I saw that all of these were morality tales, in disguised form reworkings of the moral fairy tales which he had learned at the knee of his father, the lay minister and playwright Henry DeMille. It now became essential to see all of the director's films which now existed, and I traveled to George Eastman House in Rochester, New York, where DeMille's only daughter, Cecilia, had deposited all of her father's extant works. Over many days stretching into weeks, I saw the "lost" DeMille silent films: astonishing works like *Joan the Woman*, with the great opera star Geraldine Farrar; *The Cheat*, with Fanny Ward, a film thirty years ahead of its time in terms of lighting and the dramatic use of decor; *The Whispering Chorus*, a harsh realist work of art; or *The Affairs of Anatol*, a superbly hand-tinted and brilliantly sophisticated version of Schnitzler's play. I realized that I was witnessing the tragedy of an artist destroyed: a great film director who had settled, finally, for being merely a great entertainer. There were, of course, the accomplished and not vulgar talkies—*Dynamite, The Plainsman, Reap the Wild Wind*—to set aside the many crude and violent works of the sound period, but there was little after sound came in to suggest that this had been a genius whose social comedies (films like *Male and Female* and *Why Change Your Wife?*) were revolutionary, influencing the great Ernst Lubitsch when he came to America in 1924 and making American screen comedy the envy of the world.

Once I had decided to write the story of this extraordinary

man, I was immensely fortunate in obtaining the unqualified cooperation of Cecilia DeMille (Mrs. Joseph Harper), who made available to me the gigantic collection running to almost a quarter of a million documents, of DeMille's correspondence, notebooks, production notes, and amassed research data going back to 1913 and beyond. Over several months, I worked in a cellar surrounded by the swords and shields and maces of DeMille's historical epics, or in a back pantry on a rickety bridge table, dwarfed by piled up materials many of which had not been examined by anyone for half a century. At the great DeMille mansion at Laughlin Park (now known as 2010 DeMille Drive), with its sweeping lawns and plantings of fir and pine, I found it possible not only to see in perspective through the vast collection of documents the true character of this embattled man, but to obtain a strong sense of the environment in which he lived. To this day, his handsome desk is cleaned every morning, the desk calendar turned, the papers laid out, as though, by some miracle, he will one day return; and in the outer office just as she did in his lifetime, his devoted secretary Florence Cole sits at her smaller desk fourteen years after his departure, attending to the complex affairs of the four million dollar estate, the DeMille Trust, and Cecilia's extensive business interests.

For many years I seem to have been talking to people about DeMille. There are far too many names to enumerate here and indeed many of those I have spoken to have preferred to remain anonymous. However, out of the two hundred or more I have seen I should like to single out the following for special mention: all of them have supplied me with richly fascinating information which I have woven into the warp and woof of this story of struggle: Samuel Goldwyn, Mrs. Jesse L. Lasky, Mrs. Alvin Wyckoff, Frances Marion, Adela Rogers St. Johns, Blanche Sweet, Sessue Hayakawa, Mrs. Wallace Reid, Mary Pickford, Robert Cushman, Mitchell Leisen (through the medium of a special interview with David Chierichetti), Bebe Daniels, Evelyn Scott (daughter of Beulah Marie Dix), Katherine DeMille, John DeMille, Richard DeMille, Mary Miles Minter, Leatrice Joy (through the medium of a special interview with Richard Lamparski), Barrett Kiesling, Joseph Kane, Mrs. James Cruze, Archie Stout, Ray Rennahan, Tom Allenby, Jetta Goudal, Mrs. Joseph Schildkraut, Lenore J. Coffee, Arthur Miller, Anton Grot, C. E. Toberman, Eddie Quillan, Fritz Feld, Conrad Nagel, Natalie Visart, Eleanor Boardman, King Vidor, Fredric M. Frank, Lewis Milestone, Karl Struss, Roland Anderson, Henry Wilcoxon, Gladys Jeans, Frederick Sawrin (DeMille's butler), Barbara Stanwyck, Mrs. Alan Hale, Walter Brennan, Akim Tamiroff, Paulette Goddard, Ray Milland, John Wayne, Signe Hasso, Angela Lansbury, Olive Deering, Cornel Wilde, James Stewart, Charlton Heston, Victor Milner, Anne Baxter, Edward G. Robinson, Yvonne De Carlo, Judith Anderson, Vincent Price, Pat and Mickey Moore, Curtis Harrington, David Bradley, John Wayne, and Mr. DeMille's indispensable secretaries, Florence Cole and Berenice Mosk.

DeMille stills supplied by courtesy of the DeMille Estate and Motion Picture Associates, with special thanks to Cecilia DeMille Harper.

1

Origins

Two-fifteen P.M., January 18, 1939: Canoga Park, near Los Angeles in California. A motion picture company is shooting a fanciful elaboration of the completion of the Union Pacific Railroad of seventy years earlier: two period trains drawing up face-to-face, their cowcatchers meeting; a troop of blue-clad infantry, and a brass band striking up; Irish and Chinese track workers flinging their caps in the air; Indian onlookers silent and depressed, aware of what the railroad has done to their territory. Incongruously, an ambulance drives up to the location; men in white coats carry out a man groaning with pain. His face is pale, almost gray with suffering under a patina of sun tan. He is wearing a sun helmet, a tropical jacket,

1

Cecil as a child.

puttees, and special boots designed to protect his weak heels. In one hand he carries a megaphone. He is borne, shouting imprecations, to the camera boom. With heavy leather straps, he is attached to a special platform, and with a groan of winches, he is hoisted sixty feet in the air to direct the scene. He pours ferocious scorn on a player who displeases him. Then, grinning as broadly as a schoolboy, he begins to direct the scene.

It was intensely characteristic of Cecil B. DeMille that he would put himself to the utmost test of courage: directing a gigantic epic—*Union Pacific*—after an operation, in a condition in which most men would have been content to lie motionless and admire a pretty nurse. Life, for him, was an immense test of Christian patience and endurance, which he sustained with true heroism. The public saw him as a consistently successful, entertainingly egotistical film tycoon; the critics as a shrewd and arrogant vulgarian.

Both images had a degree of truth, of course; but the central reality of DeMille, known to his family and dearest friends, was a more complex one. He was stubborn, decent, loyal, unswerving, as well as ruthless, desperate, and at his worst an unmitigated bully. His ruthlessness, desperation, and cruelty were confined to the film set; at home, for the most part, he was a model of kindness and consideration. He worshiped his wife, the adorable Constance Adams, and remained with her for almost sixty years of marriage. He was a stern but loving father, who did his utmost to blend his one daughter, Cecilia, with three adopted children: John, Katherine, and Richard. To his servants, he was the most generous and warm-hearted of men. In the studio, only the picture mattered: and many men and women suffered to that end.

We are fortunate that we can still see him, alive and robust, on the screen, both in his own sumptuously mounted trailers, his bald and square-shouldered figure addressing us from behind a vast office desk, and in such works as *Variety Girl* and *Sunset Boulevard*, a personality above all confident—though it was a confidence won from an endless battle with adversity. Like most great film makers, he began as an artist, and was gradually overwhelmed by the need to prove himself as a businessman. He was not only harassed by the need to marry God and Moloch in his work; he was harassed by the need to marry them in himself. His life struggle until he gave up as a personal artist was not only against the men who held the purse strings of the industry in New York; it was between his body and his soul.

Sturdy Dutch stock, courageous, dashing, and fierce-spirited, formed the very root of Cecil B. DeMille's character. For years, genealogists worked for him, unraveling the complex story of his father's family; his mother's origins, characteristically, did not interest him to any great extent. He was a man's man, concerned with the nature of manhood; it was what his father had bequeathed him that obsessed him for most of his life.

On his father's side, he could trace his origins back to Gillis diMil, a Flemish soldier of the thirteenth century; other oddly assorted forebears were Anthony DeMil, Abbot of Eeckhout, and Adam deMil, a shoemaker who murdered his stepfather with an ax in 1553. Many of the DeMils were drawn to the priesthood or the ministry. The family first moved to America in 1658: Anthony deMil, a baker, and his wife Elizabeth sailed to the New World aboard the *Gilded Beaver* and became active in the affairs of the Colony. The family settled in Stamford, Connecticut, during the eighteenth century, flourishing as millers and flour merchants.

DeMille's grandfather was William Edward DeMille, a prosperous mercantile agent, owner of the steamer *Pamlico*, and a settler in the Deep South. He joined the Confederate Army as a commissary, and was captured by a troop of Federal cavalry. By the time he was released after peace was declared, the family home had been destroyed by fire. The struggle of the DeMilles to survive was a harrowing one, and when Henry DeMille, Cecil's father, grew up it was to a legacy of poverty and famine.

This staunch adolescent Dutch stock was not to be defeated

by adversity. Henry DeMille was a strong and stoical boy who at fourteen was already deeply religious, determined despite severe odds to obtain an education for himself. He talked his paternal grandfather into helping finance his education at the Adelphi Academy in Brooklyn and later at Columbia College.

Henry DeMille had been fascinated by theater from the beginning of his life; but his family absolutely opposed him in that desire. While he dreamed, at first futilely, of life on the stage, he attended performances of the Philokalia Musical and Literary Association of Brooklyn and joined the Association's entertainment committee in 1872. There he fell in love with a pretty young actress, Tillie Samuel, whom he called Beatrice. After he took his Bachelor of Arts degree, setting out on a career as a teacher in deference to his family's wishes, and already determining on a career as a lay preacher, he seriously began to press his attentions on Tillie. She accepted, since her aims in life were similar to his: a dedication to propriety and rectitude, a devotion to good works. On July 1, 1876, they were married at St. Luke's Church in Brooklyn.

Both DeMille's parents taught at John Lockwood's School in Brooklyn, and lived in cheap rented rooms nearby. In 1878, their eldest son William was born, and Henry DeMille accepted a post at Columbia Grammar School. It was at this time that Henry fell under the influence of the late British poet, Charles Kingsley, author of the celebrated children's book *The Water Babies.* Deeply influenced by Kingsley, Henry invariably based his lay sermons at St. Stephen's Church in Brooklyn on Kingsley's original works. He was so profoundly impressed by Kingsley that he even thought of following him into the Episcopal Church as a minister. Although he was never actually ordained, he took extensive courses in theology and remained devout to the day of his death.

In order to eke out his meager living as a teacher, Henry began a career as a writer on the side. He published a serial in *Leslie's Weekly* and wrote a play, *Robert Aclen,* which did not achieve production but instead earned him a position as a play reader for the Madison Square Theatre.

Cecil was born on August 12, 1881, in the small town of Ashfield, Massachusetts, where his parents were spending their summer vacation in rented rooms. Shortly thereafter, Henry felt able to afford a house at Echo Lake, New Jersey, where William and Cecil would have room to play. Although Henry's life was intimately wrapped up in the vivid life of the theater, his home was run with absolutely rigid austerity. The two boys were constantly aware of religion from their earliest days, the walls of their bedroom lined with sacred texts and prints of scenes from the Bible, their life explicitly dedicated by their parents to near-poverty, chastity, and obedience.

Each day, Henry DeMille used to read the boys one chapter of the Old Testament, one of the New. With his superb speaking voice, he held the brothers spellbound. And after the Bible reading, he would read romantic novels, dwelling with particular ripeness on the details of balls, parties, lavish coronations, and funerals.

The family home, in the muddy, ill-paved little town of Echo Lake, was supposed to be haunted—a man had killed himself there. For the first four nights there, Cecil and William lay shivering with cold in an attic room, while they listened to a voice calling "Who-oo!" over and over again. One morning they discovered that the sound was caused by a branch rubbing against the house. Cecil said to his brother, "That shows how stupid fear is," and the experience taught him the basis of his stoicism in later years.

The plain, frame house and the simple dark rooms of Echo Lake were designed to support the family's frugal existence with cold comfort. Meanwhile, Henry DeMille steadily built a small reputation as a moralistic playwright, collaborating with the up-and-coming David Belasco on *Elsie Deane*. When his career as a playwright limped, he worked as an actor in stock. He left the Madison Square Theatre and later joined the Lyceum, again working with Belasco as a dramatist. It was the beginning of a long and rewarding association, encouraged by the brilliant new showman Daniel Frohman.

One of Cecil's earliest memories of boyhood was of earnest discussions between his father and Belasco, then a young man, writing their plays in longhand watched eagerly by himself and William. They began a career as commercial co-authors with the celebrated play *The Wife*, while at the same time developing a so-called "society drama" for the Lyceum, a stock company headed by Georgia Cayvan, Henry Miller, and Grace Henderson, among others. The two men made an oddly assorted pair: DeMille, thin, balding, prim and proper, his pince-nez perched on his sharp nose; Belasco, wild-haired, passionate, committed to art, his piercing dark brown eyes seeming to seek out the soul of those whom he addressed.

Though *The Wife* was the subject of a plagiarism suit as late as 1914, it was in fact drawn from a variety of previous works by the energetic but somewhat uninventive pair of collaborators. It would be tedious to relate the plot: suffice it to say that it concerned a woman who marries a Senator on the rebound; after some pressure to return to her abandoned lover, she decides to remain faithful to her husband in a pious and uplifting final scene. DeMille wrote most of the lines while Belasco acted them out on the stage. The play, poor and vulgarly written though it was, became a great success after it opened at the Lyceum on November 1, 1887. Although Daniel Frohman wanted to close it initially, Henry DeMille literally threatened him with physical violence if he proceeded in this desire. The play found its audience, following admirable reviews, and ran for two hundred thirty-nine performances.

The playwrights were now pronounced successful and Frohman packed them off to Echo Lake to write a new play, *Lord Chumley*, for the actor E. H. Sothern. They went on to write *The Charity Ball*, a theme close to Henry DeMille's heart—the story of conflict between a clergyman and his wicked brother, later adopted in certain of Cecil's films. They also collaborated on

Men and Women, produced at Proctor's Theatre on October 21, 1890.

The partnership broke up, largely due to the fact that David Belasco had fallen in love with the actress Mrs. Leslie Carter and wanted to concentrate on developing her career. On his own, Henry, with William and Cecil admitted as pupils to the Horace Mann School, began writing a translation of Ludwig Fulda's play *Das Verlorene Paradis* as *The Lost Paradise* at his home in Waverly Place, New York.

It was in 1891, when Cecil was nine years old, that his first detailed awareness of life began. His memories in later years rarely went past that period, when Henry fell in love with Pompton Lake, New Jersey, and built a lovely house there, Pamlico, which was furnished in 1892: it was three stories high, made of white-painted wood, with a marvelous sun porch and sweeping lawns dotted with bushes. It was a good house to grow up in, the garden rich with plantings of flowers, the woods nearby full of wonderful trails.

By the age of ten, Cecil's character had already begun to form. He was a sturdy boy, with a head well-set on already strong shoulders, a well-shaped chest, and well-muscled limbs. He excelled in sports: swimming, running, baseball, football, handball. He was absolutely devoted to the Bible and regarded its words as entirely beyond question. He admired courage above all things; he was a ruthless competitor in class and on the sporting field, and had a passion for the out-of-doors. He was a sweet-natured and devoted brother and son, and he adored his parents. He loved the classics, and the works of Gustave Doré: the most fingered book at Pompton Lake was the Doré Bible Gallery, a collection of illustrated sacred texts published by Belford-Clarke in 1891. Cecil loved to pore over pictures like "Ruth and Boaz," "The Judgment of Solomon," "The Sermon on the Mount," and "The Prodigal Son." From these the whole visual inspiration of his great religious films sprang.

Henry DeMille's vivid readings of the Bible continued to

impress the young boy. But one overpowering experience affected his religious development more than anything else. A visiting minister at Pompton announced he would preach on every day of Passion Week at eight o'clock in the morning. On the Monday, DeMille made his way to Pompton Christ Church on foot through icy rain. When he arrived, he was astonished to discover that nobody else had chosen to go to church that day. He sat down in a pew at the back and waited quietly. At the appointed moment the minister, red-bearded and bushy-eyebrowed, stepped up to the pulpit and smiled gently at the young boy sitting alone below him. DeMille gave the responses at the reading lesson, and listened with deep attentiveness to the brief sermon. At the offering, the minister stepped down and put the silver collection plate on the altar railing. Cecil walked up and solemnly placed a single worn nickel in the plate. In reply, the minister put his hand on the boy's head. In walking back to his seat that day, Cecil knew this man's God to be a real God, and that his faith was God-like in its monumental simplicity. It left a lump in his throat, and to the end of his life he could not think of it without emotion.

On January 8, 1893, Henry DeMille delivered Charles Kingsley's beautiful sermon "The Light" at Pompton Christ Church. It was the last sermon he ever gave. After delivering a lecture in New York, he fell seriously ill. The sickness was diagnosed as typhus. On February 10, 1893, he died, leaving William, Cecil, and their younger sister Agnes (who died as a baby) in the care of the bereaved mother.

After Henry DeMille died, Beatrice's character seemed to strengthen and develop. For all her fiber, she had lain somewhat under her husband's shadow; out of her grief she achieved a new and powerful resolution. She had begun a school at a small grocery store; she immediately removed this to Pamlico itself, and, with the support of clerics, she opened the Henry C. DeMille School in April 1893.

She raised William and Cecil with all the kindly sternness of her husband. The brothers grew to be contrasts: William was easy-going, relaxed, scholarly, untidy; shock-haired and messy, his pockets stuffed with a miscellaneous assortment of objects, he took uneasily to discipline. Cecil was determined, forceful, pin-neat, his face polished with health; he was the ideal all-rounder, an athlete with brains.

When he was fifteen, Mrs. DeMille sent Cecil to boarding school for the first time: she bicycled with him to Chester, Pennsylvania, to save the train fare, and entered him in the Pennsylvania Military College under the directorship of Colonel Charles E. Hyatt. Hyatt, like Henry DeMille, was an unswerving fundamentalist, and Cecil in the formative years of his adolescence again learned and re-learned the truths of the Old and New Testament. DeMille loved the endless dawn drills, the cold baths, the stern reminders of the dangers of falling from a high level of manly virtue. In the meantime, William was at Columbia, working on plays; and Cecil, too, was fired with an inherited passion for the theater. In 1898, he left Pennsylvania Military College in a glow of approval from Colonel Hyatt, and enrolled at the American Academy of Dramatic Arts.

He learned acting technique from the sturdy and authoritative teacher Charles Jehlinger. From the outset, they clashed— and Cecil was frequently dismissed impatiently from class. Jehlinger believed in imposing his will on the players, forcing them into a mold; Cecil believed that an actor should simply be given the gist of a scene, and then feel free to improvise, to develop ideas as he went along. Cecil got along better with the teacher of diction, Wellington Pitman, who made him drill constantly in the proper use of vowels, and gave him the haughty, slightly theatrical mode of speech, every word perfectly enunciated, that he retained until the day of his death.

Cecil graduated from the Academy in 1900, and as a result of a successful appearance in the graduation play *The Arcady Trail*, he was engaged by Charles Frohman for a role in the play *Hearts Are Trumps*, opening at the Garden Theatre, New York, on February 21, 1900. The play went on the road after ninety-three performances, touring through the Middlewest and West. Among the players who joined the troupe in Washington was an attractive young girl, Constance Adams; and DeMille was fascinated by her. She had a grave, sensitive, aloof quality he found irresistible. More important, he was enchanted by Constance's feet. He always told friends that he fell in love with her when he saw her walk up a staircase, while he was standing in a hallway. His mild form of foot fetishism, growing as he became older, was accepted by him with the usual warm self-admiration that marked most of his feelings. If anyone had had the temerity to suggest to him that he suffered from an example of *psychopathia sexualis,* he would have dismissed them from his sight.

But a foot fetishist he was, and remained; any self-respecting actress who required a role in one of his films would make sure that at the very outset he looked at her lovely feet. And even in the days of his struggle, young women understood his yearnings, and obliged.

The friendship with Constance developed into a romance, and on the last day of 1900, sitting in a bleak wind on the steps of a Boston boardinghouse, Cecil proposed, and was accepted. Her father, Judge Adams of the Supreme Court of Massachusetts, opposed the match: he had set his sights higher than a struggling young actor. But Cecil obtained a flow of work in Frohman productions, and his powers of persuasion, developed in debates at Pennsylvania Military College, were considerable. On August 16, 1902, at the Adams family home at Orange, New Jersey, the couple were married in the Episcopal faith.

Shortly thereafter, the couple left on a nationwide "honeymoon," appearing for Dan Frohman and E. H. Sothern in touring productions of *Hamlet* and *If I Were King.* From Sothern, a brilliant actor-director, Cecil learned how to group figures on the stage, how to light, and how to make a crowd scene come to life. With a minimum of financial resources, Sothern could make the panoply of the court of Claudius of Denmark or Louis XI of France dazzle and enthrall audiences.

Henry DeMille.

Beatrice DeMille.

Pompton.

DeMille (fourth from left) at Pennsylvania Military College, class of 1893.

DeMille (second from left) on Pennsylvania Military College football team, 1897.

Cecil as Florestin in The Bohemian Girl, *late 1890s.*

But while Cecil was learning at the master's knee, the business of living was, even for his stoical spirit, a severely difficult one. The cheerless lodging houses, poorly heated trains, atrocious food, and nights rendered sleepless by the ceaseless clanging of the freight trains stayed with him for a lifetime.

He felt a compulsion to follow in his father's footsteps as a playwright. With William, he wrote several forgotten works: *The Genius, The Royal Mounted,* and *After Five* among them. He also appeared with the Standard Opera Company, singing and acting in productions of *The Bohemian Girl, The Chimes of Normandy, Martha,* and *The Mikado.* On one occasion, when the conductor, Rudolph Berliner, collapsed just before a performance, Cecil took over and conducted the entire performance.

Happier than these assignments, which paid little and forced Cecil and Constance to scrape along in a demeaning state of poverty, was a chance to act an important role in William DeMille's play *The Warrens of Virginia,* for David Belasco. The play opened at the Belasco Theatre in December 1907; it was a success and Belasco encouraged Cecil to write a new play for production at the theater. Its name was *The Return of Peter Grimm.* *

DeMille prepared *The Return of Peter Grimm* on the theme of a manufacturer who dies and sees the wrongs he had committed. He returns to earth and communicates with the living. The play, though the ramifications of the plot are today absurd to relate, was a strong theatrical vehicle for the Belasco star David Warfield. Unfortunately, the question of the authorship of the play caused DeMille the most acute distress, since Belasco put his name on it and barely gave DeMille any credit for it at all. Actually, Belasco extensively rewrote it, changing the wicked manufacturer to an aged Dutch horticulturist. In July 1911 Belasco, vexed by the controversy that sprang up, issued a statement to the press, indicating that he simply paid for the

---

* During the writing, DeMille's only daughter, Cecilia, was born, on October 5, 1908, at the Adams family home at Orange.

idea to the tune of ten thousand dollars—an astonishing sum for those days.

The truth of the matter never emerged at the time, but in fact much more of DeMille's work appeared in the finished production than Belasco was prepared to acknowledge. Meanwhile, another controversy blew up over William DeMille's Belasco play *The Woman*, which opened simultaneously in New York. A barber named Abraham Goldknopf announced that he had written *The Woman* under the title *Tainted Philanthropy*, and the case was brought to trial in New York before Judge George C. Holt on August 3, 1912.

Belasco created a tremendous scene in court, sweeping in wearing his famous clerical collar and black coat, his hair like an aureole about his head, and told the judge that he would put on a performance of both plays for his benefit to prove to him that the charges were absurd. Holt acquiesced, and on November 26, at the Belasco Theatre, the great producer showed the judge *The Woman* followed by the hitherto unproduced and quite atrocious *Tainted Philanthropy*, starring Milton Sills and Helen Freeman. The audience screamed with laughter at the insane concoction, and the barber lost his case.

In that year, Beatrice DeMille began developing a successful career as a literary agent and obtained a distinguished list of clients as a result of her own and her two sons' absorption in the theater; among those clients were Beulah Marie Dix, Zoë Akins, Wilson Mizner, Mary Roberts Rinehart, and Charles Klein. It was through his mother that Cecil in 1911 formed the extraordinary friendship which was to last until the day of his death: with the producer of musical shows and former vaudevillian, Jesse L. Lasky.

Born in 1880, Lasky had been solo cornetist in the San Jose Juvenile Band in California, played vaudeville, and became the manager of the magician Hermann the Great. He began booking acts continually between 1906 and 1910, building up a fortune of one hundred thousand dollars which he lost in the disastrous collapse of his show, *Folies Bergere*, put on in competition with Ziegfeld's 1910 *Follies*; among his cast was a young woman called Mae West. In 1911, a twinkling-eyed, pince-nezed charmer with an extraordinarily attractive outgoing manner, he discovered a possible way to repair his fortunes: he had an idea for an operetta, *California*, set in his native state, and went to see Beatrice DeMille about the possibility of having William write the libretto. She explained that William was too busy working on a new production with Belasco and recommended Cecil instead. Lasky refused to consider this alternative, but she pressed him to discuss the matter with Cecil before giving his final refusal.

The meeting, in a back office, was an extremely uncomfortable one. Cecil was coldly contemptuous of a mere vaudevillian and Jesse was distinctly less than overcome by Cecil's reputation as a playwright. Urged by nods and winks from Mrs. DeMille, Cecil politely expressed an interest in the rambling plot Lasky unfolded; gradually the ice began to melt; and within an hour the two men had become less guarded and almost on friendly terms.

By the next day, they had agreed upon a collaboration: Robert Hood Bowers composed the score for the work, and William LeBaron the lyrics. They spent pleasant times together with Jesse's wife, Bessie, his sister, Blanche, and Blanche's husband, a glove salesman named Samuel Goldfish. *California* was a success, and Cecil and Jesse collaborated again, on *In the Barracks* and *The Antique World.*

To all intents and purposes, Cecil's life was a pleasant one in the years 1912–1913. But in fact, it was a depressing existence lived on the edge of poverty and failure, an unsteady tightrope walk over an abyss. Cecil, Constance, and their little baby Cecilia barely made ends meet in their humble rooms, and when any large sum was needed, they had to pawn the family silver and even their clothes. The dreary, horrible grind of everyday living weighed upon Cecil's soul: life seemed to consist of endless washings and ironings and monotonous, unsatisfactory meals; a constant fight against city grime; a stiff collar turned to conceal the rim of dirt which collected on it; shoes worn until they were full of holes and let in the rain. Buying a new suit involved endless scrimping and saving, and if a typewriter broke down, it was a disaster. Hanging over everything was the threat of illness, of being unable to support his family, and the even greater dread that Constance would conceive again.

In this miserable life, without any of the fugitive glamor DeMille experienced in the theater, in the grind of days and months and years, his character was finally forged. Hunger toughened him; his stoical character as a boy hardened and broadened. He found consolation in his body: hard as rock, rippling with muscle, it was constantly subjected to punishment in cheap gymnasiums and free pools. He found consolation more than ever in religion, and in Doré: if some new book he longed to read was unavailable at a library, or beyond his meager purse to buy, he would sit up late by candlelight to save the electricity and pore over Doré, and dream. And once a week—joy of joys—he would take his family to a matinee, sitting in the second balcony, enjoying the pleasures of a new show, or occasionally, through his mother or Belasco, obtain better seats to an evening performance.

By mid-1912, he was a little more prosperous, thanks to help from Jesse and Sam Goldfish; and he began to think that with his savings, he might go to Mexico and join the army to fight for Pancho Villa, or sail to the South Seas and find a life of adventure in Tahiti, or the gold fields of Australia. Dreams were better than reality. He lived in them so fully that Constance often grew impatient with him, but neither realized that a far greater dream than any he envisaged was to open up in the years to come.

2

Hollywood

Every day that fall, DeMille met Jesse and Sam for
luncheon—at their expense—at the Claridge Hotel dining room, flanked by ferns in huge brass pots under the
imitation Adam ceiling. Other conversations were held in
various Greenwich Village drinking places and in the forests of
Maine where they traveled by canoe along an arm of the
Penobscot River and tramped across virtually untrodden territory near Kidney Pond. With his passion for the wild, DeMille
enjoyed these expeditions, but he longed for more distant
adventures. He told Jesse over lunch one day at the Claridge
that he was going to leave Broadway, and take off for Mexico,
where he might be able to earn some money writing about the

Cecil with Jesse Lasky and
visiting actor David Warfield, 1919.

local conflicts taking place there. Jesse had an even more adventurous notion: Cecil could make movies. Lasky recorded in his memoirs *I Blow My Own Horn*: "[Cecil's] eyes gleamed, and before I was over the shock of hearing my own unconsidered suggestion, Cecil put out his hand, grabbed mine, and said, 'Let's!' " As they strolled down Forty-fourth Street to the Lambs' Club after lunch, they ran into Dustin Farnum, who had recently appeared with that diminutive precursor of Shirley Temple, Mary Miles Minter, in *The Littlest Rebel* for Charles Frohman. They walked into the Lambs' Club together. Jesse said casually to Farnum: "We're going to make a movie. And who knows? It might be the biggest picture ever made. Would you like to star in it?" Farnum looked across the Lambs' Club members' room and waved to the author Edwin Milton Royle, who had written the successful Broadway play *The Squaw Man*. Farnum, who had appeared in the 1901 revival with William S. Hart, smiled and said that if Royle would agree to the play being filmed, he just might consent to play the lead. Lasky crossed the room, whispered something to Royle, and Royle's face lit up. By late afternoon, he and the others—including an attorney, Arthur Friend—were drinking happily together, very much in business.

The contract which formed the basis of the Jesse L. Lasky Play Company was drawn up by Lasky himself in pencil on the back of a Claridge Hotel menu. It made Lasky the president, Samuel Goldfish the business manager—he would secede all interest in the glove business—and DeMille the general stage director. Later, the title of the company was changed to the Jesse L. Lasky Feature Motion Picture Company, and Lasky rented offices to house it in the Longacre Theatre Building, third floor, at 220 West Forty-eighth Street. Fifteen thousand dollars was raised with the aid of Bessie Lasky's family; of the partners, DeMille was the only one who was unable to contribute a single cent.

The partners still met daily at the Claridge, deciding from the very outset that they must obtain the rights to as many plays as possible. Since they were unknown, clearly their properties must be known. In order to secure the absolute cooperation of Royle, he was offered the job of head of the story department in New York. Lasky told the trade publication *The Moving Picture World* that December: "[We want the stories to be] melodramatic, with great action and plenty of heart interest. Will we have a scenario department? Yes, indeed. We will not engage a stock company. We will engage special casts for each play, and for a star a man or woman as the story may require."

As soon as DeMille's friends learned that he was deserting the stage for movies they were absolutely horrified. William DeMille was appalled, seeing no future in the "tawdry medium" of motion pictures. With his obstinate nature, Cecil was spurred on still more to the new adventure by these adverse reactions, and at once prepared to leave for the West.

Lasky at first suggested that the picture should be shot at Fort Lee, New Jersey, then a popular site for Westerns, but DeMille looked distinctly unenthusiastic, and spoke about shooting a picture in "the real West." Lasky's second proposal was "somewhere in Indian country, somewhere like Flagstaff, Arizona," and at that DeMille brightened somewhat. Dustin Farnum, however, was far from anxious to leave Broadway, in case he should have another offer for a stage show. Rather desperately, Lasky offered him five thousand dollars cash as a surety and to cover his initial expenses on location. Lasky also had to buy up, with the aid of Bessie's brother and uncle, all of Farnum's stock. DeMille left for Arizona with a cameraman, Alfredo Gandolfi, an experienced film director, Oscar Apfel, Dustin Farnum, and Farnum's secretary, Fred Kley.

DeMille arrived in Flagstaff on December 18. The weather was fine, but he disliked the location—it was far too built up.* He proceeded at once to California. By the time they crossed the border into California, DeMille and Apfel had reworked the story of *The Squaw Man* into a satisfactory motion picture plot.

---

* The conventional story that it was raining in Flagstaff is discredited by newspapers of that day.

An English army officer, James Wynnegate, is in charge of a
trust fund raised by members of his regiment for the relief of
the dead members' widows. The Earl of Kerhill, who is serving
under his command, embezzles the money; Wynnegate nobly
pretends to be guilty in order to protect the name of Kerhill. He
sails for America in a trading schooner which catches fire in
mid-ocean. Along with a handful of passengers, Wynnegate is
rescued by a steamer, and arrives in New York. He changes his
name to Carston and goes West, where he buys a ranch. He is
almost murdered by a bitter opponent, Hawkins, but he is
rescued by the action of a devoted Indian girl, Nat-U-Rich,
whom he marries. Meanwhile, the Earl of Kerhill, injured
fatally in a polo game, signs a confession clearing Wynne-
gate/Carston's name. During some final melodramatic compli-
cations, Nat-U-Rich commits suicide and Wynnegate/Carston
marries the widow of the Earl of Kerhill.

The party arrived at the old Santa Fe Railroad Station in
downtown Los Angeles on December 20. They were met by
prior arrangement: two splendid locomobiles arrived from the
Alexandria Hotel and two liveried chauffeurs drove them
through the arid business section to their luxurious destination.
Almost at once they were besieged by offers of places in which
they could make films. The most attractive offer came from two
men called Burns and Revier, who said they had "a fine
laboratory" in a district called Hollywood. DeMille and Dustin
Farnum drove along bumpy roads to Hollywood—a dusty,
flower-filled backwater whose streets were flanked by bedraggled palm trees—until finally they arrived at something looking
like a large dilapidated shack. "The fine laboratory" was in fact
a barn at 6284 Selma Avenue in which a man called Stern had
tethered up a horse and parked a carriage. DeMille's heart sank
when he saw it, but he had no time to look for anything else: he
was due to deliver a finished picture to New York by February
15. He signed a lease, which contained a proviso that the horse
and carriage should stay just where they were.

The group moved to the Hollywood Hotel on Hollywood

Boulevard and Highland Avenue. Bessie Lasky described it as it looked a few months later on her first view of California. "A dismal summer hotel filled with unwanted summer boarders, their aged bodies looking blank and useless, rocking on the porch, filling the air with futility and gloom." One somnolent clerk in a green eyeshade occupied the front desk, the elevator groaned arthritically, and the rooms smelled of dried fat behind their motionless pale green blinds. When DeMille turned on his bath, a small trickle of dark brown water emerged from the tap. Outside the window, a dead tree stood, filling him with a sense of hopelessness.

He, Farnum, and the others pulled themselves together sufficiently to drive around and explore the place they had chosen for themselves. The air was filled with the scent of orange blossoms and the stench of burned film. Most of the buildings were single-story clapboard structures, peeling under the sun. Toward the ocean, Westwood and Brentwood were no more than rolling meadows covered in alfalfa and pepper trees. Roads often petered out, making the hiring of horses a necessity.

DeMille fell in love with Los Angeles at once. With his painter's eye he was captivated by the Pacific light, the intense black shadows with their razor-edged outlines against glittering stone, the warm-hearted, sun-wrinkled people with their harsh frontier manners. He began engaging artisans: a signpainter to put up a board outside the barn on Selma and Vine reading "Jesse L. Lasky Feature Play Company," a carpenter to construct a wooden partition in the barn which fenced off a small office, a girl, Stella Stray, to do the typing on her own typewriter.

Once he had finished work on the studio, DeMille and Oscar Apfel left on an extensive search for locations and shot some scenes. They traveled two thousand miles, to the Uintah country in eastern Utah and up the Green River to Ah Say, Wyoming, looking for ideal sites. While doing so they agreed to divide the film-making chores: DeMille would direct the actors;

Apfel, with the cameraman, Alfredo Gandolfi, would pose them and arrange the compositions. DeMille was excited by the release from the convenient confines of the stage. He told a correspondent of the New York *Dramatic Mirror* later: "Imagine, the horizon is your stage limit and the sky your gridiron. No height limit, no close fitting exits, no conserving of stage space, just the whole world open to you as a stage; a thousand people in a scene do not crowd your accommodations. It was a new feeling, a new experience, and I was enamored with the way Mr. Apfel went about focusing his camera, getting his actors and actresses within range of the lens and the way in which our cameraman followed every move, studied the sun, tried to dodge a cloud, edged his camera into a more advantageous position, and then the artists."

Almost at once, DeMille learned the technique of film direction. He learned not to huddle his players in a small corner of the screen, improvising an approximation of the proscenium arch, but to dispose them against the magnificent landscapes of the West. He used mountains, boulders, deep valleys, all as part of a canvas; he became, in a sense, a landscape painter. "The baize," he told the *Mirror*, "was the sand of Gila, the outskirts of the great American desert. Our perspective was the upper chain of the Rockies, and our ceiling piece was God's own blue and amber sky. I felt inspired, I felt that I could do things which the confines of a theater would not permit."

Back in California, he and Apfel began shooting the sea sequences of the hero's journey from England. These were an immense hazard. A hurricane raged down the coast, wrecking ships off San Francisco, and swelling the Sacramento River to flood point. In the great wind's wake, it left heavy seas off San Pedro, where DeMille built a replica of the ship which was to take the film's hero from Southampton. He was forced to postpone shooting of the sequence of the ship's departure from England for several weeks; instead he spent much of the preliminary days fighting his way through bargain sales at Barker Brothers, "America's Largest, Most Completely

Stocked, and Best Equipped Home Furnishing Establishment,"
and at the Broadway Department Store (a "White Sale")
obtaining props for his sets.

They were difficult days, and DeMille's first weeks of
shooting were extremely desultory. Bit by bit, he began to put
together his cast. He had already cabled for the beautiful squaw
Red Wing (as Nat-U-Rich) and Joseph E. Singleton as the
Indian Tabywanna, since these individuals had actually been
the models upon which Edwin Milton Royle had based the
characters. The female star (as Lady Diana) was Winifred
Kingston, a fair-haired, blue-eyed English girl of twenty years,
who had appeared on the London stage under the direction of
Sir Herbert Beerbohm Tree and in New York under Charles
Frohman. Almost as soon as she arrived, she fell in love with
Dustin Farnum, and they began an increasingly passionate
affair during the shooting.

Late in January, the company returned by caravan seven
hundred miles to the Green River in Wyoming, where Royle
had set his actual drama. They shot for ten days. Back in
California, the most hazardous part of the filming took place on
January 14, when DeMille was directing the burning of the
abandoned schooner near Catalina. In order to show the final
explosion, one hundred sulphur pots, stored on the boat deck,
had to be ignited. DeMille arranged the pots and lighted them
himself, when nobody else proved willing to do so. Something
went wrong, and the ship exploded, throwing him into the sea,
and capsizing the crew boat which was anchored twenty feet
away to starboard. He was dragged unconscious, and suffering
from minor burns, into the boat. Next day, he was up at dawn,
to hire a new vessel and start—with the aid, this time, of
members of the Los Angeles Fire Department—an entirely
new, and on this occasion successful, sequence.

Away from the rigors of filming, DeMille settled into a
comfortable routine. He spent the first weekends driving
around Hollywood, proclaimed by a huge sign as "The Gem of
the Foothills." He explored the romantic Cahuenga Pass and

Laurel Canyon, roads winding through the crests of low-lying hills to Lookout Mountain. Hollywood had already begun its boom: in the past year one million dollars worth of houses had been built, and deposits at the Hollywood National Bank had risen to $650,477. Even sleepy Beverly Hills had begun to show some signs of activity: stately homes valued at ten and fifteen thousand dollars had begun to emerge in the fields and dunes, and the Rodeo Lands and Water Company had started to beautify the area with lovely plantings of trees.

It wasn't New York, of course. Shops closed after eight P.M., most lights were out by ten, and "nightlife" was a visit to one of two movie theaters. Nevertheless, DeMille plunged with pleasure into such social life as there was, attending a Grand Masked Ball given by Mr. and Mrs. Yslas at their fine home at 1232 Lake Street, where he and the other guests pelted each other with imitation snowballs filled with confetti and colored streamers, a Yama-Yama Dinner Dance given at the Midwick Country Club, and several of *thé dansants* at the Alexandria, where Arend's Orchestra played. Meantime, every spare moment was absorbed in building a stage in a lemon grove adjoining the barn, a wide platform of pinewood put together by DeMille himself and a team of laborers, with canvas screens to diffuse the sun.

Exasperated by the inefficiencies of the Hollywood Hotel, DeMille moved in late January to a house at 6136 Lexington Avenue, with a wolf—bought from an advertisement in the *Los Angeles Times*—as his sole companion. He began work on the studio: The stage was forty feet by forty feet, surrounded by a lemon orchard. Gradually, during the next few months, DeMille began to develop the whole complex. In this he was aided by his production staff, George Melford, James Neill, and Frank Ricker. DeMille supervised the construction of carpenter shops, which produced sets of startling authenticity; *The Moving Picture World's* Hollywood reporter, visiting one of the sets being built for a production which DeMille directed, remarked on the thoroughness of "a five-room floor, consisting of kitchen, butler's pantry, dining room, living room and hall, besides a staircase and entrances to two rooms up one flight, the whole of hand-mitred construction and filling the entire glass-walled stage." For city backgrounds, DeMille reigned over the exact reconstruction of the corner of Forsyth and Houston Streets, New York, with a ginmill, a perfectly reproduced saloon, and a block pavement actually made of stone. He renamed a local street Lasky Lane and lined it with dressing rooms.

His customary garb on the set was a flannel shirt, khaki trousers, and puttees; his high boots, which became a fashion for directors, were inspired by a fear of snakes, which still crawled in the gardens of his home, and by the need to support his weak heels. His schedule was so brutal that after the first visit to the parties downtown and the sales purchases at the New Year's sales, he only made two other visits to the city. He rose before dawn, rode to the studio with a boxed lunch, worked with grim intensity all day, then returned home to pore over the scripts, which he invariably wrote or rewrote himself, until the small hours. He cut *The Squaw Man* as he went, squeezing in the harrowing work of giving the film a fluid continuity between his other assignments. Bit by bit, he learned the art of juxtaposing scenes for maximum dramatic effect, knowing just where to place a climax and where to cut it off; in some cases, he found, cutting completely altered the whole mood of a picture for the better.

At DeMille's urgent invitation, Belasco's stage designer, Wilfred Buckland, came to Hollywood with the express intention of applying to the design of motion pictures the same rules which governed the art of painting. He accepted the very small sum of seventy-five dollars a week in return for his services, a salary that was not increased even three years later. From the beginning, he collided with DeMille. He wanted to group the figures on the screen, while DeMille felt that the function of the art director was only to design the backgrounds. This was entirely against Belasco's concepts. Not only Buckland but the

Alfredo Gandolfi, cameraman, and Mr. DeMille with a real wolf, January 22, 1914.

The Squaw Man (*1913*).

William and Cecil.

entire workshop involved in the construction of sets was bitterly dissatisfied in that early period. Quite often required to work eighteen-hour stretches, seven days a week, they had a tendency simply not to turn up on a set when needed, a matter of extreme aggravation to DeMille. They became exasperated by the habits of the Director-General: a chair brought to him to sit on by some minion each day, large, medium, and small megaphones for long distance, medium, and close-up shots, and an infuriating habit of cracking a whip when he was angry. DeMille regarded his employees as soldiers in an army of which he was Chief of Staff.

Not only were there hazards of nature to cope with, but of human beings as well. Somebody unknown in those days seemed bent upon DeMille's professional destruction. One morning, when he entered the laboratory, DeMille stumbled over a heap of film negative of *The Squaw Man* upon the floor; it had been severely damaged, almost certainly trampled on, and it was completely unusable. After that, DeMille slept in the laboratory, armed with a gun and an umbrella to keep the rain off when the roof leaked.

Toward the end of shooting, DeMille brought Constance and Cecilia from New York. Farnum and Winifred Kingston insisted that he move to a better house, which he rented, at thirty dollars a month, in the Cahuenga Pass. The road from the house was so bad that DeMille began riding to the studio on horseback. One day a shot rang out from the underbrush on the mountainside, startling his horse, which reared violently. DeMille drew his gun, but he could not detect anybody hidden by the roadside. A few days later the episode recurred at almost exactly the same spot. In the meantime, threatening letters poured into his office, assuring him of immediate death if he proceeded with the picture.

In spite of everything, DeMille managed to finish the picture by late January. By this time, Jesse and his wife, Bessie, had arrived and were staying at the Hollywood Hotel with Sam Goldfish, married to Jesse's sister, Blanche. The film was sold to the States Rights' Market for forty-three thousand dollars. But at the first screenings in New York and Los Angeles, the film jumped alarmingly, and in whole sequences all that could be seen were the actors' feet.

At the suggestion of Goldfish, the entire film, negative and positive, was taken to Philadelphia for examination by an expert named Sigmund Lubin, who was supposed to know more about film stock than anybody in America. DeMille traveled to Philadelphia with Lasky and endured a torment of suspense while he waited for a verdict. According to DeMille's version, Lubin found that the reason for the jumping film was that the sprocket-punching machine DeMille used was incompatible with current projection standards. According to the historian Terry Ramsaye, who interviewed Lubin in the 1920s, the company had used two different cameras, with two different frame lines, and a simple reperforation job would settle the problem. Leaving Lubin's office, DeMille and Lasky danced along the sidewalk, overjoyed that the problem had been solved. The trade showing in New York was a great success, and even the skeptical William deMille was won over. That gifted press agent William Reichenbach took charge of the publicity, brilliantly launching *The Squaw Man* on the public consciousness.

DeMille's next assignment as a director—he was producer of Oscar Apfel's *Brewster's Millions*—was *The Call of the North*, based on Stewart Edward White's novel *Conjuror's House*. The noted star was the courtly, distinguished stage actor Theodore Roberts, who rapidly became known as The Grand Duke of Hollywood, a forerunner in style of George Arliss. Roberts, who was in his early fifties, had played Tabywanna in the stage version of *The Squaw Man* in both of its New York stage productions. DeMille himself had appeared with him in stock at Elitch's Gardens, Denver. DeMille cabled Roberts in San Francisco, where he was appearing in a play called *Sheriff*, and invited him to appear as Galen Albert, the head of a Hudson's Bay station in Canada. The film's other important star was

Robert Edeson, who had starred in *The Call of the North* on the stage. His performance in *Strongheart*, under the direction of Henry B. Harris (who drowned on the *Titanic* in 1912), had also been distinguished. Edeson's contract with Lasky was an extraordinary one. It specified that the supporting players "must be as near the robust types inhabiting the Canadian Northwest as it is possible to procure"; that Lasky agree to send the entire company to Moose Factory, Canada, during the severest part of the Canadian winter for reasons of authenticity; that in the event of the weather not being severe enough at Moose Factory, Mr. Edeson would be able to select a location as far as Meridian Fifty North; and that real Tiger Tribe Indians appear. Clause five of the contract somewhat repetitively insisted that "it is expressly understood that the Jesse L. Lasky Feature Motion Picture Company agrees to maintain the entire company in the location selected by Mr. Edeson until the weather is of sufficient inclemency to make the picture and give it the proper atmosphere of rigorousness." Clause six still more fantastically said that Mr. Edeson "would work under the direction of the producer in the location selected"—what would have happened if he had declined to do so was far from clear.

Of Edeson's requirements, few proved practicable. Eighteen actual Tiger Tribe Indians were engaged and, after special permission was obtained from the Canadian government, imported. Canoes from a museum in Montreal were borrowed to ensure authenticity. But the film could not be shot in Canada at all, and certainly not in the dead of winter: Lasky needed a new release in a hurry, and it was far quicker and cheaper to shoot the picture in the eternal snows above Big Bear Lake, California.

So far from fulfilling the terms of the contract with Edeson, DeMille had strict instructions to shoot the film in high summer. A flotilla of trucks followed the unit crammed with salt, which was to substitute for snow. Instead of shooting in raging blizzards, the film was made at ferocious one-hundred-degree temperatures. DeMille asked Edeson if he wouldn't like to sacrifice authenticity for comfort by taking off some of the heavy clothes suitable for the Canadian far north. Edeson obstinately refused. The makeup ran down his face under the hot sun; when reminded that people in the far north rarely sported tans, he said that snow-tans were common, and he would "not depart from reality by one iota." He suffered grimly for his pains. One major problem was the direction of scenes involving the ferrying of pelts down river by canoe. DeMille was at his wits' end: he had never paddled a canoe and didn't know anybody who had. He was utterly perplexed when, of all people, Stewart Edward White, the author of the novel on which the film was based, turned up on location and showed DeMille exactly how to manage.

The Call of the North was a classic film: the story of a free trader who hunts the men responsible for wronging his father; he is trapped by the Hudson Bay Company as a trespasser and sent on La Longue Traverse, a journey through trackless wilderness without food and weapons, followed silently through the trees by an Indian known as "The Shadow of Death." His son, also played by Edeson, continues his grim pursuit.

DeMille here worked with the former actor Alvin Wyckoff as his cameraman—a genius whose command of natural light, of the vaulted forest paths and lakes of Big Bear, was nothing short of miraculous. The film was suffused with DeMille's love of the wild, and when Goldfish and Lasky saw it in New York they threw their hats in the air. The moment the screening was over, Goldfish cabled Edeson: DON'T EVER COME BACK TO NEW YORK / PICTURE IS GREATEST EVER. Edeson replied jubilantly: I WON'T / LET ME DO WESTERNS TILL I DROP. He became a very successful star of many subsequent pictures in Hollywood.

In those first months of 1914, the very essence of DeMille's approach to a subject was speed. Unlike Griffith and Ince, whose films had a stately, measured quality, DeMille believed in extreme rapidity of plot development. He improvised a good deal on the set and on location, and allowed the actors leeway for additional interpretation. He was not always a benevolent despot: he was capable of a cold rage which could reduce an actress to tears and make strong men put up their fists. His charm usually dissolved all opposition: when he wanted something, and there was no other way to get it, he calculated his smile with unerring precision to move a dissident spirit.

After *The Call of the North*, Lasky assigned DeMille to direct an appropriate sequel, the first screen version of Owen Wister's immensely popular novel *The Virginian*. In this film, Alvin Wyckoff insisted DeMille use a pattern of shadows to illustrate a scene of a hanging: the hanging was not actually seen, only the shadow-play of hangman, noose, and struggling, rope-bound victim. In this picture, too, Wyckoff introduced coated lenses which enabled DeMille to shoot directly into the sun without showing reflections, and a special technique of showing a darkened room lit only by a single match. As early as 1914, Wyckoff was writing articles for learned publications on the problems of lighting in different weathers and for different dramatic situations.

For *The Virginian*, with Dustin Farnum and Winifred Kingston (their romance developing rapidly), DeMille staged some exciting rescue scenes. In one, Farnum was supposed to rescue Miss Kingston from a stagecoach sinking in the middle of a river; as he did so, she fell flat on her face and narrowly avoided drowning. In another, she had to play a scene with a rattlesnake which, by accident, had not had its poison sacs removed. She escaped without injury.

The Call of the North and *The Virginian* were released out of sequence, the second on August 15, the first on September 7, 1914. With three pictures in release, all enjoying an enormous initial success, DeMille became a household word in the industry, already mentioned in the same breath with Ince, though not yet (quite) with Griffith. Critics praised his sense of realism, his flair for landscape, and even his approach to comedy, though this last was in fact very primitive and unsophisticated. His life continued to be entirely devoid of the glamor which even at that early stage in the history of

Hollywood seemed to be expected by the public of its idols. He continued to live in his rough-hewn cottage in Cahuenga Pass, eating the simple meals prepared by Constance, riding to work with Cecilia behind him in the saddle, avoiding all social life, austerely devoted to work, though always sparing some time to play with Cecilia and tuck her into bed. He enjoyed this Spartan existence, evidently feeling himself to be something of a Western pioneer, and the caravan trips to location were a great joy; he felt like an early settler, a quietly martial commander of a wagon train, with his standard line of five trucks, three cars, and a few actual wagons for the period scenes. At camp, he was something of a solitary while his cast and crew reveled in fireside stories; by the light of a hurricane lamp he would withdraw to his tent at sundown, poring over the next day's script pages line by line, his meals brought in to him on a tray.

For the summer, Jesse and Bessie Lasky returned to join the young film-making group; thereafter, they traveled frequently between the coasts, often renting private cars for the purpose. When Lasky came back to Hollywood, he had great difficulty in finding it; the taxi driver had never heard of it. Finally Lasky just said, "Drive me down Vine Street until you see a barn," and he reached his destination just as DeMille walked out with the company for a lunch break.

That September, DeMille adopted the five-year-old, handsome but delicate foundling son of a man called Ralph Gonzales, and called him John. Constance had been told by doctors she could not have any more children. She had withdrawn primly from the marriage bed, and she felt, with Cecilia, that Cecilia should have a little brother. John was welcomed as one of their own.

That fall, Jesse ordered—reluctantly, and under protest from the tree-loving Bessie—the grove adjoining the barn cut down and replaced by a glass stage measuring one hundred by eighty feet, and a plant for making all the props needed. He also acquired a lease of twenty thousand acres outside the city, dubbing it the Lasky Ranch. This magnificent site included almost everything that could be needed for a picture production: six thousand-foot mountains, capped with snow and fringed with forests of fir and pine, desert with picturesque cactus, a street that could be used for a variety of purposes. He bought forty head of horse, ordered them trained to take heavy falls, engaged ropers and crack riflemen, and tested more in the Keene Camps area of San Jacinto, including several former members of the Texas Rangers. By the time he returned early in December 1914 to New York, four companies were shooting simultaneously: DeMille was making *The Girl of the Golden West*, Oscar Apfel *Cameo Kirby*, Frederick Thompson *The Goose Girl*, and George Melford *Young Romance*. Contrary to the depressed figures of the theater world, Lasky found the movie people boisterous and full of beans. "It was the only place where I could get away from the moans of show business," he told the *New York Telegraph.*

On September 30, 1914, William deMille had finally broken his promise and left for Hollywood to join his brother, and to head the scenario department there. Interviewed at the railroad station while changing trains in Chicago, he announced that he would also be involved in Cecil's film production of his play *The Warrens of Virginia.*

When William arrived, Cecil was at the Lasky Ranch shooting *The Rose of the Rancho*, with the gifted stage actress Bessie Barriscale, later to make a great hit in the Thomas Ince company. He sent Constance to greet his brother, who, after checking into the Hollywood Hotel, immediately drove up to the ranch. William was astonished to see Cecil, in sunglasses, blue flannel pants and puttees, absolutely covered in dirt and sweat, while around him was a scene that looked as though time had slipped a notch: a group of women in floppy hats and crinolines, sitting exhausted in the sun sipping pink lemonade. Cecil's greeting to William was: "Here, Bill, put on one of these cowboy rigs and get on a horse. We need an extra man for the attack of the Gringos." William noted that Bessie Barriscale also looked marvelous: she had been the star of one of his earliest plays at the Twenty-eighth Street Theatre. One by one, various old friends from Broadway days emerged from the shade of a tree to shake his hand. Uniformly dirty, brown-skinned and wild-haired, they were barely recognizable. At the end of the day everybody showered in hastily-rigged-up canvas showers, changed into sporting clothes, and climbed into their Model-Ts or more elaborate autos for the twenty-mile ride back to Hollywood. Next day, Cecil showed William his office, and soon after that he was told to whip up a script for a new film in two weeks.

It was while making *The Rose of the Rancho* that DeMille met the woman who, more than any other, was to influence his work as a film maker and who was to capture his sexual interest more intensely than anyone else at the time: the film actress, writer, and director Jeanie Macpherson. She was in every way a remarkable woman: courageous, forceful, fierce-tempered, dominating, the very exemplar of the qualities DeMille most admired in anyone. Her life up to the time she met him had been a brave struggle against circumstances which would have crushed a weaker character. Born in Boston in 1887, she was of mixed French, Scottish, and Spanish descent. Her family was wiped out financially just as she was completing an expensive schooling at a lycée in Paris. She had shown some ability as a singer and dancer, and managed to obtain work as a teenage member of the chorus at the Chicago Opera House. Later, she worked in a very minor role in the Sir Johnston Forbes-Robertson company of *Cleopatra* both in New York and on an extensive tour. She was almost continuously out of work after that, living in extremely reduced circumstances in order to pay for singing lessons. A slightly better role in support of Robert Edeson in *Strongheart* was encouraging; and, astonishingly, she even managed to secure a feature role in the musical production of *Havana* on Broadway, starring James T. Powers. Her immense will power triumphed over only moderate abilities as singer and actress; she even managed to barge her way into D. W. Griffith's flourishing new Biograph Studio in New York. When he refused to see her, she sent him a letter which read: "I want a job. If you catch me on a Scotch day I will make money for you, and if you catch me on a French day I will act for you." Intrigued, he telephoned her himself and asked which day it was now. She replied: "A French day." He said: "Put on a pretty dress and come over here." She had a masochistic streak, enjoying the agony of shooting. One of her favorite phrases was, "Only a thoroughbred can take a good whipping."

She appeared in minor roles in a number of Griffith productions, moving to Universal when she received a slightly better offer. There, in Hollywood, she wrote her first script for a Western entitled *The Tarantula.* When the print was destroyed in a fire, and the director went to New York, Universal told her she could direct a new version from her memory of the original.

It was not beyond her powers. By now, her character had been firmly developed. An emancipate, she took on men as her equals in the life-struggle. Though not quite beautiful, and somewhat frumpish and mannish in her dress, she still had considerable allure: her flashing blue eyes, electric personality, and air of being totally available worked effectively on the men with whom she dealt. The suggestion she gave of a school marm who underneath pulsed with the vitality of a real woman, of a perennial virgin asking to be relieved of her virginity, earned her immediate professional success.

This was fortunate, because her talents were extremely limited. When she met DeMille, she decided to capture him with all of the considerable skill at her command. Knowing that he loved a quarrel, and that he had a passion for moral courage, she decided the only way to interest him was to infuriate him. She made arrangements to shoot a scene of *The Tarantula* when he was laying out sequences of *The Rose of the Rancho* in the same area. He received a note from her saying, "Kindly vacate at once. J. Macpherson." He sent a note back by the same messenger, "Go chase yourself." Next day, she arrived at the barn and told him to get out of the area he had invaded. He refused, and when her unit turned up, he had his men chase them off with shotguns.

When *The Tarantula* was finished, Jeanie was out of work. She decided at once to seek a job from DeMille himself.

She returned angrily to the barn (he described her later as "a funny little tornado with a nose that turned up, and hair that curled up, and a disposition that turned up, too"). She behaved rather as though DeMille were a butler whom she was considering for a job. She acted as though seeking work with him was the greatest possible way of flattering him and that she was the greatest actress in the world. He listened to everything she had to say without glancing up. Finally he gave her a brief flickering regard, and continued with his work. She finally lost her temper, shouted "Well!" and slammed out. Two days later she returned, swept into the office and shouted, "I'd like you to apologize to me for your rudeness the other day!" DeMille stood up and told her exactly what he thought of her. She told him she had written him a letter attacking his brutishness. Then she stormed out again.

A third time she returned, and informed DeMille that if he knew what was good for him, he would at once send her to Europe as his permanent representative. He told her that instead he would engage her at twenty-five dollars a week to take dictation in longhand. She raged and stormed until at last he managed to quiet her with, "Well if you really want to act for me, I'll give you just one day's work." She accepted. At the end of the first day's work, he gave her a ten dollar check, double the usual rate. She burst into his office yet again, flung the ten dollar check on his desk, and screamed, "My price is one hundred dollars or nothing!" "Then it's nothing," DeMille snapped, and put the check in his pocket. Finally, after a series of battles, she accepted the job of longhand stenographer at the twenty-five dollars a week he had offered her in the first place.

He began by dictating a scenario to her. Every few minutes she would stop him and say, "But you can't do that—you must do it this way." Bit by bit, he became aware of her dramatic insight, calling her "You clever little devil." Finally he gave her the chance to help with the script of *The Unafraid*. She brought it in, and he told her, "You write like a plumber!" She rewrote the script six times until it satisfied him. Within six months she was writing late into every night, dropping with physical exhaustion on the floor of his office.

The reason she had accepted the job of stenographer in the first place was, of course, in order to seduce her celebrated employer. We may well imagine what occurred when she was collected off the office floor and tenderly laid out on an available bench or sofa. At all events, by mid-1915, the romance was the talk of the studio. Jeanie's office was next to DeMille's, a fact which scandalized Los Angeles. He also stopped over at the Ambassador Hotel with her, and she was a frequent guest at his home. Fiery, passionate, difficult, they were locked together from the outset. Their quarrels were bitter and long, but they loved each other deeply. It was an extraordinary professional and personal association, the most profound and piercing of DeMille's life.

Late in 1914, DeMille was seemingly producing and directing a film every month. When he "produced" it simply meant that, every few hours, he would take a break to work on a new script and another director, usually Oscar Apfel, would handle the actual shooting which DeMille had drawn up. It says something of his intense energy at the time that between cutting sessions on other pictures he found it possible to direct much of *The Ghost Breaker*, the American cinema's first feature-length ghost comedy, about the mishaps of a Kentuckian amateur sleuth, Warren Jarvis (H. B. Warner), who goes to a haunted castle in Spain to investigate the disappearance of various heirs to a fortune. With the aid of Buckland, DeMille and Oscar Apfel brilliantly re-created a whole Gothic ambience: a sinister crypt, a shadowy winding staircase, and a paneled library, the panels of which slid back to disclose an extraordinary, cobwebbed labyrinth of stone corridors. Asked by the director how money

Fannie Ward and Sessue Hayakawa in The Cheat (*1915*).

Fannie Ward in The Cheat (*1915*).
(*Note Alvin Wyckoff's "Lasky Lighting."*)

Jeanie Macpherson, Constance, DeMille, and Lasky
(*trip to New York, 1919*).

could be found to illustrate a sea voyage, DeMille simply snapped "Show the funnel," and an assistant was sent to San Pedro to shoot the funnel of a departing President Line ship.

The opening scenes of *The Ghost Breaker*, showing a ghost at large, were superbly achieved in double exposure, pointing the way to the treatment of phantom presences in many films to come. DeMille's insistence on realism almost shocked Lasky: in a scene in which Warner was trapped in a dungeon, DeMille had water coming through cracks in the floor and actual rats crawling all over Warner's body. The "rats" were found by the prop man, Bill Bowers, after a two-day search in downtown Los Angeles. Actually, as DeMille later discovered to his annoyance, they were large white mice, dramatically painted black.

Late in 1914, DeMille began to pour out new movies with the regularity of a conveyor belt. He directed *What's His Name?* in which Cecilia DeMille appeared as a little girl who brings together a warring couple in New York State; and *The Man from Home* with Anita King, shot on location near San Francisco. More elaborate and ambitious, *The Girl of the Golden West* and *The Warrens of Virginia* made a magnificent pair of Westerns. They were followed by a string of less successful films, in one of which—*The Wild Goose Chase*—Ina Claire, fresh out of the Ziegfeld Follies, destined to be one of the great Broadway comediennes, was utterly wasted as a runaway heiress. All she remembers of her role is running round and round a block in the dusty Hollywood streets, getting sorer, hotter, and dirtier by the minute.

Ina Claire detested DeMille, and the feeling was mutual. But his most harrowing experiences in 1915 were with the tempestuous Fannie Ward, the legendary beauty whom London and New York society had taken to their collective bosoms, and for whom he had had a special vehicle, *The Cheat*, expressly written by Hector Turnbull.

The Cheat was a beautifully constructed story of a deceitful woman. Edith Hardy is a worthless social butterfly, who gambles on the stock market with charity funds. When the money is lost, she is terrified of confessing its disappearance to her husband. A wealthy Burmese ivory king, Hara Arakau, lends her ten thousand dollars to compel her to sleep with him. When her husband gives her that exact sum, she tries to return it to escape from her bargain, but the ivory king turns on her and brands her. She shoots him, but only wounds him in the arm. Her husband assumes the charge of attempted murder, but Edith confesses her guilt in court. Hara Arakau is nearly lynched by the spectators.

Fannie Ward was born Fanny Buchanan in St. Louis in a year officially given as 1878*; she had been taken up by London society when she made her debut there in 1894. Her famous jewelry collection was valued at half a million dollars. DeMille hired her chiefly because she was the epitome of the "socially accepted" actress, and her part called for a society woman who is threatened with absolute ruin. He cast her with the gifted Japanese actor Sessue Hayakawa. When he drove over to her cream stucco villa in Hollywood and offered her the role, she said: "But Mr. DeMille, I am a comedienne. I have never played emotional roles." He told her: "Which is exactly the reason I want you to play in *The Cheat.*" As he had planned, that put her on her mettle, and she accepted; what she had not realized, of course, was that another reason he had cast her as *The Cheat* was because he was convinced after seeing her at parties and on the screen that she was very deceitful.

DeMille found Miss Ward far from amusing to work with. Considerably older than her published age, her face was so caked in makeup, which she adamantly refused to remove, that it was only with the greatest difficulty she could be photographed to look like a real woman. Her hair was vividly dyed blonde—an affectation DeMille found intolerable. She affected "baby vamp" mannerisms then fashionable, while being neither a baby nor a vamp. Her spoiled, ferocious tantrums drove him

* It was actually 1872.

beyond endurance, and whenever she gave an interview she contrived to say nothing of interest to the interviewers at all.

Miss Ward quarreled incessantly with Sessue Hayakawa. Thirty-five years later he told Fred Watkins, a writer for *Films in Review* (June–July 1956): "It was a pleasure to brand Fannie Ward. . . . She was very temperamental, complained about everything, and treated Jesse Lasky like a prop boy."

She insisted on having an entire wardrobe designed, not by Claire West, DeMille's designer, but by Martial Armond of Paris. Worse still, her husband, Jack Dean, interferred constantly with work on the picture, and—though he had only a modicum of ability—insisted DeMille hire him as her co-star.

Despite the problems of shooting, *The Cheat* was a brilliant success. Supported by Alvin Wyckoff's careful lighting, with burning white faces shot against intense darkness, the director brought off many extraordinary scenes: the branding, the shooting of the ivory king, his figure outlined in shadow against a paper screen stained with blood, the astonishing trial scene, horrific in its impact, cathartic in its final release. As the heroine and her Burmese suitor, Fannie Ward and Sessue Hayakawa were staggeringly good.

As if Miss Ward were not enough of a problem, Sessue Hayakawa proved difficult too. His bull-pup, Shoki, meaning "Destruction," had an alarming tendency to follow its master to the studio, invade the set, and bark at the players. Hayakawa objected constantly to the character he was playing, correcting DeMille maddeningly on details of Burmese clothing, etiquette, and behavior. DeMille pacified him by praising his previous films: *The Typhoon* and *The Wrath of the Gods*.

After completing *The Cheat*, DeMille at last found a house that seemed worthy of his growing reputation. He was saving thousands out of his share of profits arrangements with the studio, and his virtually untaxed thousand-dollar-a-week salary, of which he had frugally preserved almost two thirds. It seemed time to invest in a home. The new house was high up in an area called Laughlin Park, in the Los Feliz district of East Holly-wood, about thirty minutes from the studio. The park had been named after Laughlin, a dry goods man, who had made a fortune downtown and had bought the hill with its beautiful plantings of fir and pine for subdivision, supervising the building of houses for various prominent citizens. The agent who negotiated the sale was Charles E. Toberman, a brilliant young real estate man.* Toberman drove over to DeMille's office at the Lasky Studio and described to him glowingly the beauties of Laughlin Park. DeMille went up that weekend with Constance to have a look, and they fell in love with the landscaped slopes, the house with its handsome colonial pillared portico, and above all the enormous conifers which DeMille adored. He paid $27,893 for it, payable over ten years. They spent months furnishing it in the slightly dramatic, baroque style DeMille favored. He began to hire a household of servants. Frederick, the butler, was an inestimable help, but some of the servants proved unreliable: a French chef ran off with the chambermaid, a cook from the Philippines chased the milkman with a knife and had to be let go. It was years before a suitable complement to Frederick appeared, and proved to be a pillar of the household: Marie, the excellent and indomitable cook.

In addition to the splendid home in Laughlin Park, DeMille bought a place called "Paradise," snuggled in the Sierra Madres just off Little Tujunga Canyon. It had six hundred acres of farmland, where he raised alfalfa, apricots, apples, grapes, and peaches. Following a fire which destroyed part of the property in 1916, he built magnificent cabins for himself and his family, and a redwood guesthouse, constructed so skilfully that two giant oaks put their branches through the roof and formed pillars in the living room. A mountain lion prowled continu-ously through the grounds, deer nibbled the crops—but De-

* Toberman is still alive at the age of ninety-two, with over forty million dollars in Hollywood property in his hands.

Mille would not allow them to be shot—and chickens and geese kept up a constant din. The clubhouse was superbly designed by Wilfred Buckland: the living room was sixty by thirty feet, furnished in Indian style, with a huge stone fireplace. The furniture was made of logs, Navajo Indian blankets were strewn vividly about, the lights were arranged up genuine giant totem poles. A victrola had three thousand records. Later an Aztec pipe organ was installed at a cost of twenty-five thousand dollars, each pipe painted and carved with Aztec bas-reliefs. The walls were decorated with trophies—a moose head from Canada, a grizzly, the head of a prize-winning swordfish. After guests had a hike and a swim in the pool, tables were brought in by cohorts of servants and chairs lined up on either side for a resplendent feast. The place had no telephone; after all, there were no telephones in Paradise itself, were there?

At the same time, DeMille bought a beautiful locomobile—dove-gray, with red leather seats—which he loved to drive himself to the studio; Constance always used a chauffeur, but he always eschewed one. He liked to chug up to the Lasky barn, startle extras cuddling in the orange grove with his horn, and then yell a friendly and encouraging greeting to them as he roared past leaving a powerful trail from the exhaust. Years after the locomobile had seen its best days, he insisted upon using it.

Constance ran the household at Laughlin Park with meticulous skill and flair. Refusing him access to her own bed, she bore DeMille's romantic liaisons with absolutely saintly tolerance. Each morning she rose early and prepared the menus, drawing up a long list of matters to be attended to. Meals were strictly punctual. Though neither she nor DeMille attended church, they preserved a severely Christian household in which DeMille ruled like a benign despot. Often—after 1919 three times a week—films were run after dinner, not always suitable for young children, though both John and Cecilia seemed impervious to the horrors that occasionally flashed across the screen. They laughed hysterically at the posturings of stars like Valentino, and were even irreverent about the behavior of a woman many believed to be Lasky's mistress, Agnes Ayres.

Entertaining, at that time and later, was strictly a family affair. DeMille detested social gatherings and almost never hobnobbed with visiting aristocracy, authors, composers, or—except when, like Dustin Farnum and Wallace Reid, he counted them among his personal friends—movie stars. He loved holidays, because they meant immense and joyful gatherings of every available member of the DeMille clan. They would sit around the fire, aged from eight to eighty, playing complicated games, matching up in intelligence tests, laughing uproariously in paper hats. It was in these glowing evenings that he could forget the grinding misery of film making and the boring, exhausting pressures from Lasky and Zukor in the East.

Jeanie Macpherson was the one interloper in the house, an oddly formidable, forceful figure, with her hair Scottishly prim in spring-tight coils about the ears, flat, glossy, black, and parted down the left side as precisely as a schoolboy's. The children used to giggle uncontrollably when she came into a room and said something in her sharp, school-mistressy voice. DeMille was speechless with fury when that happened, but Constance sat quietly, her lovely hands folded, and concentrated grimly on some invisible object right in front of her nose.

Throughout 1916 there was a great deal of concern about the running of the studio workshops. The extreme pressure of work told on the men, and Wilfred Buckland was forced to write DeMille an urgent series of memoranda on this. On July 31, 1917, he wrote to DeMille: "The men in this department are almost universally dissatisfied, discontented, disheartened. For the time being the *esprit de corps* of these men which made the reputation of the Lasky Studio what it is, has been practically lost. One of the many indications of this is the incident of last Sunday, when forty of our regular mechanics who had been called to work found some excuse for failing to appear."

Buckland was also deeply unhappy: he wrote in a memorandum (November 30, 1917): "I came to the Hollywood studio
under a *serious misapprehension.* I was seeking an opportunity to
picturize in a more 'painter-like' manner, supplying to Motion
Pictures the same rules which govern the higher art of painting.
This my life-long association with artists, coupled with thirty
years' stage experience as actor, stage manager and producer
peculiarly qualified me to attempt." He went on to point out
that he had accepted a lowly seventy-five dollars which in all
the boom years since December 1913 had not been increased
by one cent; he pointed out that he had refused several offers
for work by others; but he insisted on having a say in the way
that figures were shot, in their grouping and lighting. "Had I
known I was wanted merely to design sets, I would never have
joined the company, but would have sought the opportunity I
wanted elsewhere." From the receipt of that letter on, relations
between DeMille and Buckland were extremely strained, and in
1920 DeMille relieved him peremptorily of his post.

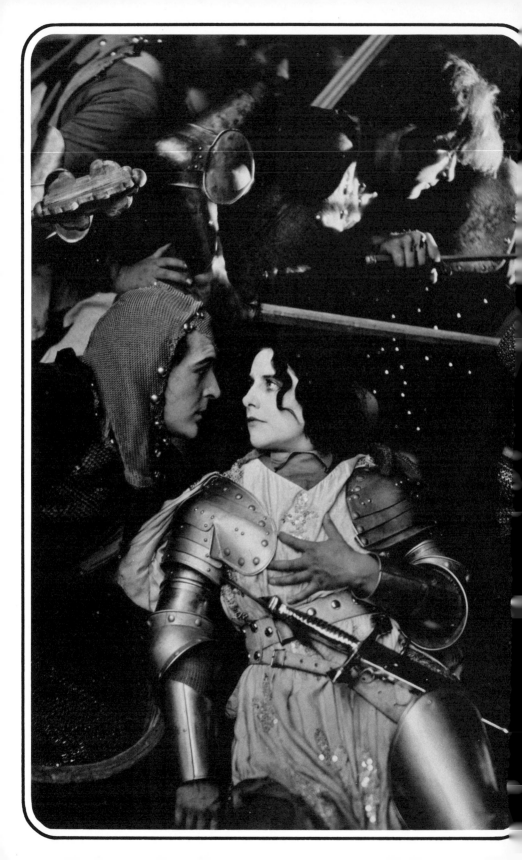

3

Gerry

The most important event of 1917 was the filming of *Joan the Woman*, with Geraldine Farrar. The great opera star had made pictures with DeMille in 1915 and 1916: *Maria Rosa, Carmen,* and *Temptation.*

Miss Farrar had been talked into the idea of Hollywood by the distinguished theatrical manager Morris Gest one Sunday night in the winter of 1914 at a party in her house at 1 West Seventy-fourth Street in midtown Manhattan. Gest said casually, and all too aware of what 10 per cent of movie earnings meant, "The only way to live forever is on the motion picture screen." She drew Gest aside and said: "I have seen some motion pictures and I am very impressed. Let's talk it over."

DeMille chiaroscuro: Wallace Reid and
Geraldine Farrar in Joan the Woman.

Seizing on the fact that her recording of *Carmen* had sold over a million copies, Gest suggested that story would be the ideal subject for her film. After a discussion that went on for most of one night, she agreed. Gest called Jesse L. Lasky for a luncheon appointment at the Hotel Astor. They talked about Farrar for several hours. That night, the two men went to the Met to see her in *Madame Butterfly.* At a late night supper at the Knickerbocker, Gest said suddenly: "What would you say if I told you that I could get Miss Farrar for your photoplays?"

"I should say that you were a liar," Lasky replied.

"Well, what would you do if I *could* get her?"

"You put the question wrongly. What *wouldn't* I do?"

At that moment, according to Gest, Lasky said that he wouldn't pay Miss Farrar by the month, the week, or the day, but by the minute. "You can tell her that for every minute of daylight she is in Southern California, whether she is at the studio or not, I will pay her two dollars—and a royalty, and a share of all profits." Gest walked to 1 West Seventy-fourth Street in a jubilant mood to convey the news. Miss Farrar said: "It's done—if you'll have someone play me three themes from Rimsky-Korsakov's *Scheherazade* every day on the train to California."

A few weeks later Miss Farrar and her entourage set out for Hollywood. Included in the party was the celebrated young New York man-about-town Jimmy Sullivan, who was brought along partly to give sexual satisfaction to the star, and partly to provide endless piano performances in the private car. He played the piano almost constantly during the journey, providing Miss Farrar with an uninterrupted flow of jazz melodies as well as the obligatory Rimsky-Korsakov. Clad only in a *negligée,* the star frequently astonished her companions by climbing on top of the Bechstein grand and performing an expert buck-and-wing while Sullivan vamped away in fast ragtime. After some hours of this, a brakeman, who had joined the train while it crossed the Arizona desert and was standing on the rear platform of the car, was heard to say loudly to himself: "Is that dame nutty?"

At times, Miss Farrar changed from jazzy abandon to bursts of temperamental rage: the dust that blew through the windows, the burning cinders and blast-furnace heat of summer drove her beyond endurance, and her language was enough to embarrass a storm trooper. She was mollified, though, when she arrived in Los Angeles and found a red carpet sprinkled with flowers at the station, a large chorus of school children singing a greeting, and the Los Angeles Mayor stepping forward to shake her hand and lead her to the magnificent Hispano-Suiza which awaited her.

Over the protestations of Lasky and Goldfish, DeMille insisted on casting her, not in *Carmen* at once, but in *Maria Rosa* opposite a fine actor, the tall and handsome Wallace Reid. *Carmen* would be made next, and released first. The reasons were twofold: DeMille felt that if Miss Farrar plunged straight into *Carmen* she would simply be too "large" in her approach, too operatic for the screen in a role she had made famous on the opera stage. Also there was the problem of a possible breach of copyright of Bizet's opera, since the owners of the Bizet estate were demanding an immense sum for its use: finally, rights to the Merimée novel were obtained by Lasky for a much more rational figure, and no material from Bizet was used.

Despite the rude remarks of *Photoplay* which greeted her on her arrival ("The Mona Lisa without her smile; a Stradivarius without its strings; children of a deaf and dumb institute at play"), Miss Farrar adored Hollywood. DeMille entertained her at Laughlin Park and walked her through his gardens. She was given a lavish bungalow surrounded by two acres of lovely lawns, as well as a special dressing suite at the studio with private reception rooms, dressing room, and bathroom, the walls hung with chiffon drapes and Venetian mirrors. Since she refused to be watched while she was working, a private corridor led from her rooms to the closed set. Her contract specified that she would not work more than six hours a day, the period to be broken into morning and afternoon sessions of three hours each, with two hours at midday for a complete rest. DeMille was exasperated by this arrangement, but could do nothing about it: Lasky's word was law. His frequent cables of complaint were cheerfully ignored.

Despite her own, and DeMille's, pious declarations to the contrary, from the moment Geraldine Farrar arrived in Hollywood she was as fiery and difficult as at any of her rehearsals with Toscanini in New York. After expressing delight with her dressing rooms, she declared them unsuitable for a lady of her station and had a complete bungalow redesigned by Wilfred Buckland. She fought bitterly with Jeanie Macpherson, demanding—to DeMille's extreme annoyance—endless changes in her scripts. Her servants at the house Lasky had so expensively rented for her were replaced almost every week. She deliberately outraged Hollywood by courting and winning an equally temperamental, but quite untalented actor, Lou Tellegen, who had been Bernhardt's lover and co-star, and had the body of an Adonis.

Miss Farrar's main—and most justified—cause of complaint as she began vigorously playing in *Maria Rosa* was the makeup then used in motion pictures. She had to wear ghastly white grease paint, with an overlay of Rachel powder, and garish blue or green eye shadow. Her lips had to be white. The primitive Klieg lights were so ferociously hot that her eyes swelled up and streamed, forcing her to retire to a darkened room for hours. Dressing her for the part of Maria Rosa was an anguish for DeMille: he had to avoid all white, because it reflected the light with an intolerable harshness; silver and gilt ornaments had to be covered in a special cream which prevented severe reflections. Everything had to be in soft pastel shades. Worst problem of all, when he ran Geraldine Farrar's first rushes he was horrified to see that her gray eyes completely disappeared as the film would not register them. "I had the sightless orbs," she wrote in her memoirs *Such Sweet Compulsion,* "of a Greek statue." DeMille called her in to see the dreadful sight, and she screamed with rage, literally clawing at the screen. DeMille managed to pacify her—just—by promising her an improvement in the next day's shooting. He had his assistant director hold a square of black velvet behind the camera, and this prevented the eyes from getting washed out. But she still looked as though she were completely toothless when she was smiling.

It was during the shooting of *Carmen* that Miss Farrar introduced a custom which was to be the rage of Hollywood. She had been so used to singing the role that she felt it would help her if she could have Bizet's score played to her during the playing of the scenes. DeMille was terrified that Bizet's relatives might get wind of this, invade the set, and charge breach of copyright—even though, in a sense, the performance was "private." So he instructed the pianist Melville Ellis to play some other of the star's favorite numbers, mostly in the field of jazz, while she acted the scenes.

During the shooting of *Carmen,* DeMille devised a brilliant dramatic idea. Knowing that Jeanie hated Geraldine, he decided to give her the chance of a lifetime and cast her as Geraldine's rival for the hand of the handsome Don José. In a tobacco factory scene, the two women indulged in a ferocious leg-biting, hair-pulling, and scratching duel. Unfortunately, though, the plan backfired. DeMille had forgotten—despite the visual evidence staring him in the face—that Miss Farrar had the biceps of a champion wrestler. She almost mangled Jeanie, who came out of the fight weeping, bleeding, and looking as though she had just fallen into a bear pit.

DeMille's methods of directing became thoroughly sophisticated with the Geraldine Farrar films. He discussed with his star and supporting players the meaning of the scene, then instead of rehearsing them, told them to behave spontaneously, living rather than "acting" the parts. He knew instinctively that screen acting was "being," not "performing" in a theatrical sense. In later years Miss Farrar wrote in her memoirs, her problems with the director forgotten, "Mr. DeMille understood my enthusiasm and left me free to express natural impulses whenever my feeling prompted them. The experience was wholly enjoyable, and the gay studio crowds, the departures to the woods and parks for 'location' scenes, took on the delight of a picnic outing. After the responsibility of a long singing season and anxiety over a troublesome and delicate larynx, this was a carefree haven indeed for me."

Joan the Woman, the story of Joan of Arc, was the most ambitious of the DeMille/Farrar films, a masterpiece of dramatic action. DeMille had only three weeks of preparation on the picture, two of which were consumed in reading, which left only one week to prepare the rough synopsis of the scenario. In addition to this, he had to place a costume order consisting of 43,300 items, and, with Jeanie Macpherson, supervise every one of them for authenticity. Once into the picture he shot from ten A.M. to seven P.M. each day, attended from seven to eight P.M. to the business of the day, dined at eight, and then worked on the scenario from eight to one A.M. He wrote to Lasky on July 12, 1916: "Macpherson is doing splendid work on the scenario and Wyckoff is outdoing himself on the photography. All departments are keyed up to the highest pitch." He was again aggravated by Farrar: after agreeing to postpone shooting for two weeks because of extra work, she then announced that she expected to be paid for the lost time, and demanded—and got—ten thousand dollars. DeMille wrote in the same letter to Lasky: "She seems to have lost a little something of the great spark of genius that animated her last year . . . also, she has gotten pretty plump." In addition to the problems of the picture, he was constantly quarreling with his brother William who, he felt, was incompetent. There was also the vexation of a very difficult merger of the studio with the coldly brilliant showman Adolph Zukor's Famous Players in New York that month. The situation in the scenario department on both coasts was desperate, with a number of writers fired after bitter quarrels, and enormous difficulties experienced in finding new ones. Nearing collapse, Lasky took off that summer for a hunting and canoeing trip, and when he got back DeMille reported that things were worse than ever. Tension increased in September because Adolph Zukor refused to work with Sam Goldfish at all, and told Lasky point blank that he would have to choose between them. Lasky studied them carefully, weighed the situation, and decided to dislodge Goldfish. On September 14, Goldfish resigned, sparing Lasky the unpleasant necessity of asking DeMille to vote against him.*

Despite everything, though, DeMille pressed on with the production of *Joan* in July and August. With Alvin Wyckoff, he spent several weeks developing the largest motion picture camera used up till that time. Capable of shooting in deep focus, with foreground and background objects equally clear in the same shot (some twenty-five years before deep focus was supposedly invented by Gregg Toland for Orson Welles' *Citizen Kane*), the camera could also encompass, with its wide-angle lenses, a magnificent panoramic view of the events. These covered several miles of the Lasky Ranch, where, with Wilfred Buckland's indispensable help, DeMille built villages, towers, castles, and a replica of Rheims Cathedral, all taken from photographs which his business manager John H. Fisher had obtained in France. Many of the weapons, and the model of the armor worn by Joan, were bought at enormous expense from museums. DeMille insisted—with Wyckoff's enthusiastic support and over the demurs of others at the studio—on shooting night for night, using double exposure effects for the visions which seized Joan, and actually placing the star in close proximity to fire for the final burning scene. Hand-tinted scenes were beautiful in their lyricism: a glade lanced with golden sunlight where Joan drove her sheep, actual moonlight shots

* Zukor's power grew by degrees, and within a year he was controlling the weaker Lasky's every move.

Alvin Wyckoff with Cecil on Joan the Woman.

The Inquisitors: Joan the Woman.

Geraldine Farrar in Joan the Woman.

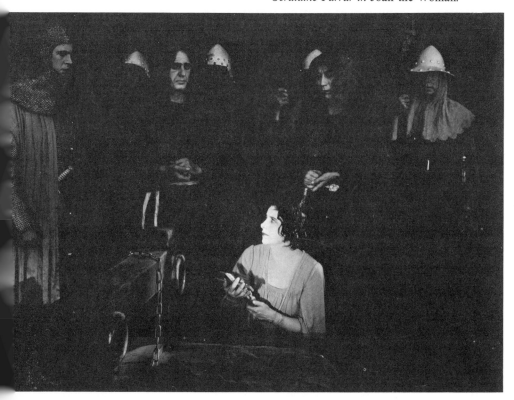

Jeanie on location: The Little American.

tinted an eerie pale blue-gray, the leaping crimson flames of the finale. When Joan sees the French army raise one thousand swords manfully in honor of her, the hand tinting created the effect of burning white light emerging from silver blades. Scenes had a sickly green or purple tint as masses of men struggled in a muddy, verminous moat, or fell, pierced by authentic period arrows, from their high ladders placed against the castle walls.

Jeanie Macpherson did not hesitate to show Joan as a vulnerable woman, longing for sexual fulfillment from the soldier she loves, but deliberately rejecting him in favor of serving Christ. Her forewarning of her own death was brilliantly created by both writer and director: Joan shrinks from fire every time she sees it. As she rides through a green glade, a deathly gray figure of Azrael accompanies her, unseen by her bodyguard. But the greatest stroke of genius occurs at the end. We see the square where Joan is to be burned absolutely empty, at daybreak. Gradually, the screen begins to shine with gold, as pale sunbeams creep across the monochrome cobblestones of the square. A carter appears, dragging some sticks. One by one he places them around the stake. Gradually a few people start to arrive, a mother with her children, two lovers, an old man hobbling on a crutch. They have come to see the burning. And in a cell not far away, Joan is more woman than saint, paralyzed with fear at what is to come.

The film was notable for its introduction of the telephone as an aid to the direction of scenes. To prepare fourteen hundred men in a battle scene spread over twelve acres DeMille had twelve assistant directors equipped with a standard operator set each, a device which enabled him to communicate with them at every part of the field. As a result, he was able to trim the rehearsal time from two days to eighty minutes.

One problem during shooting was that Miss Farrar—who was hefty enough to wear a suit of armor—was terrified of horses. She had to be lifted, in a near fainting condition, on and off her mount, her horror of being on a saddle increasing when she had to carry, not only a massive broadsword, but a heavy fleur-de-lys banner as well. On one occasion, when the trumpets sounded for the beginning of a scene—a dramatic stroke DeMille thenceforth adopted as a standard for many of his silent films—the horses galloped off, leaving her hanging in ungainly fashion from her saddle. The actor Jack Holt, an expert horseman, followed her across the Lasky ranch, reigning her terrified horse to a halt. As a result of this mishap, DeMille used a fine horsewoman, Pansy Perry, for all the long shots of Joan in action. But the scenes of siege, with Joan scaling a ladder in armor with the immense banner held high, were still an endurance test for the temperamental star.

During the attack of the army on the fortress of La Tourelle, DeMille, to ensure authenticity, offered a bonus to the English if they captured Joan and to the French if they prevented the capture. The English won. During the fight, one of the French, ardently protecting the star, accidentally knocked her helmet off with his broadsword. That night a delegation of French and English soldiers threw the offender into the air in a blanket three times. DeMille also offered a bonus to any man who could fall in full armor off a forty-foot wall into a moat. No one volunteered. That night DeMille said laughingly to Miss Farrar in her dressing room: "I guess the men are afraid to do it. We will have to cut that scene." He was overheard; that night twenty-five extras sent him a note promising to fall off the parapet. If anything went wrong with the shot, they should forfeit the bonus. Next day two hundred men plunged off the wall, leaving nobody on the wall left to shoot.

Miss Farrar's worst ordeal was the burning at the stake. She was actually bound to it while the logs piled around it were set on fire. Her body had been soaked from head to feet in a special solution which rendered her fireproof, and she had cotton, soaked in ammonia, stuffed into her nostrils and mouth until she felt violently ill. For some shots she was placed in tanks filled with oil, which were also set on fire, but she was only slightly singed. She went through these severe ordeals with stoical courage, but at the end, when she saw the wooden figure representing her shrivel and burn as the flames reached it, she collapsed, dragged herself to her dressing room, and vomited again and again.

When she left Hollywood at the end of shooting, the star was given a magnificent present to which every single member of the cast and crew contributed: a mirror carrying a crest of fleur-de-lys, with a silver bas-relief of Joan of Arc on the handle and a complete list of every single person who worked on the picture. On the last day of shooting, she walked onto the set and was amazed to see every member of the cast lined up. DeMille called her attention to a disarranged strand of hair, and she asked Lucy, her maid, to bring a mirror. It was covered in a towel. When Lucy removed the towel, the star saw the superb gift. The scores of people on the stage applauded and cheered and she burst into tears, flinging her arms around her new husband, Lou Tellegen, as he emerged from her dressing room.

By October 1916, DeMille was happily engrossed in cutting *Joan the Woman,* and promised Lasky delivery by New Year's Day, 1917. He wrote jovially to Lasky on October 7: "I am awfully glad that you can come West for the running of *Joan.* At that time, we will go off somewhere and with a couple of pipes sit under a tree and I will tell you what I really think of you." Generally, though, the correspondence between the two men had grown so formal that Lasky scribbled at the foot of one letter (November 14, 1916): "How in H—are you anyway? This business stuff has surely 'got' me! Judging by the formal tone of our correspondence, when I meet you at the depot, it will be 'How do you do Mr. Lasky, Glad to see you, Mr. DeMille!' " Lasky was constantly feeling that the huge business of the new industry, the endless agony of finding writers and directors to cope with the boom, was driving him into becoming a gray, lifeless machine. DeMille commented on the foot of his reply of November 21: "I enjoyed the footnote on your letter received today. It is the first sign I have had in six months that you were a regular fellow. I was beginning to lose hope."

Lasky—with Zukor behind him—exasperated DeMille by forcing him to cut the picture down to eight reels, or eighty minutes, for general release following the mixed reception given by preview audiences in New York. DeMille suggested rather desperately in a letter to Whitman H. Bennett, a distribution executive of the Lasky office in New York (June 2, 1917): "In the strong Catholic communities, those scenes relating to the Catholic church might best be spared; while in Protestant portions of the country, it might be desirable to retain such scenes." But he begged for the retention of the World War I framework, in which a soldier in the trenches (Wallace Reid) dreams of his life with Joan long ago. Rather than going through the ordeal of cutting it himself, he asked that this be done in New York. His remarks reflected the savage criticism of the film by various Catholic groups across the country.

DeMille's great disappointment of 1917 was that *Joan the Woman* was not doing well. He suffered from fallen arches and general exhaustion, and was almost beside himself with distress. He constantly rampaged about Lasky's failure to promote the picture properly, but there was no gainsaying the fact that, despite ecstatic reviews, the picture simply was too artistic for the general public, and costume pictures were out of favor in 1917. In August, Lasky wrote that he had acquired *Old Wives for New,* a modern story which would provide a welcome change after the flop of *Joan.* DeMille said he was interested provided Farrar could have no possible role in it.

Aside from *Joan the Woman,* DeMille's main concern in 1917 was the Lasky contract star Mary Pickford. Jesse Lasky wrote to DeMille on January 11, saying that he had sent by Twentieth Century Mail a copy of the play *Rebecca of Sunnybrook Farm* as a probable vehicle for the star. He wrote: "We are to meet Pickford this afternoon and I will wire you the result of the interview. This much is certain—we will not allow her to go to the coast unless she consents to be managed and guided by you in everything pertaining to her plays as well as the choice of her stories." He strongly approved DeMille's idea of writing a Western for her, since "she has done about everything else." He indicated that the public was tiring of "typical Pickford stuff" and a change was needed. "This is a task really worthy of your steel and the same applies to Jeanie." He foresaw that the popularity of the star would wane, and "I trust I have aroused your fighting blood." On January 19, Lasky referred to a wire sent by Cecil offering, as well as the Western subject, a "modern story set somewhere in Belgium," but Lasky preferred the Western for the time being. At first DeMille found a subject based on the vigilantes, with Elliott Dexter in the lead.

Mary Pickford left for the coast on February 10, 1917. She was to receive eighty thousand dollars for eight weeks as against Farrar's twenty thousand dollars for the same period. Right up to her departure, Lasky was urging DeMille to make *Rebecca of Sunnybrook Farm,* but the suggestion was never adopted. Despite several attempts to lick the story, he and Jeanie were forced to give up. They recommended work on the vigilante story, called *Other Men's Shoes,* until Lasky ruled that out. Lasky also gave instructions that Miss Pickford must be kept on the coast, since if she were in the East her pictures would cost 40 per cent more. And anyway there was no room for her, as Lasky's studio at Fort Lee was jammed to capacity all summer. In March, Lasky was suggesting a story called *The American Girl,* intended to typify the spirit of the American girl in time of war, and adapted from a story called *The Girl of the First Empire,* which William deMille had picked up.

Mary Pickford quarreled with DeMille from the outset. He wrote to Lasky shortly after her arrival (February 19, 1917): "If she refuses to work we are convinced we have a perfect law suit against her for heavy damages, etc. We will instantly stop paying her immense weekly stipend, which will be a relief. She has eight months more under this contract and for that period we could get an injunction so that she would not work for anyone else. We feel that by the end of eight months we can get along without her and prefer to do so rather than give her a further increase of her salary which is of course the main object of her kicking up a row at this time."

From then on DeMille's experiences with Mary Pickford were considerably less than happy. She had established herself as the adorable sweetheart of every young man in America. Her power was absolute and beyond question, and DeMille was determined to make her bend to his will. It was not an easy task. *Other Men's Shoes* became *The Romance of the Redwoods*, shot in Northern California, near Santa Cruz, the story of a young orphan who joins her uncle there in the 1849 gold rush period. Miss Pickford objected to DeMille's ruthlessly unglamorous treatment of her. But he directed several sequences expertly: the wagon train attack at the beginning, in which Indians kill the girl's father; Mary playing a spinet in the lonely cabin in the redwoods; the scene in which she prays, illuminated by a single gas lamp. Wyckoff's lighting was consistently beautiful to watch. The second Pickford film, *The Little American*, was very elaborate: it encompassed the sinking of the *Lusitania*, magnificently achieved, scenes of World War I, and a romance in which the young girl is torn between American and German lovers. Although DeMille admired Miss Pickford's courage in the scene in which she struggles in a sinking ship among debris and confetti, shot off San Pedro, he continued to the end to be aggravated by her star mannerisms, and he was very happy indeed when the association terminated.

The United States' entry into war in 1917 caused DeMille to help form a Home Guard regiment, beginning with seventy-five men, all armed with guns, and recruited from the rank and file of the Lasky studio. DeMille was captain, William was top sergeant. The local authority under Captain T. E. Duncan issued the gallant little group uniforms, and at a special ceremony held on her return from *The Romance of the Redwoods* location, Mary Pickford presented the unit with a specially designed flag. In many cases members of the group went to serve on the Western Front. Few of them came back.

To DeMille's lasting regret he was not able to release himself for active duty. To the end of his life he regretted not having been able to serve on the Western Front.

Late in 1917, Geraldine Farrar returned to Hollywood for two new features, *The Woman God Forgot* and *The Devil Stone*. It was in *The Woman God Forgot* that DeMille first met and became closely bound to a great friend, Theodore Kosloff, who played an Aztec warrior. Kosloff had all of the qualities DeMille admired in a man. He was fearless and superbly built—limbs like those of a Michelangelo carving, and a flawless pair of shoulders. His noble profile and aristocratic bearing were almost overpowering. A Russian, formerly a brilliant ballet dancer who had danced with Nijinsky, he had formed his own company, and, falling in love with Los Angeles in 1915, set up a ballet school there. In *The Woman God Forgot* he was splendid as Guatemoc, a corruption of Guatemozin, an imperial warrior of the Incas, while Miss Farrar was Montezuma's daughter.

Still more importantly, DeMille featured in *The Woman God Forgot* a lovely, gentle young girl called Julia Faye, who played Geraldine Farrar's lady-in-waiting. Julia Faye, introduced to DeMille by Wallace Reid at a party earlier that year, fell in love with him at once, and he with her. Constance endured the situation with her usual saintly tolerance. Though she left Laughlin Park briefly that fall, saying she would come back when Miss Faye was no longer heard from, she decided against that move and returned humbly. Jeanie Macpherson was furious at Julia Faye's appearance on the scene, however. She and Julia quarreled constantly; at one stage Miss Macpherson threw an inkwell at her rival and it shattered into pieces on the wall of DeMille's office. Later, he put the entire scene into his film *Why Change Your Wife?*

Julia Faye was born in Richmond, Virginia, in 1894; she was raised in Chicago, and educated at the University of Illinois. She broke into movies in her teens, with no experience whatsoever; she succeeded in impressing D. W. Griffith at a casual screen test, and appeared in a bit role in *Intolerance*. Her powers of persuasion were so considerable that she managed— although not even achieving the cast list of *Intolerance*—to play the role of Dulcinella in Chester Withet's version, made in 1916, of *Don Quixote*, with De Wolf Hopper in the title role. She later joined the Mack Sennett Company, playing with a degree of charm and élan; she was drawn to DeMille's attention by a magazine article which unequivocally stated, "Miss Faye has the prettiest feet and ankles in America." Aside from her feet, she was not a beauty; but her Southern drawl, easy sophisticated manner, and great charm captivated DeMille, and from the moment he saw her feet, he was absolutely enslaved.

She had the utmost skill in soothing his savage breast in the years to come. Her wit, grace, and sheer style fascinated him, and she bore with great distinction the role of back street mistress, of a witty, beloved companion who must always be unable to obtain the blessing of the church on her relationship. DeMille, presumably, squared his conscience by telling himself that it would have been far crueller, as well as distinctly unwise, to divorce Constance; for some quarter of a century, Julia was in fact his spiritual as well as his physical wife, although almost no detail of their intimate relationship survives.

One aggravating thing happened during the filming of *The Woman God Forgot*. The last great battle on the teocalli, or Mexican step pyramid, described in the book which most inspired DeMille, Rider Haggard's *Montezuma's Daughter*, was extremely difficult to stage: so much so that even with his disdain for human weakness he was forced to have a doctor standing by, with an ambulance and a team of nurses and orderlies. When some of the players fell as though mortally injured, a group of socialites from New York began laughing hysterically. DeMille thrashed them verbally, and had them removed from the set.

After the unremarkable *The Devil Stone*, which wrote an inglorious finis to Miss Farrar's Hollywood career, DeMille turned to a new work, *The Whispering Chorus*. The stark plot of

Mary Pickford in Romance of the Redwoods.

Mary Pickford and Ben Alexander (age 6) in The Little American *(1917).*

With editor Anne Bauchens on the Catalina location for Male and Female. *Right: Thomas Meighan and Gloria Swanson.*

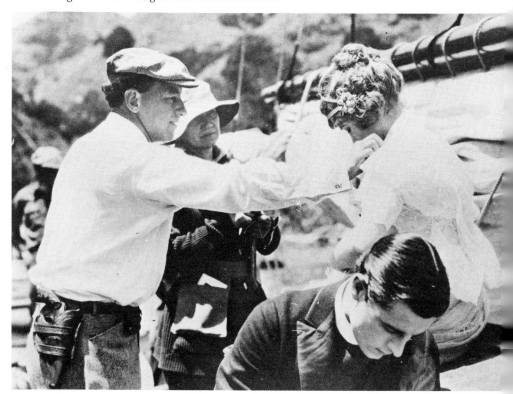

this film very deeply influenced the makers of the film *Nora Prentiss*, made at Warner Brothers almost thirty years later. A man, trapped in a situation in which he needs money desperately, renders a corpse unidentifiable by cutting its face about, then dresses it in his clothes and flings it in a river. Later, he is accused of murdering himself. He is executed in the last scene. Raymond Hatton was the star. DeMille and Alvin Wyckoff together worked out extraordinary effects: in multiple exposure, faces float around Hatton in the darkness of successive rooms, symbolizing the contradictory promptings of his thoughts. This device, worked out with Alvin Wyckoff, was brilliantly imaginative and years ahead of its time.

DeMille spent most of 1918 churning out a series of potboilers, including a very limp remake of *The Squaw Man* designed to "keep the presses busy." It was a depressing period, but he was happier when, after the war ended in November, he busied himself with a version of Sir J. M. Barrie's very successful play, *The Admirable Crichton*. Negotiations with Barrie in London were slow: Lasky and Barrie could not come satisfactorily to terms for several weeks. DeMille filled in the time by reading Joseph Conrad's novel *Victory*, which Lasky had pressed upon him as a possible vehicle for Thomas Meighan. But he did not enjoy it; he wrote dismally to Lasky on January 23, 1919: "I have, by gluing myself to it, managed to read two hundred ninety-three pages of *Victory*. On page two hundred ninety-eight, I have found the first thing of interest. It may be from here on it will improve; but Conrad's dry and uninteresting style is a hard test for the nerves." Next day, he wrote that he had finished the book and had absolutely no interest in filming it. His letter to Lasky crossed one in which Lasky announced triumphantly the successful purchase of the Barrie property.

DeMille abandoned Barrie's original title at once. Both Jesse's telegrams and letters misspelled the title "Admiral Crichton," and DeMille was afraid the American public might become equally confused. He changed the title several times:

finally, he awoke at Laughlin Park one morning at three A.M. and addressed the little sheeted group on the sleep-out porch with the cry, "*Male and Female*!" "Oh, go to sleep!" Constance snapped, but he never heard her. He had already made his way up the stairs to his study, and begun working on a script outline for Jeanie to develop.

Barrie was enchanted by the new title. When told of it, he exclaimed, "*Capital!* Why didn't I think of it myself?"

DeMille and Jeanie worked all that winter on the delicious story of the wealthy castaways on an island who managed to preserve their absurd rituals intact. Originally, DeMille wanted to cast Elliott Dexter as the butler, Crichton, who proved himself supremely resourceful and the true leader, reversing the social roles. But Dexter fell seriously ill, and DeMille was forced to replace him with Thomas Meighan.

As a setting for the picture, DeMille settled with some difficulty on the attractive natural setting of Santa Cruz Island, off the California coast. He was also concerned with the casting of the female star opposite Meighan. Fortunately, he made an ideal choice in a diminutive but spunky young girl, Gloria Swanson, whom he had admired before she had joined him two pictures earlier in Sennett comedies and in Triangle productions. She herself had experienced some difficulty in easing herself out of Triangle, because they needed her at a time when the company was falling apart.

A major asset to the production was a gifted young man named Mitchell Leisen, whom Jeanie Macpherson had discovered; though he was not very experienced, DeMille was sufficiently impressed by his sketches to invite him to design the costumes for important flashback scenes, in which Gloria Swanson was seen in Babylon. As sketch artist for the advertisements, DeMille engaged a brilliant young eighteen-year-old, Walt Disney.

The journey to the island of Santa Cruz was rough, and Thomas Meighan and Gloria Swanson were helpless with seasickness on the way across. Miss Swanson's distress was increased by the fact that two gila monsters, specially obtained for the picture, had gotten loose on the deck. After an urgent search, they turned up only a few feet from Miss Swanson beside some tackle, helplessly seasick themselves.

Meighan, who had always wanted to play Crichton since he saw the play in London, delighted DeMille and the whole crew with his impromptu wit. During a scene in which Gloria Swanson sank her teeth into his arm, he said: "Have a little pepper and salt, Gloria?"

DeMille had great fun with the island, and Wilfred Buckland brilliantly executed his ideas. The ship's steering wheel became a chandelier for a roughly built hut, shells were used for crockery, skins, as in the DeMille office, were used as carpets.

The company was an extremely happy one all through shooting. But both Meighan and Swanson were faced with unusual tests of courage. DeMille was determined to offer live animals in the flashback scenes to Babylon. He wanted a title, "The Lion's Bride," followed by a shot of Gloria lying in a lion pit, being very gently pawed. Fortunately, the sexual implications of the scene escaped the vigilant attention of the New York office.

DeMille told Miss Swanson to lie flat on her face and not stir or show the slightest fear while the lion—trained to perfection by a special trainer—ran its paw affectionately over her head and back. She obeyed without a tremor. DeMille, who had admired a boyish cap she wore, called her "Young fellow," in admiration also of her great courage. "Don't worry young fellow," he said to her as she entered the pit. "We have a sharpshooter here, and he will kill the moment the lion starts to savage you."

The scene went off without a hitch. At its end, Miss Swanson walked steadily over to DeMille, then suddenly burst into tears.

Meighan was faced with an equally severe test of courage. He had to be shown killing a leopard with a bow and arrow and draping it over his shoulders. DeMille refused to kill a leopard or use a stuffed one for the scene. Instead, he obtained a leopard from the Selig Zoo and chloroformed it. Meighan was supposed to take the leopard, fling it over his shoulder, and say to Gloria a typical Macpherson line: "I know I have paid through lives and lives, but I loved you then and I love you now." Just as he was halfway through the line, the leopard started to come round. Meighan said, "I know I have paid through lives and lives—Mr. DeMille, that damn thing is waking up!"

Male and Female enchanted the New York office when it was finished. Lasky cabled excitedly, and even Zukor sent a note of cold approval for the project. Now an important Lasky sales executive, John C. Flinn, cabled DeMille on September 23: HAVE JUST SEEN MALE AND FEMALE / A THOUSAND CON- GRATULATIONS / IT IS NOT ONLY THE FINEST PICTURE IN EVERY PARTICULAR OF LOVE STORY AND SPECTACLE THAT YOU HAVE EVER MADE IT IS THE FINEST PICTURE EVER PRODUCED / OUR WHOLE DEPARTMENT IS KEYED TO A PITCH OF INTENSE ENTHUSIASM. The picture was graceful, witty, absurd, with a particularly fine sequence in which Gloria Swanson emerged from the surf in dripping wet satin. Barrie, though somewhat put out by the Babylonian sequence, enjoyed the picture enormously, overlooking Jeanie's excruciating titles and enjoy- ing her deft reconstruction of his plot.

Overjoyed after the dry spell of the previous seasons, DeMille rushed into a new social comedy, *Why Change Your Wife?*, which had originally been planned by William deMille. He cast Thomas Meighan as a hapless male over whom two women— Gloria Swanson and Bebe Daniels—fight like tigers. Mischie- vously, he told Jeanie to include scenes in which she reflected her loathing of Julia. By this stage, all three were more or less friends, the two women had reached a state of armed truce, and DeMille moved as casually between the two women as a Roman Emperor. At times, they even arrived simultaneously at Paradise, which was preserved as a sacred retreat at weekends. It was already four years since DeMille had been seen at Laughlin Park on a Saturday night.

Why Change Your Wife? was certainly DeMille's most personal, most autobiographical work. In one scene, the two women fight and fall on the floor, tearing each other's hair, in an excess of mutual sexual jealousy and frustration which astonishes even today. The film specifically advised against divorce, in long and hortatory titles, indicating that a wife might be stern and upright, but she should not put too much of a leash on her husband. What Constance DeMille thought of this production and its arguments has, perhaps fortunately, not been recorded.

Somehow, during the rush of film production, DeMille found time to get in some serious flying experience. Ever since the Wright Brothers' flight at Kitty Hawk, he had been fascinated by the possibilities of air travel. Like many others of his generation and income, he had been anxious to fly for the thrill of flying, and he also felt that airborne cameras would in time become very important in making motion pictures. At the time he was rejected for army service he was told that if he became a pilot the army was so hard up for men who could fly that they would virtually enroll any volunteer regardless of age.

During 1918, DeMille took extensive lessons with the expert aeronaut Al Wilson. He was fascinated by the experience. His godlike leanings were satisfied at least temporarily by the thrill of soaring over Los Angeles, trying to make out Laughlin Park or Paradise, then sailing happily all the way over to San Diego or Catalina. The wind in the struts and the deafening roar of the motors were music to his ears. He immediately decided to buy a plane. While the war was on, this was almost impossible; virtually everything that could be lifted a few feet from the ground had been commandeered. But he finally located a Curtiss JN4-D which had crashed in Ontario, killing its pilot, and had been reconditioned. It was bought by an agent and shipped to Hollywood. But no sooner had DeMille obtained his pilot's license and applied for—and won—a commission in the Air Corps, than the Armistice was signed.

Shortly thereafter, on December 18, 1918, Al Wilson came to DeMille with an interesting proposal. He said that if DeMille would lend him his plane for a day, he would earn him a handsome profit. DeMille agreed, and Wilson took various passengers to various areas and back for ten dollars. DeMille's profit was three hundred dollars for one day. When Wilson returned from the final flight, DeMille shook his hand and said, "Al, we're in business!"

The sightseeing tours became overwhelmingly popular, and they had to be doubled in Christmas week. Intoxicated with excitement, DeMille bought eight planes, which were not only in constant demand by tourists and local folks, but were hired by the film studios as well. And businessmen used the planes to cut the traveling time to San Francisco or San Diego by as much as 80 per cent.

At the outset of 1919, DeMille was taking Jeanie (who herself, not to be outdone, later became an aviator) and Julia—with whom he once romantically became lost in a fog over San Diego—on joy-rides. In May, DeMille and a group of associates formed the Mercury Aviation Company, the first official commercial airline in California's history. Mercury built fields in San Diego, Long Beach, Pasadena, Bakersfield, Fresno, and San Francisco. DeMille introduced advertising in the sky: during a political campaign, he ordered the dropping of "dodgers," and he scattered leaflets everywhere advertising the new Rosslyn Hotel. He arranged for the aerial mapping of the greater Los Angeles area, and for a fire-watching service, with fires reported to district foresters.

Flying became a fascination, a dream fulfilled. On May 18, 1919, DeMille was overcome with pride as he supervised the holding of the first Air Memorial Day, in honor of the eight hundred forty-one flyers lost from the air service in World War I. DeMille flushed with delight as he watched the flight parade of military planes in formation, a simulated air rescue, a sham battle, demonstrations of wireless communication between planes and the ground, altitude trials, races, aerial acrobatics,

Airman Tony Lynch, Jeanie Macpherson, Cecil B. DeMille—1918.

DeMille with members of the Mercury Aviation Company, September 9, 1920.

and parachute jumps. DeMille himself piloted one of the planes, and Lieutenant Jimmy Doolittle performed some stunts.

In 1920, DeMille heard of an all-metal plane which had been built in Germany. He arranged for Mercury to buy the first metal cabin plane to be used in the United States from the Junkers Aircraft Corporation. On August 11, 1920, Captain Eddie Rickenbacker and John Larsen, American distributor of the Junker Company, triumphantly flew the Junkers Goose into DeMille Field Number Two at the conjunction of Fairfax and Wilshire boulevards.

It at last became possible, with the arrival of the Goose, for passengers to toss away their boots and breeches, fur-lined helmet, and goggles, though, characteristically, DeMille continued to wear them. On September 9, John H. Fisher, DeMille's manager, Harry Chandler, publisher of the *Los Angeles Times*, and two other businessmen, Guy Cochran and John B. Miller, arrived at the airport, and DeMille and a co-pilot flew them to San Diego for lunch at the Coronado Hotel.

When the star Bessie Barriscale missed the train which was to take her to San Diego for the opening of the play *Arizona* with an all-star cast, Jeanie suggested she should fly on the Mercury airline. Piloted by Lieutenant Robert E. Haynes, the two women, equipped with uniforms and goggles, made the trip easily. Later, DeMille flew over Los Angeles, Hollywood, Edendale, Glendale, and other suburbs flying a flag which announced the excellence of the new mayoral candidate, Meredith P. Snyder. He frequently took to the air with Jeanie, and on several occasions was lost—as with Julia—in heavy fog. He told the *Los Angeles Examiner* (August 25, 1920): "I myself, when very young, laughed with derision at the thought of a horseless carriage, and in my youthful stupidity made the remark that one never would be invented. Now, I hear on all sides the same stupid remark made with regard to aviation which once I made concerning the automobile, and which my great-great-grandfather made regarding the locomotive. In spite of this common disbelief in the practicality of aviation we are on the verge of a great aerial age."

The obsession with flying became so extreme in the fall of 1920 that both Lasky and Zukor begged DeMille to desist. They felt that the quality of his work as a director was beginning to fall off, and that if the obsession proceeded to develop he would be finished as a creative force. Though he argued bitterly with them, at heart he knew they were right. On September 15, 1921, he admitted his defeat after almost three glorious years of his new life. On that day, the Mercury Aviation Company sold out to the Rogers Airport group, and ceased to exist.

4

The Twenties

The outset of the twenties saw DeMille not only prepared for the new era, but a precursor of it. Already, in his sex comedies and melodramas, particularly in *Don't Change Your Husband* and *Why Change Your Wife?*, he had foreseen with amazing prescience the tenor of the times. People were talking about "the facts of life," skirts were getting shorter, and necklines more daringly down. In the carefully chosen words of William deMille, writing in his memoirs *Hollywood Saga*: "C.B. decided that this was not the opportune time to picturize the Elsie Books." Cecil learned that a combination of daring costumes, lavish sets, and bathrooms (already his trademark) of rich vulgarity could excite the public as backgrounds of stories

81

Party on the Seaward, *c. 1924.*

of infidelity and reconciliation, of divorce and illicit passion, provided, of course, that True Love triumphed in the last reel. And he often liked, after *Male and Female*, to add a sequence set in ancient times: audience reactions to seeing their favorite stars, not only in contemporary clothes, but dressed in the styles of ancient Rome or Babylon, were so ecstatic that he could not have ignored the demand even if he had wanted to.

His team was ideally organized to meet the public's needs. His office, dramatically situated at the very end of a corridor, decorated with animal skins and huge lamps, broadswords from the Farrar vehicles and sumptuous rugs and brocades, was the focus of constant day-and-night conferences between the members of his personal entourage and staff. Jeanie Macpherson was the most important of all: with her prim air and clock-spring curls, her flaring temper, she was a furiously obsessed presence at these meetings. She constantly rewrote script pages, ringing the characters in red, and marking in the margin particular features of the personalities being dealt with. Often, she differed with her lover and master, and their language became vividly purple. Over his protests, she absolutely refused to change a line once he had finally approved a script. She tolerated Julia Faye's presence as "studio reader" at these meetings, but she wasn't entirely happy about it even after an agreement to a truce had been reached. The other members of the team could only observe the curious *ménage à trois* with amazement, constantly fascinated by its tensions and its surprising essential unity.

Wilfred Buckland, near breaking point when his salary still remained minimal and his treatment by DeMille abominable, sustained a loyalty that was only to be broken the following year after a particularly severe row. His sets were as good as ever: particularly his bathrooms, correctly described by William deMille as "shrines." Claire West's costumes continued to dazzle, despite frequent collisions with her rising and very ambitious new assistant, Mitchell Leisen. Alvin Wyckoff continued to provide the lighting designs, each exquisitely fashioned sketch presented to DeMille for his grudging approval. Anne Bauchens, a loyal editor who had worked with him from the beginning, was always present to help "edit in the script," suggesting swift transitions before a foot had been shot. William deMille frequently dropped over from his own office-library (with its brass-studded walls, candles in antique parchment shades, and mullioned windows) to join in the discussions and supervise an obstreperous Jeanie in her work.

DeMille's obvious value in the new decade had not escaped the now proliferating movie companies: First National, eager for his services, had offered him one million dollars a picture, and United Artists three hundred thousand dollars. He decided, rather against his better judgment, to stay where he was; he felt he owed it to Lasky, who begged him not to leave at a time when the company had run into financial difficulties. The chief thorn in his side still was Zukor, who had a severe reluctance to "indulging" DeMille at all. After some considerable—and heated—correspondence between DeMille's brilliant attorney Neil McCarthy and the Famous Players office, DeMille was reluctantly granted a weekly salary of sixty-five hundred dollars against a gross budget of two hundred ninety thousand dollars a picture. In a series of telegrams he begged Zukor to reconsider the budgets for the productions. He pointed out that costs had risen incalculably since the time of *Joan the Woman*, and that it was no longer possible to produce a motion picture of real quality for the figure of little more than a quarter of a million dollars. Zukor adamantly refused to be swayed by these arguments.

DeMille decided that he had best form his own company, to protect himself if relations with Zukor became strained beyond the endurance point. In 1920 he formed Cecil B. DeMille Productions, with its headquarters at Laughlin Park, and Constance DeMille, Neil McCarthy, and Constance's stepmother Ella King Adams as full partners, each investing heavily in the company.

In 1920 also, DeMille made his first picture with a religious theme. Still a fundamentalist so far as the Bible was concerned, yet convinced that God was not an individual being but a force for good, he decided to infiltrate religious ideas into the rich productions he planned for the new decade. He made the carefully titled *Something To Think About* in 1920, starring Elliott Dexter and Gloria Swanson, in which a wealthy cripple falls in love with the blacksmith's daughter he has helped to educate. She reneges on her promise to marry him, and runs away instead with a city worker, who is killed in a subway train crash. The cripple agrees to marry her platonically; she falls in love with him; and she is aided by the religious faith of a housekeeper, played by Claire McDowell. DeMille's showmanship saved the film from becoming unendurably maudlin, but critics emphatically dismissed it. Even the normally sympathetic *Variety* called it "confused and foggy," and DeMille was sufficiently aggravated to send a lengthy memorandum of reproach to the editor.

After *Something To Think About*, DeMille obeyed Zukor's behest for more and quicker productions by rushing out a remake of *The Golden Chance* (1915) as *Forbidden Fruit*. Its only point of real interest was the re-creation of a Cinderella ball, dressed with incomparable elegance by Claire West. But it was DeMille's next production, *The Affairs of Anatol*, based on Arthur Schnitzler's play *Anatol*, that really established him as a great film maker of the 1920s.

On a visit to Hollywood earlier that year, Somerset Maugham had suggested *The Affairs of Anatol* to DeMille, who had listened without much interest. Later, Maugham repeated the story of Schnitzler's play to Lasky in New York—and Lasky took heed. In October 1920 DeMille was still mulling over the possibility of the project, while Lasky went ahead and bought the rights. He telegraphed DeMille on October 9 that he felt a number of stars had appeared too frequently in DeMille pictures and that this should be "a sort of sentimental farewell appearance of Swanson, [Bebe] Daniels, [Wanda] Hawley, and [Agnes] Ayres." DeMille wired Lasky on October 10, IT WILL BE

TOO DIFFICULT TO FILM. But Lasky was insistent, and suggested the alternative title *Five Kisses.*

Reluctantly, DeMille proceeded to make the picture in color in 1921. Elliott Dexter, despite a slight limp following his illness, was able to appear opposite Gloria Swanson and Wallace Reid, who gave an admirable performance as the New York sophisticate Anatol DeWitt Spencer. Adapted freely from Schnitzler's characteristically bittersweet play, it was an intensely sophisticated film, ingeniously scripted by Jeanie, Beulah Marie Dix, Elmer Harris, and Lorna Moon, the current mistress of William deMille, using Granville-Barker's British translation as a guide. Spencer is unhesitatingly shown as a ruthless philanderer, his character prefiguring the personalities of the Lubitsch comedies which followed later, and were deeply influenced by this production. Abandoning his wife on their honeymoon, Anatol sets up a Follies girl as his mistress, installing her in a lavish apartment to the great annoyance of her Ziegfeldian employer. She immediately proceeds to be unfaithful to Anatol with a wealthy older man, Gordon Bronson, played with expert lechery by DeMille's old friend Theodore Roberts. On the rebound, Anatol—infuriated by his mistress' infidelity—returns to his wife, wins her back, and embarks on a second honeymoon. But again he is unable to resist philandering, and makes off with a girl who promptly relieves him of his wallet. Back in New York, he enters the luxurious bordello of Satan Synne, "the wickedest woman in the world," the rooms bathed in scarlet light. At the end of the picture, Anatol is thoroughly informed about the ways of women, but resolutely refuses to face up to the truth. "Truth is dead," he says in a final title. "Long live illusion."

Physically, the film was DeMille's most tasteful production up to that time. He was aided immeasurably by the hand-tinted photography of Alvin Wyckoff and Karl Struss: images bathed in gold or scarlet or blue, the focus unusually deep so that background figures emerged as clear as close-up faces, discreetly ceilinged sets which gave a sense of total reality. Above all, though, he had the help of Paul Iribe, a brilliant French designer with a leaning toward Art Nouveau, who arranged the entire picture like a series of Beardsley illustrations to Oscar Wilde. Lasky sent the suave and elegant Iribe to DeMille following Wilfred Buckland's inevitable resignation, with instructions DeMille use him; correcting DeMille's vulgar streak, Iribe created an ambience so dazzling, so intoxicating, that many art critics discussed the picture in serious journals. And when DeMille saw it, after the long discussions and wranglings during the production, he embraced Paul Iribe in gratitude.

On February 3, 1921, Somerset Maugham cabled Lasky that he was furious about *The Affairs of Anatol* being started as he had told DeMille the full story and had in fact been commissioned by Lasky to write it. Both DeMille and Lasky ignored Maugham's charge and Maugham finally dropped it.

Aside from the making of *The Affairs of Anatol*, 1920 had a pleasant experience to offer: the adoption of a lovely, nine-year-old girl, Katherine Lester, the Canadian-born daughter of an Italian-Swiss mother and a British father. Her father had been killed in the Battle of Verdun and her mother had died of tuberculosis. She had been placed in an orphanage of which Constance DeMille was a director. She used to come home often with Constance, and sit gravely reading books; frequent visitors to the house like Ella King Adams, Ella's sister Margaret, and Beulah Marie Dix, were impressed by the gentle dark-eyed child, and DeMille needed no pressure from those women to arrange for her adoption.

Katherine fitted in well with the other children: Cecilia, eleven, who was becoming consumed with a passion for horses, and the mechanically-minded John, nine, who teased the girls constantly. All the children (John included) were at the Hollywood School for Girls, which took some boy pupils as well. Katherine and Cecilia, with their great friend Natalie Visart, loved to go riding in San Fernando Valley and at Griffith Park, where there were fine stables.

In 1922, there was to be another member of the family: a

Bebe Daniels and Wallace Reid in The Affairs of Anatol.

DeMille with Constance at Laughlin Park (mid 1920s).

At Laughlin Park with John, Constance, Cecilia, and Katherine.

tiny, fragile baby boy, discovered suffering from rickets in Neil McCarthy's parked car outside the DeMille estate. The thin, twisted figure was taken into the house and carefully tended, and gradually under the family's vigilant care restored to normal health. DeMille called him Richard, not formally adopting him until 1940.

In 1921, DeMille acquired a yacht befitting his status as a newly rich man. In 1917, he had obtained a fifty-seven-foot cruiser, the *Sea Bee*, and later a speedboat, the *Defiance*, which he entered in races off San Pedro, and a hydroplane, the *Hummingbird*. But it was in 1921 that he really fulfilled a romantic dream, and bought the magnificent ocean-going yacht *Seaward*, a twenty-nine-ton gross register, Gloucester-type schooner one hundred and six feet overall, carrying auxiliary power, a crew of seven, and quarters fitted for eight.

He enormously enjoyed the peace of yachting, frequently spending the weekends, not at Paradise, but sailing around Catalina Island or down the coast toward Mexico. Neither of the films he made that year particularly interested him (*Fool's Paradise* and *Saturday Night*), and indeed he told both Lasky and Zukor in a series of memoranda that his extremely tight budgets meant that he was forced to reduce the quality of these productions. He was particularly annoyed by having to produce *Saturday Night* for one hundred fifty thousand dollars, and warned Lasky in a letter dated September 10, 1921, that he would have to make this a substandard picture. Lasky agreed to double the budget, but wrote to DeMille more than once that fall telling him that the studio was aggravated by his extravagance, that money was so short the eastern studio had been closed, and that the high-handed demands of Neil McCarthy were becoming an exasperation.

To escape these problems DeMille spent as much time as possible on the *Seaward*, sunning and swimming, often with Julia or Jeanie as a companion. These days away from picture making were the happiest of an otherwise uninteresting year.

But finally even the *Seaward* didn't provide sufficient escape.

Tired out by the constant snipings of his New York confrères, DeMille decided to go to Europe at the outset of 1922. He had never seen it: when he had needed research for earlier pictures, John H. Fisher had gone for him, and he had fretted over the long expense sheets. This time he decided he would go himself, with Paul Iribe as his interpreter, and his Japanese valet, Yamabe. He described an odd little incident in Paris in his memoirs. Visiting Maxim's with Iribe, he picked up a beautiful young girl and went with her to her house. When they reached the bedroom he told her he had no wish to sleep with her but would prefer to talk. She smiled and opened a door. He was astonished to see her husband and children enjoying a late-night supper, and he joined them happily for the meal and for a conversation that continued for several hours.

In Rome, DeMille and Iribe were invited to see Pope Benedict XV at a private audience. When they arrived at the Vatican they were coldly received and virtually asked to leave. They looked at each other in astonishment: they had dressed precisely according to the dictates of protocol, and were scrupulously punctual. But they had overlooked one detail: the Pope had died that day.

Returning to Paris, DeMille felt an unbearable pain in the heels of his feet. Stoical as ever, he refused to acknowledge it. Then suddenly he began to feel pains in his chest, suffered violent attacks of coughing and vomiting, and went down with a high fever at the Ritz. Unable to sleep, he felt as though he were stifling, and he realized reluctantly that he was desperately ill. The French doctors diagnosed his illness as inflammatory rheumatism, contracted in the catacombs of Rome, and complicated by severely infected tonsils, which he had never had removed. He was rushed to the American Hospital for an emergency operation. He barely survived; weak and ill with exhaustion, he sank to a mere hundred and fifteen pounds. He was barely able to walk when Iribe and Yamabe transferred him to a boat train, and thence to the *S. S. Berengaria*. The crossing was from beginning to end a nightmare. He was put in the ship's hospital. Two days out, a tremendous storm struck the liner. His hospital bed, not nailed to the floor like the ship's furniture as a whole, crashed jarringly up and down as the ship yawed and plunged. DeMille was evacuated to a second officer's cabin, where he lay in a delirium, alternating between hemorrhages and bouts of seasickness. When he got to New York he was a limp, partly paralyzed ghost, barely able to recognize Lasky, who came to the boat. He was very far from certain, in his abyss of pain and misery, that he would live.

Somehow DeMille managed to pull himself together sufficiently to make the long train journey to California. It was a severe ordeal, and when Constance and Cecilia came to fetch him off the train, he was still limping and exhausted as though he had had a severe stroke. Back at Laughlin Park, his recovery was painfully slow. It was a tedious spring, his activities restricted, his contempt for his own weakness causing him to be irritable even to those closest to him.

But at last, by April, he was on the mend, and he could actually walk to the end of the garden without hobbling. Sitting up in a wicker chair, his arm in a brace, basking in the California sunlight, he began to read again, and to send the first of a new stream of cables to New York.

While he recovered from his illness, DeMille suffered a severe shock. He was told that while he was in Europe William Desmond Taylor, a distinguished director of Famous Players and a pleasing acquaintance, had been shot dead under mysterious circumstances in his apartment. Both Mabel Normand and Mary Miles Minter, Lasky contract players, lay under grave suspicion, and there was talk that Miss Minter's mother, Mrs. Shelby, had committed the murder dressed as a man. In addition, the Fatty Arbuckle case dragged on, following the plump comedian's arrest on a manslaughter charge over the death at the Hotel St. Francis in San Francisco of a girl called Virginia Rappe. In his travail, DeMille felt the anguish of the truth: the character of Hollywood he and many friends had sought to conceal—desperately evil, cruel, and degenerate—

had at last slipped out, and no one would ever be able to hide the truth again. When DeMille was firmly on the mend, he met for the first time the Postmaster-General, Will Hays, whom he and other industry leaders unhesitatingly supported as guardian of the industry's morals and of its public image by appointing him President of the Motion Picture Producers and Distributors of America.

Despite his attempt to make a haven out of Laughlin Park, DeMille felt the reality of Hollywood come very close to his front door that spring. Theodore Kosloff, now one of his most intimate friends, called him in terror saying that he had received a Black Hand letter demanding he leave ten thousand dollars in a leather bag near a railroad track or he would be murdered. DeMille arranged for the Pinkerton detectives to watch the spot when the bag was delivered, but at the last minute Kosloff lost his nerve and failed to appear. Shortly afterward, a second meeting was arranged, the members of the Black Hand appeared and snatched the bag, and the detectives gave chase, firing at them. But the criminals made a completely successful getaway.

As if that were not enough drama for the ailing director, he was faced with a robbery as well. In late April, he woke one morning to discover that his magnificent solitaire diamond, the Blue Lagoon, had been stolen from Paradise. The Burns Detective Agency worked on the theft, and after a few days the diamond was mysteriously returned, left on the floor of DeMille's office where it was found at midnight by a Japanese janitor.

Among the novels DeMille picked up during the period of recovery that summer was one called *Manslaughter*, by Alice Duer Miller. He had Lasky buy it for him, and Jeanie came over to the house daily to work with him on the screenplay. It was the story of a jazz-mad girl whose dangerous driving causes the death of a police motorcyclist in an accident. She is jailed for manslaughter, and is so sobered by the experience that she rejects her life of gaiety. One afternoon, sitting under a sun-umbrella in the lovely garden at Laughlin Park, Jeanie said: "Why don't I go to jail?" "Are you serious?" DeMille replied. "Oh, yes, it would be such a marvelous way to be sure of the authenticity," she told him.

She made the arrangements by letter with family contacts in Detroit. She left at once for New York and then proceeded to Michigan. Under the name Angie Brown, she arranged to steal a fur neckpiece from a friend who was staying at the Hotel Statler, Detroit. She arranged in advance with a police official known to her family and to Famous Players-Lasky that she would be placed at once in the Detroit House of Correction so as to obtain adequate background for the production. The reason she chose this particular prison was that it was the only jail in the country which incarcerated petty criminals along with killers.

Stopped by the house detective in the lobby of the Statler after her friend reported the "crime," Jeanie was placed under arrest and tried. Before the judge, she gave her pseudonym and declined to pay the ten-dollar fine. She was immediately removed to the cellars and transferred to a police van. Her plan almost collapsed when a friendly officer said he would try to have her released as it was a first offense; fortunately, the man who could assist in this plan could not be found.

Dressed in a faded gingham overall, long woolen underwear, and paint-stained shoes, Jeanie was led in handcuffs to a cell on the second tier of the block. Windowless, it measured six feet by six feet by five feet, furnished only with a broken-down chair, tin washbasin, pail, and pitcher. Oddly enough, her first experience was seeing a film in the prison chapel. It was a cheap, wretchedly-made documentary about the Panama Canal. In the midst of it, a girl yelled out, "My Gawd, can't they give us a love story?"

Supper consisted of moldy bread, bitter coffee, and a large dish of prunes, followed by soup served out of sticky, greasy bowls. Jeanie woke up in the night to feel vermin crawling over her. She was unable to sleep, kept awake by the sounds of women quarreling, screaming, or making love. After three days of this misery, she had lost twelve pounds and was sick with hunger and loss of sleep. She summoned her police official friend and demanded to be released. When she returned to Hollywood she broke into tears as DeMille greeted her off the train. She told reporters carefully invited by the Chief: "I have plumbed the utmost depths of human degradation. I have seen women's souls stripped naked. . . . I wouldn't go through that experience again for any amount of money. But I wouldn't sell it for an even greater sum."

An assistant, Cullen Tate, traveled to New York to photograph interiors and exteriors of the Auburn, New York, women's penitentiary. For details of the interior of the courtroom, Neil McCarthy was engaged as special assistant. J. M. Bailey, superintendent of the Bureau of Identification of Los Angeles County, was secured to pass judgment on all details of costumes, procedure, and settings.

Characteristically, DeMille instructed Jeanie to add a flashback to ancient Rome. An entire corps of researchers was engaged to settle on details of the food served at Roman banquets, the rules governing gladiatorial combat, the clothing and arms of Roman ministers, and the proper choreography for a Roman ballet. Theodore Kosloff trained an immense corps, combining his own students with those of the Denishawn company. DeMille used the picture for a moral purpose, not only preaching against the perils of the newfangled speedsters, but against the whole tenor of the times: a slogan read: "A Drama of the Mad Age! Is the Modern World Racing to Ruin on a Wave of Jazz and Cocktails?"

The film was expertly photographed by Wyckoff, who made exhaustive experiments with experimental lighting for the production. He told a correspondent of the magazine *Table Talk*: "In the story the heroine is sent to prison. In the prison scenes she is at first bitterly rebellious and then later becomes normal and almost happy. These changes in temperament of the character we emphasized by lighting. Where she was in the bitter mood I resorted to lighting that emphasized the hard shadows and brought out all the bitterness in the face of the principal character. As she changed in the story, the lighting was altered until at the finish her face was luminous both in action and illumination."

DeMille was delighted with the picture, and with the central performance of Leatrice Joy. Paul Iribe's prison sets, based partly on Cullen Tate's photographs and partly on Jeanie's notes and sketches, were inspired. And the heroine's collision with a motorcycle rider was startlingly accurate: the stuntman concerned behaved with a bravery even DeMille could not fault.

Manslaughter pleased both the New York office and the public, and DeMille finally shook off the last effects of his illness in August. On the fourteenth, with his manager, John H. Fisher, he set off on an extended bear-hunting trip to escape the summer heat of Los Angeles. They traveled by train to Searles and the Sand Canyon Park Station, where he joined his guide, Chester Wortley. They climbed the side of the High Sierras on horseback—an exhausting ordeal in view of his comparative weakness that summer. At one o'clock, they had a delicious lunch prepared by Fisher himself. They crossed a beautiful valley and camped at sundown, Fisher entertaining the little party on the mouth organ. DeMille wrote in his diary: "The night was gorgeous—clear as crystal—and a wonderful moon. Not a sound except the wind in the pines. Sat about the campfire and talked for about an hour—turned in at 9:15 and slept nine hours."

Next day the group rescued a couple of horses which had gotten away in the night, crossed the second divide at fifty-eight hundred feet, and entered the Long Valley region. Climbing an almost sheer path up the other side of the valley was a

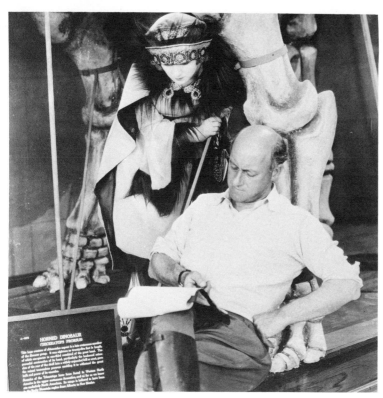

With Anna Q. Nilsson on set: Adam's Rib.

Primeval forest of Adam's Rib.

With art director Paul Iribe on cruise to Tiburon, 1923.

Lasky publicity montage: Jeannie's Dreams.

hair-raising experience. Just as they were picking their way along a narrow ledge a black grizzly loomed up, seemingly out of nowhere.

DeMille wrote: "Instantly, there was pandemonium. Each horse started frantically away in a different direction—some up and some down. Mine decided to go home . . . Fisher had his gun across his saddle horn when his horse went down. He threw himself clear from his horse and slid halfway down the mountainside, leaving various parts of his anatomy in little chunks by the wayside. As luck would have it, he slid almost to the bear—who was equally stampeded. Fritz [an assistant guide] shot the bear." Later, DeMille had an exciting encounter with two rattlesnakes, which he bagged and took home for office trophies.

DeMille was sufficiently famous now for every detail of the trip to be made public. He enjoyed becoming a "figure," not merely another Hollywood director.

By the fall of 1922, the Cecil B. DeMille jokes were flying thick and fast. Herbert Howe wrote in the *New York Times*: "Even if some exhibitor cut off the DeMille name and coat of arms I'd suspect who the director was as soon as I saw a pink heart in a subtitle—or a rosebud. Then if a mistaken wife ambled on wearing one of those gowns that fall off as soon as you kiss the secret spring under the shoulder blade, my suspicion would approach conviction. Then a flashback to the primeval garden of Baltz and Budweiser with nymphs draped in the hardest working tiger skins in captivity . . . Cecil can't fool us even when he has the bathroom door closed." He was quoted constantly: one widely circulated story was that when Nita Naldi, the famous vamp, first arrived at the studio, he looked at her ankles climbing the stairs and said, "Who are those?" DeMille's dislike of most screenwriters was widely publicized: when the writers Peter B. Kyne, Stewart Edward White, and Gouverneur Morris bitterly attacked the compromises and vulgarities of Hollywood, DeMille led a mass Hollywood attack on them, calling them "an anvil chorus" and adding characteristically: "I'll take the taste of sixty million people to that of this handful of authors. These gentlemen are placing themselves in the class of people who said there would never be a railroad. They are looking at a gigantic, stupendous art—the greatest the world ever knew—and because they didn't succeed in it they are standing up and saying—'There ain't no such art.' Who do you think the chambers of commerce will be building statues to twenty years from now? The man who started the film art or the contemporary *literati?*"

His fulminations made national newspapers, a fact he gratefully relished. His investments in real estate also caused widespread comment: he bought the corner block on Sunset Boulevard and Wilcox Avenue for a hundred and forty-four thousand dollars, and his oil interests grew daily.

After finishing *Manslaughter* that summer, DeMille turned down Lasky's suggestion of a version of *Bluebeard's Eighth Wife*, a comedy which had starred Ina Claire on Broadway as "too light," toyed briefly with a detective story, *Suspense*, and finally settled on a subject honoring the "flapper," which Jeanie Macpherson had written. He decided to link it with elements in Jack London's novel *Before Adam*—without paying permission fees if possible. He wrote to Lasky on June 30, 1922: "How does the title—DUMB AND BOBBED—appeal to you?—It would be damned and screamed at, like MALE AND FEMALE was . . . people would flock to see it." He sweated it out waiting for Lasky's reply for two weeks. Then on July 6, the answer came that Lasky enthusiastically approved the subject: I FOUND FLAPPER BEING DISCUSSED ABOARD, he cabled. But in a following letter he absolutely ruled out the title *Dumb and Bobbed*, "a horror—a tongue twister no one will understand." DeMille wired Lasky on July 7 that he was already deep into scripting and had chosen the cast: Elliott Dexter, Milton Sills, and Theodore Kosloff among them. Lasky suggested the title *Glorifying the Girl*, but DeMille protested bitterly at that, and settled finally, with Lasky's approval, on *Adam's Rib.*

In October, DeMille established a private luncheon suite at the Lasky studio, with a kitchen, dining room, range, and a black chef. A special telephone was at his table. Here, with William and Jeanie, he spent long hours working out the details of *Adam's Rib*, which they devised as a typical parallel story in which a love affair conducted in a museum of ancient history is matched to an affair of life in prehistoric times. Typically, DeMille showed women as ruthless, predatory, thinking only of making themselves sufficiently beautiful to snare an available man. Typically, too, his fanaticism for detail insisted on a complete replica of the Smithsonian Institution. The script effortlessly combined the current interest in paleontological discoveries, the advent of the flapper as the central figure of the "emancipated society" (at one stage the heroine hangs her hat jubilantly on the head of a brontosaurus), and the righteous attitude of the public toward gold diggers.

His cast included Anna Q. Nilsson, Milton Sills, Julia, and a new actress, Pauline Garon. To announce Miss Garon to the world, and to show his own recovery as complete, he gave an immense party, at which over one hundred Paramount executives and salesmen, led by Jesse, Mr. and Mrs. Thomas Ince, Chaplin, Dustin Farnum, and eighty Los Angeles socialites gamboled until dawn.

Cullen Tate went to the Smithsonian where with the aid of specialists he had exact plaster copies made of various primitive heads. Professor Frank Speck's discoveries in the Trenton Gravels formed the basis of the prehistoric scenes. Dried heads of Jivaro Ecuadorian Indians were used as models for the prehistoric masks used by the actors in the flashbacks. As a setting for the scenes of primitive man, a complete redwood forest was built by Wilfred Buckland on the soundstage, with lath and plaster boulders and rocks and lavish plantings of real moss. One hundred and twelve by two hundred and fifty-two feet, it had a two-hundred-foot running stream, an eighty-foot waterfall, a pool, a fallen tree, and a cave. Twelve thousand ferns and six tons of Oregon moss were used in the forest, which took four hundred plasterers and carpenters two months working in round-the-clock shifts to complete. Asked by a *Los Angeles Times* reporter (November 15, 1922) why he did not use a real forest, DeMille predicted a whole cycle of studio film making by saying: "I have been in the real forest four times. The trees are wonderful but it is impossible to put their real beauties adequately on the screen . . . in our constructed forest we have all the beauty of the redwoods . . . we can light them with daylight and with scores of spots and arcs set at vantage points on the ground and in the rafters."

Adam's Rib was remarkable, among other things, for unleashing DeMille's foot fetish to an unprecedented degree. "Eves in every age have adorned their feet with protective covering of rare and unique beauty," ran an early press release. Advertisements for the film showed primeval men and women adorning their feet with tiger skins, flowers, twigs, and leaves. "Today," the posters read, "a shoe must be more than well constructed, it must have style, for the 'Sons of Eve' are just as fastidious in the selection of shoes as are the 'Daughters of Eve.' " Many shoe stores offered competitions for the best limericks written about footwear, and countless boot repairers featured posters from the film in their windows. Julia Faye even posed for photographs, released by DeMille across the country, of her feet.

The publicity was extravagant in every direction. The Lasky studio set up what it called an Adam's Rib Society for the suppression of false propaganda critical of the modern Eve. Local school teachers eager for publicity were encouraged to send chain letters to everyone they knew inciting anger against men who failed to take women seriously. When certain shops shut, selected assistants put up signs reading, "Closed, gone to see *Adam's Rib*." Cashing in on the Coué craze, many posters read, "I'm getting better and better every day, I've just seen *Adam's Rib*." Photographs were released of Elliott Dexter taking a large pair of pliers to a dinosaur's tooth.

At the tail end of shooting, Barrett Kiesling, DeMille's new and vigorous young publicity man, devised a stunt whereby a

competition would be held in the *Los Angeles Times* for the idea
of DeMille's next picture. A thousand dollar prize was offered
for the best idea. The stunt obtained immense publicity, and
was won by several people who selected the Ten Commandments as the theme. DeMille was intoxicated by the idea, and
had Jeanie start sketching an outline immediately.

After he and Anne Bauchens had finished cutting *Adam's Rib*
in the fall, DeMille had the pleasant experience of arranging the
secret wedding of Elliott Dexter and the socialite Nina Chis-
holm Untermeyer at Laughlin Park. The ceremony, before a
select group of friends, was presided over by the Reverend E. P.
Ryland. The following month, a massive Famous Players-Lasky
convention was held in Los Angeles; DeMille flung open his
house for a festive party, followed by a still more lavish affair in
the ballroom of the Alexandria Hotel, at which Zukor, Lasky,
Sid Grauman, and the witty Marcus Loew, the head of Loew's
Inc., gave entertaining and inspiring speeches to the delegates.
DeMille laughed loudly when Loew, whose daughter was
married to Zukor's son, said: "I have known Adolph Zukor for
more than twenty-five years, and during that time I have never
had an even break with him; we could never agree on anything
until about three weeks ago, when we both became grand-
fathers at the same time. That's the time we both agreed."
DeMille was busy that winter with the *Cecilia*, a splendid
power launch built to his specifications in the Lasky Studio
workshops, under the supervision of Ray Prewitt. Twenty-three
feet and made of mahogany, she was to be used not only as a
racer but as a fast tender for the *Seaward*. She was driven by a
BMW motor of three hundred horsepower, and would be
entered in the Gar Wood speedboat races in 1923. DeMille also
built up a large collection of shrunken heads, which one
waggish commentator suggested "might soon feature those of
Jesse L. Lasky and Adolph Zukor." The nucleus of the
collection began with *Adam's Rib*, as he wanted to show the

stars carrying shrunken heads in the primeval forest. By December, 1922, it had grown to two hundred specimens.

In November, DeMille was making plans to do a Shakespearean adaptation, as well as *The Ten Commandments*, but Lasky, perhaps wisely, vetoed that idea. Instead, DeMille began making elaborate plans for a vacation on board the *Seaward*: a six-week cruise to Tiburon, a barren island in the Gulf of California. With him on the trip went the big-game hunter Carmen Runyon, John H. Fisher, Paul Iribe, Dr. Frank Watson, the wireless operator Joseph Kane, and Captain William Bethel of San Francisco.

Just before leaving, on January 2, 1923, DeMille entered the Los Angeles Yacht Club motorboat race in his launch *Cecilia*. He started out confidently with his mechanic, Alfred Fear. Suddenly the carburetor backfired and the gasoline tank blew up, hurling both men violently into the water. Fear blacked out completely, and DeMille had to hold his head above water to prevent him from drowning. When the referee's schooner picked them up, Fear was still unconscious, his face black and scalded, and DeMille's eyebrows and eyelashes had been singed off. The *Cecilia* was a total wreck.

On January 7, DeMille and his party left on the *Seaward*. At first they enjoyed perfect weather, cruising lazily through sapphire waters to Ensenada. They wandered happily through the streets of that polyglot town, then took sail the following morning through a sea swarming with thousands of sharks. At Cedros Island, they enjoyed superb fishing and managed to kill and skin a few seals. At Turtle Bay, they found a tiny settlement of three thatched huts, talked to the occupants, and shot some wild duck. DeMille, stripped to the waist, enormously enjoyed exploring the skeleton of an old ship on the beach, and discovered an hourglass which firmly marked the ship's date as early nineteenth century.

At Magdalena Bay, the party found a marvelous landlocked harbor. DeMille wrote in his diary (January 17, 1923): "It is so large it could easily hold all navies, an ever-present menace to the United States if it is not kept neutral." The travelers entertained local citizens on board, studied the white bones and ruined houses of an abandoned whale station, and saw huge turtles. Next morning, Paul Iribe helped DeMille harpoon some immense blanket rays weighing in at seventy pounds, and two powerful hammerhead sharks, which were tied to the rear of the motorboat. Whales, rainbows, and clear, sunny, perfect days marked the slow voyage down the coast. Paul Iribe kept the log, remarking one evening on "a silhouette of palm trees in black, against the purples and orange of the setting sun."

The happy friends traveled on, encountering on the way a new school of whale which seemed to dance in phosphorescent waves. They put in at La Paz, and sailed on to San Joseph and Carmen Islands, where they had wonderful catches of bass and yellowtail. Finally, they were on their way to Tiburon; they learned that the inhabitants were not cannibals, as they had supposed, but simply very primitive, seldom visited because of the violent storms that swept around the island, and the half-mile-wide Infernal Channel, separating the island from the mainland of Sonora, Mexico, known as the most dangerous crossing in the region.

During the crossing of the Channel, a tremendous storm suddenly swept down on the voyagers, forcing them to send an SOS to the shore stations. DeMille cabled his secretary Gladys Rosson: NORTHWEST GALE HAS MADE IT IMPOSSIBLE TO REACH TIBURON / HOURS OF DRENCHING RAIN AND HAVE BEEN BLOWN CLEAR ACROSS THE GULF / SEAWARD IS BEHAVING SPLENDIDLY BUT THIS WIND AND SEA WOULD STOP ANYTHING.

Back in Ensenada, forced to retreat without seeing Tiburon, DeMille learned that the yacht *Eloise*, with one hundred prominent business and professional men of Los Angeles and San Francisco, was in grave danger as a result of the storm. He intercepted the first SOS calls and immediately saw to it that a rescue party rendered assistance to the crippled vessel before he returned to Hollywood.

Back from the exhausting thwarted voyage to Tiburon, DeMille had to shoulder another burden, in many ways more severe than any he had been faced with before. He learned upon returning to Laughlin Park that Wallace Reid had died of the effects of morphine on January 18. For a year, DeMille had been aware of Reid's terrible suffering. The shocking degeneration of the strapping, magnificent, six-foot-three giant of *Joan the Woman* and *The Affairs of Anatol* had grieved DeMille deeply. In 1920 Reid had begun his first addiction, driven by a bad back and by the pressures of work at the studio. Denied his daily ration of drugs by physicians, the star had to be incarcerated in a home to "dry out." DeMille had visited him there and had been appalled to see him reduced to a gray, miserable skeleton, weighing just over one hundred pounds. As he heard the news he felt weighed down with an unbearable grief, not only because of what had happened to Wallace Reid, but because of what was happening to the simple, rural Hollywood of his younger days.

It had been a hard year. The sickness in Paris, the harrowing voyage home, the explosion of the *Cecilia*, the storms off Tiburon, and now Wally Reid's death. And he learned to his dismay that *Adam's Rib* had not only received very bad reviews—about which he cared nothing—but that it had been a complete box-office failure.

And this was not all. That difficult February, he had to face a minor and major scandal which aggravated him almost beyond endurance, and, coming on top of everything else, almost broke his powerful spirit.

5

The Ten Commandments

As if he had not enough to contend with that winter, in the very midst of preparing *The Ten Commandments* DeMille was faced with what could have been an enormous and ruinous disaster. A blackmailing group of attorneys on both coasts threatened him with the exposure of a supposed affair between Gloria Swanson and Marshall Neilan, director of the Mary Pickford vehicle *Stella Maris*, conducted in Europe and at a hotel in downtown Los Angeles. Unless the sum of one hundred fifty thousand dollars was released immediately the news would break and the star would be ruined. She was married at the time to the restaurateur Herbert K. Somborn. A frantic flurry of telegrams ran between Los

107

The Exodus: The Ten Commandments *(1923)*.

Angeles and New York on this extraordinary and nerveracking matter. Will Hays telegraphed DeMille on February 18: LET THERE NOT BE A SHADOW OF DOUBT THAT IF THIS AFFAIR BECOMES KNOWN THE PRINCIPAL STAR WILL BE BARRED FROM PICTURES AND PERMANENTLY KEPT FROM THE SCREEN. Notes scribbled on yellow paper by DeMille indicate that a meeting between him, Swanson, her husband, and others involved was held at his house. He cabled Lasky on February 14: HAVE HAD LONG TALK WITH IMPORTANT ATTORNEY REPRESENTING HUSBAND OF STAR IN PRODUCTION NUMBER 273 / SCANDALOUS PUBLICITY BOMB WILL EXPLODE WITHIN WEEK OR TWO DAYS / ACTIONS IN EUROPE WITH DIRECTOR OF STELLA MARIS WILL RECEIVE FULL PUBLICITY / STRONGLY ADVISE IMMEDIATE RELEASE OF ANY PICTURE ON HAND THAT MIGHT BE INJURED BY VERY UNFORTUNATE PUBLICITY / PLEASE TREAT MATTER VERY CONFIDENTIALLY AS ONLY AFTER GREATEST DIFFICULTY I HAVE OBTAINED PERMISSION FROM INTERESTED PARTY TO TELL YOU LADY HERSELF DOES NOT KNOW STORM IS ABOUT TO BREAK / C. On February 20, he cabled Lasky again: MEETING LASTED ALL NIGHT / BELIEVE OUR PRINCIPAL SAFE / PARTICULARS LATER / C. On both coasts, Paramount representatives went to hotels obtaining depositions from managers that the star and her friend did not share rooms while staying there. Finally, DeMille agreed to settle with the blackmailers, and acting on instructions from Lasky, began to consider an immediate vehicle for Swanson to quash any scandal that might leak out. The check stub—dated March 22, 1923—indicates that the account for these purposes was labeled *Suspense*, the name of a long-planned but abandoned picture. DeMille's last cable to Lasky (dated March 6) read: MATTER WILL BE FINALLY SETTLED TOMORROW NIGHT / HAVE CLOSED FOR TWENTY FIVE THOUSAND. He was speechless with rage as he handed over the check that night.

Meanwhile, on February 27, DeMille received another shock. Federal Authorities seized the *Seaward,* claiming that her master, Captain McNeary, had illegally smuggled eighty quarts of fine liquor bought in Ensenada. This was not only in defiance of customs laws, but it was in defiance of prohibition. Fortunately, it emerged that DeMille had known nothing of the purchase, but McNeary was heavily fined before the *Seaward* was released in March.

DeMille recovered slowly from the debacle of the captain's arrest. He enjoyed appearing in a bit role in James Cruze's *Hollywood,* a gentle satire of the film colony in which nearly every significant figure in the industry played a scene. He was shown in his office, signing stars to a contract in the presence of Jeanie Macpherson and Lasky players. He also organized a stunt in which a bathtub was stolen from the home of Virginia Valli and various clues—including a solid silver faucet—were left scattered across the city to keep the police busy. The tub was finally found lying in the main entrance of the Lasky building. But not before DeMille had arranged a meeting of the Chamber of Commerce in the Hollywood Bowl to discuss the existence of a "Bathtub Ring."

DeMille left much of the writing of *The Ten Commandments* to Jeanie that February and early March. It was an unusual problem for her. At first, she tried to develop the story by covering a number of epochs. She wrote in an article in the *Chicago Tribune* published two years later (May 9, 1925): "I worked for several weeks on these lines with growing dissatisfaction. Something was wrong. In episodic form the story didn't have the right 'feel.' It was bumpy. It started and stopped, ran and limped. The thread or theme of it seemed subtly broken every time we commenced a new episode. It became evident that the usual failure of episodic drama would be the fate of *The Ten Commandments* unless we changed our plan."

She told DeMille on March 9 that she had thrown out the entire story and was starting again. She would, she said, only pick up one theme from her original draft. This was the story of two brothers, one of whom mocks the Ten Commandments and the other defends them. She decided to add a new character: the boys' mother. She wrote in *The Tribune*: "What (might) the mother of two such boys be like?—An old lady I had known all my life came to mind. A thoroughly good and honest woman, who believed everybody should believe as she believed, or else they were all wrong. A woman who kept the Ten Commandments, it is true, but who kept them in the wrong way. A woman who was so busy interpreting the letter of the Bible she had forgotten its spirit."

She conceived of the woman as a bigot, hammering religion home; this had the effect of driving her son into the professing of atheism. "The love motive," Jeanie wrote in 1925, "comes into the story in the shape of a modern girl who doesn't know what the Ten Commandments are all about. She neither believes nor disbelieves them; she is just as ignorant of their meaning and considers Elinor Glyn a great deal more interesting . . . once these four totally dissimilar people, all represented by individuals I had met or known of at various times, came slowly into distinct focus, I realized that drama must come from the weaving of their actions and reactions upon each other, and the first solution of my problem had been found: i.e., the translating of the Ten Commandments into terms of modern, everyday life, with modern, everyday people." The film thus became an attack on bigotry, somewhat tendentiously worked out through a quartet of characters. But she felt that the story was not quite complete as it stood; that it needed to be focused through a group of figures which could illustrate the origins of the Commandments themselves. DeMille was delighted when she suggested to him the idea of the Book of Exodus, as a source of the prologue. She wrote in a memorandum to him (March 5, 1923): "As the sins of Pharaoh and his horde of horsemen are avenged by the down-crashing waves of the Red Sea, which parted to let the Children of Israel, with their clear faith, pass through, so does an emotional Red Sea engulf our modern Dan McTavish, who has attempted to raise his puny voice against immutable laws."

Once DeMille participated in the writing after the shock of the Swanson affair, the story really began to grow, to flourish and take shape. He and Jeanie worked steadily on it all through March. While Jeanie toiled over the massive job of construction, Paul Iribe and Claire West were exhaustingly busy researching the story.

DeMille sent his assistant, Mrs. Florence Meehan, on a twenty-thousand-mile trip to Egypt, Palestine, Syria, India, Malay States, Siam, the Straits Settlements, Burma, Kashmir, China, Persia, and Japan, using as means of transportation fourteen different steamers, jinrickshas, camels, elephants, bullock carts, sedan-chairs, and muleback. She bought Egyptian and Hebraic costumes, a suit of Persian armor one thousand years old, silks, swords, tapestries, earrings, and rubies brought by her from the giant ruby mine of Mogok, Burma. Among her many real-life adventures, enough for a sizable book, was one incident in which she woke at two A.M. in her hotel in Penang to feel two hands stealing under her pillow. She jumped out of bed only to be overpowered by two Malay desperados who made off with some valuable emeralds she had bought from a town up the Irrawaddy in Burma the week before.

Cashing in on the recent discoveries of Tutankhamen in Egypt, DeMille had minute details written and photographs taken by the Cairo offices of the Lasky Company. They discovered, among other pieces of information, that the Egyptians had a form of ten-pin bowling (then the rage in America), that an Egyptian word brick was "the equivalent of ten pages of modern prose," that a form of gunpowder existed two thousand years before gunpowder was "invented," and that Egyptian aristocrats liked to wear false mustaches and beards. Details of female cosmetics and soaps were minutely studied. Paul Iribe, working virtually round the clock, did a magnificent job of the sketches, surpassing himself in the meticulous re-creation of the period. At a cost of twenty-five thousand dollars, DeMille had the gigantic Aztec pipe organ improved at Paradise for Dr. Hugo Riesenfeld to work on preparing the score. He sent a copy of the Bible to every single person on the Lasky payroll, with the words, "As I intend to film practically the entire book of Exodus . . . the Bible should never be away from you. Place it on your desk, and when you travel, stick it in your briefcase. Make reading it a daily habit." Comment from the press was irreverent: a writer for the magazine *Screen Classics* suggested DeMille now film the telephone directory, the Seven Deadly Sins, the canned soup classics, the Congressional Record, Blackstone, and the Queensberry Rules.

For the prologue, DeMille cast Theodore Roberts as Moses —a magnificent choice—Charles de Roche as Ramses II, Julia Faye as his wife, and Estelle Taylor as Miriam. For the modern story, DeMille cast Richard Dix and Rod La Rocque as the two brothers, with Edythe Chapman as their mother and Leatrice Joy and Nita Naldi in other roles.

By mid-April, the picture at last was ready to begin shooting. Zukor was terrified by the costs involved, particularly after the failure of *Adam's Rib*, and after reading the final draft of the screenplay, he told his subordinates he wished he had never approved the commencement of the project. He sent Lasky to Hollywood to check on the expenses, and on April 17 heard from Lasky that a budget in excess of seven hundred eighty thousand dollars had been prepared. On April 19 he cabled Lasky: I NOTE COST RUNS FAR OVER SEVEN HUNDRED THOUSAND / THIS IS A BIG SUM TO UNDERTAKE TO PUT INTO A PICTURE WITHOUT BEING ABSOLUTELY SURE IN ADVANCE THAT IT WILL BE A SUCCESS / NO BIG STORY TO MY WAY OF THINKING CAN EVER BE A SUCCESS WITHOUT HAVING PLENTY OF LOVE AND ROMANCE / I AM SURE THAT WITH ALL OF THE THRILLS THAT THERE ARE IN COVERED WAGON* IF IT DID NOT HAVE LOVE AND ROMANCE IT WOULD NOT HAVE THE APPEAL / CECILS PRODUCTION WILL IN ALL LIKELIHOOD HAVE AN EGYPTIAN AND PALESTINE ATMOSPHERE / IT WILL HAVE TO HAVE A TREMENDOUS LOVE INTEREST IN ORDER TO OVERCOME THE HANDICAPS OF ATMOSPHERE. Lasky handed DeMille the telegram; DeMille took three weeks to reply. He cabled Zukor on May 10: I CAN ASSURE YOU TO THE

---

* *The Covered Wagon*, directed by James Cruze, was the studio's greatest current success.

On location off Guadalupe: The Ten Commandments (*1923*).

BEST OF MY BELIEF THE PICTURE WILL HAVE THOSE QUALITIES OF
LOVE ROMANCE AND BEAUTY WHICH YOU RIGHTLY SUGGEST ARE
NECESSARY TO ANY PICTURE.

Zukor still wasn't satisfied, grumbling in another letter and
cable that DeMille wasn't answering him quickly enough; he
finally forced DeMille to drop his normal 50 per cent guaran-
teed share of profits. DeMille in fact offered to waive his salary,
or cut it in half, in order to be allowed to make the picture
exactly the way he wanted, and Zukor impolitely refrained
from answering this offer.

Further trouble came in May, when Elek J. Ludvigh, the
stern Lasky company lawyer whom Zukor trusted absolutely,
sent a series of memoranda charging DeMille with gross
overspending and lack of thrift. By now the budget had risen to
one million dollars. While Neil McCarthy tried to argue Zukor
to a standstill in New York, Ludvigh tried to do the same thing
with DeMille in Hollywood. Finally, DeMille told Lasky in
Hollywood: "See if Zukor will sell me the picture for one
million."

While Lasky returned to New York to discuss the offer with
Zukor, McCarthy hurried back to help DeMille raise the
money. Jules Brulatour, head of Kodak, and Joseph Schenck
and A. P. Giannini of the Bank of America, agreed to raise a
million dollars at once. But at that stage Zukor had decided to
proceed with the picture, convinced by the enthusiasm of its
prospective buyers that perhaps *The Ten Commandments* was a
property he should hang onto after all. Nevertheless, he kept
the firmest rein on the budget.

Not only were relations with New York more strained than
ever. DeMille had constant battles with Alvin Wyckoff: partly
because he was aggravated by Wyckoff's insistence on low-key
lighting for the Egyptian scenes, which DeMille felt would
obscure too many details of Iribe's sets, but also because
Wyckoff was involved in the nascent union for cinematographers, of which DeMille bitterly disapproved. Finally, they
parted company in late April.

DeMille then hired Peverell Marley, a very young assistant, as a cinematographer, sternly lecturing him on the need for clarity in "DeMille lighting." He later engaged the brilliant Bert Glennon, George Melford's cameraman Edward Curtis, J. F. Westerberg, and Archie Stout for the task. Cullen Tate was engaged as usual as assistant director; he performed a sterling job of handling the location problems.

As a setting for the Egyptian scenes, DeMille was forced by Zukor's tight-fistedness to abandon Egypt itself. His scheme to show the Israelites crossing the real Palestine was also frustrated. After several days of vexing delays, he managed to obtain permission from Zukor to shoot instead in Guadalupe, a wind-swept desert area near Santa Maria in Central California. A giant landlift of materials began as Paul Iribe started to construct the city of Per-Ramses in the sands. Great walls, towering gates a hundred and three feet high, and an avenue of sphinxes rose up between the dunes. Meanwhile, in Hollywood, DeMille began complex plans of operation; as excited as a child, he was enjoying, despite the depressing frustrations of Zukor's messages, the feeling of being a kind of Ramses himself.

DeMille arrived in Santa Maria in May, put up Constance and Cecilia at the local hotel, and began to supervise the building of the immense location establishment known as Camp DeMille. The cold was almost unbearable, and he feared a recurrence of the illness which had brought him low in Paris, but fortunately his constitution stood up to the severe winds that whistled and howled over the dunes. He returned to Hollywood on May 10.

Shooting began in Hollywood on May 14, in Paul Iribe's stunning set of the throne room of Ramses II (at first DeMille wanted to make Tutankhamen the pharaoh who banished the Israelites, until historians rudely pointed out that Tutankhamen had had nothing whatsoever to do with it). Then, under the coordination of Captain Alfred Barton, who had been six years with the Army of Occupation in Europe, the vast military operation that was to be the making of the prologue to *The Ten Commandments* began.

Twenty-five hundred actors and forty-five hundred animals went by train on the expedition, the most extraordinary safari of film history. Camp DeMille operated as a complete entity. It even had three dozen cows to supply milk, a hospital run by army surgeons, a field telephone system, a jazz band and dance hall, a restaurant capable of serving seventy-five hundred meals a day, and a complex series of horse-drawn sleds used for carting supplies. A construction gang of five hundred carpenters, four hundred painters, three hundred eighty decorators, and a similar number of electricians and landscape gardeners toiled for two months to build the set, which was twenty-five hundred feet long, with buildings three hundred feet high. By midsummer, most of the set had been finished. A portable electric light plant was hauled in, one capable of lighting ten circuses. Searchlights and great batteries of arcs were produced for the night scenes. Next came the wardrobe department, with thousands of costumes made specially by Claire West for the production. Two hundred camels arrived and were housed and watered. Every day when the actors went on the set wagonloads of seventy-five hundred sandwiches followed them in trucks. The bread was sliced by electric machines and men spread on the butter with paint brushes. Three men, working very fast, were engaged full time simply twisting the necks of the paper sandwich bags. A giant fleet of one hundred thirty-two trucks was engaged to run back and forth between the camp and the local town hauling in supplies, removing garbage, and handling the camp laundry. The cost of all this staggering effort was forty thousand dollars a day.

Each tent was equipped with electric light, two army cots, a bench, two washstands, two basins, a bucket, and a dresser. The layout was exactly the same as that for an army camp. At the eastern end of town were the administration tents, two huge mess tents, storerooms, the cameramen's quarters, and the emergency hospital. On the west side, in the lee of the great sandhills which protected the location from the ocean breezes, were the wardrobe headquarters, property rooms, and a large school tent where every morning at dawn lessons were given to the sixty-five children. At night, the same tent housed vaudeville and circus acts or weekly boxing matches. To the north was the vast sandhill on top of which DeMille had erected a magnificent Oriental marquee, palatial in design and decor, where he lived like Saladin. A complete garden of blue lupins, laid out at a cost of seventeen hundred dollars, surrounded the marquee, and a special flag designed in his own honor fluttered from the top, a deep blue with white letters spelling out his name. In the lowlands to the north were corrals for upwards of two thousand animals—among them, horses, goats, chickens, geese, burros, camels, and dogs, and a fine pair of black stallions bought at a cost of ten thousand dollars to draw Pharaoh's chariot in the pageant. Among the thousands were twenty-eight special managerial and personal assistants to DeMille, a personal domestic staff of twenty-eight, two troops of the Eleventh States cavalry and a battery of field artillery from the Presidio at Monterey, ninety-seven army cooks and helpers from Fort McArthur, laborers, sheep and cattle herders and animal trainers, makeup men and costumers, and a whole colony of newspaper and magazine writers. Streets were named after company executives, the wide boulevard from the center of the camp named Lasky Boulevard. The names of every single one of the thousands appeared on boards at the end of each street with the exact address. Each street also had callboards indicating exactly what were the requirements for each successive day's shooting. Giant slides were used for shifting the cameras, drawn by horses through the sand, and massive hay wagons bumped over the dunes carrying the thousands to their appointed task.

The mess tents sat fifteen hundred people each, one for men and one for women. An immense projection room was built onto the men's tent with a projector which showed each day's rushes to the director's personal circle. There was a separate tent which served only Kosher cookery to two hundred twenty-four orthodox Russian, Polish, and Palestinian Jews working on the production.

The moral life of the camp was rigorously prim and proper. A large police and police matron corps patrolled the separate camps, no man being permitted into the female section and vice versa (wives or husbands of married camp members had been left firmly at home). Prohibition laws were rigorously observed and bootleggers and professional gamblers driven out by DeMille's special police.

Hallett Abend of the Los Angeles *Sunday Times*, who visited the scene on June 10 and 11, described it: "There is much fog and little sunshine, and when the wind sweeps across the sand at sixty miles an hour the coarse sand sweeps with it in a knee-high cloud that stings and bites bare legs and sandaled feet. Though the scenes were supposed to be taking place in intense heat, the wind was so bitter that the cast and extras had to huddle in blankets to keep warm before a scene began."

Abend noted that because the shivering Israelites in their flimsy loincloths had to look as though they were soaked in sweat, five hundred gallons of glycerine were sprayed onto them from giant tanks. Each morning they had to be completely stripped and covered from head to foot in special oils which gave them the appearance of being almost black with sunburn; two young men had been sent weeks before to the beach to determine the exact extent of sunburn on white or olive skin after several days exposure; they were paid enormous bonuses for the agony they suffered.

DeMille missed nothing. An extra giggling or chewing gum would be thunderously denounced from on high. When the Exodus started, it had barely taken six steps when he called a halt, signaled by a special fanfare on the trumpets composed by Hugo Riesenfeld. He had seen through his field glasses one little girl with red hair. He descended, talked to her, and ordered a close-up made of her. Now the Exodus could proceed. But then a curious thing took place which not even DeMille or the entire corps of the Hollywood publicity departments could have foreseen. Completely unrehearsed, the Jewish extras began singing in Hebrew the ancient Hebraic chants "Father of Mercy" and "Hear O Israel the Lord Our God, the Lord Is One." DeMille burst into tears.

The film's most dangerous scene was the giant pursuit of the Exodus by the charioted army of Egypt, played by members of the Eleventh Cavalry. They made a heroic spectacle in their golden tunics, metal cuirasses gleaming in the sun, their gilded helmets tossing with multicolored plumes. In the van of the chase was a span of black thoroughbreds which DeMille had bought in Kansas City for fifty thousand dollars. When the stampede was over, four men lay in the sand, severely injured. Horses were lamed. Sand swirled with the wreckage of broken chariots ground up by the horses' hooves. One horse ran screaming about, its flank ripped open, the flesh flapping like a red scarf.

DeMille had insisted upon a thirty-piece Palm Court orchestra, playing martial music, to sit in a special enclosure just off camera "to keep everyone in the right mood." It was conducted by the unfortunate Rudolph Berliner, DeMille's childhood friend who had been installed comfortably as Director of the Palm Court orchestra of the Ritz-Carlton in New York for the past few years. The flying horses headed, many of them riderless, straight for the band, which gallantly went on playing in evening dress, seemingly more frightened of DeMille than of the advancing horde. A moment later the chariots and horses crashed into them, leaving a heap of broken instruments and badly bruised men and women.

Even when they were not being subjected to severe bruises and cuts, Berliner and his orchestra were constantly in distress, playing in the teeth of a gale which blew sand into the trombones and trumpets, clogging them up, and into ears, eyes, and mouths.

The crossing of the Red Sea was a particularly difficult problem. The special effects man, Roy Pomeroy, achieved the actual parting in Hollywood, using a bent steel tray painted to represent a landscape into which thousands of gallons of water were poured, then photographing the tray and reversing the shot. But to show the Israelites traversing the real landscape was really a major effort. Special fences had to be built so that the extras would not wander out of the camera's range. In order that the fences would not throw shadows, the scene had to be shot at the exact moment of high noon. The members of the Ritz-Carlton orchestra in their tuxedos and flowing black dresses, though badly damaged by the ordeal with the chariots, gamely struck up the Largo from the New World Symphony of Dvorak to inspire the great throng. Then, just as the cameras were about to turn, DeMille realized that the ocean was visible in the frame lines.

He knew he would have to shift the cameras, but he only had a few minutes until noon. Then, looking out to sea, he was fascinated to see a large bed of seaweed floating on the waves. Through his largest megaphone, he ordered everyone to follow him as he rushed into the waves, emerging dripping wet to spread the seaweed along the sand. "It will look as though the Red Sea really did open up, leaving weed everywhere," he bawled at the Israelites. Soon everyone had gone into the sea, fetched the weed, and spread it. DeMille climbed back onto his elevated platform and the Ritz-Carlton òrchestra again played Dvorak's Largo against the wind. Although it was the wettest Exodus in history, it emerged splendidly on the screen.

After completing the work at Guadalupe in June, DeMille returned to Hollywood to shoot the Destruction of the Children of Israel, the scene in which God shows his wrath over the worship of the Golden Calf. Twelve giant airplane motors created an artificial sirocco in the studio and dynamite blasts gave an impression of lightning. The effect of these charges was to send Theodore Roberts, playing Moses, tumbling from his rocky perch, Estelle Taylor somersaulted backwards, and the Golden Calf was smashed to pieces and had to be replaced by a stand-in.

On the set of The Ten Commandments:
Theodore Roberts, DeMille, and publicity man Barrett Kiesling (1923).

Rod La Rocque, C. B., and Ricardo Cortel
on location at Catalina: Feet of Clay.

Jeanie and C. B. on location at Catalina for Feet of Clay (*1924*).

After completing this sequence, DeMille moved his tents to Muroc, California, arriving by caravan at midnight. In this location, on the bed of an immense dry lake in the Mojave Desert, he shot the headlong dash of two hundred fifty Egyptian chariots against the Israelites.

When the great sequence of chariots rushing over the edge of the sand cliff began, the drivers suddenly proved unwilling to proceed. DeMille was disgusted. In order to shame them, he told Cecilia to seize the reins of her pony and ride it with all the skill of her eleven-year-old horsewomanship down the slope. She obeyed with great delight, and made the perilous descent without a flaw. The charioteers, flushing with shame, immediately followed her.

Disobeying strict orders, Tom Allenby of Melbourne, Australia, staged an impromptu stunt. He plunged in his chariot over a two-hundred-foot sandcliff, simultaneously pushing another actor out of the way in his own vehicle and in the subsequent collision hurtling forty feet in the air. Allenby came down uninjured, except for minor cuts and severe bruises, in the sand.

From the Mojave Desert, DeMille shifted his base of operation to San Francisco for some of the modern sequences, shooting for three days (July 23–25) in the Church of Sts. Peter and Paul, which was then being constructed, using a platform two hundred feet up. An immense crowd gathered to cheer Leatrice Joy as she made her way to the top of the spire by workman's elevator—an open platform swung on an iron cable which rocked perilously during the ascent. DeMille was at the top waiting for her, with a battery of cameras equipped with telephoto lenses to shoot the broad sweep of the view: the humpback hills, the bustle of Market Street, the blue bay, and Alcatraz in the distance. Before the company left town, one hundred fifty members of the Washington Grammar School Alumni Association gave a deluxe reception for Moses, honoring the fact that Theodore Roberts had been captain of the Washington Grammar Cadets in 1875.

DeMille also shot scenes at Balboa Beach, showing the journey of the Israelites after the parting of the Red Sea, and at Anaheim Landing, where the host was shown being stopped by the Pillar of Fire.

All through the shooting of *The Ten Commandments*, feeling built up against DeMille, especially on Zukor's part. Zukor, in a memorandum to Lasky dated August 13, said that he felt DeMille should waive his normal guarantee since he had enormously exceeded the agreed upon negative cost of the picture—it was six hundred thousand dollars and by June 23 costs had reached one million two thousand. ("As the matter now stands, we do all of the gambling while he gets his advances and guarantees.") Zukor also complained of the fact that DeMille had for years insisted on obtaining a second negative for his own use, which the company paid for. Lasky was caught between two fires, trying to appease his old friend while forced to carry out Zukor's instructions that DeMille be disciplined.

During the cutting of the picture with Anne Bauchens, DeMille saw a dream fulfilled in the completion of the community of Fernangeles, in the San Fernando Valley, a town which he had conceived from the outset, helped build from the ground up, and sold to individual buyers in a series of masterly strategies. He gave hundreds of free tickets to the opening of *The Ten Commandments* to people who visited Fernangeles. To celebrate the occasion, he wore elaborate clothing at the opening—a green sports shirt, green-dyed jodhpurs and pants, and one of the world's five green diamonds set in a ring of green gold. He also acquired a major stockholding in the Biltmore Hotel that winter, and added to his directorships important roles on the boards of the Bank of Italy and the Trust and Savings Bank of Hollywood, of which he rapidly became Vice President. He was also Vice President of the newly opened Commercial National Bank.

He became president of a real estate syndicate which

developed San Fernando Valley, earning him millions. He began lavish improvements to Paradise, served his guests off solid gold plate, gave each lady guest a present of jewels or furs, and had armed guards at the gates and storm cellars built.

That fall, on October 8, Beatrice DeMille, Cecil's beloved mother, died. She had been ill for several weeks at her home at 2026 Argyle Avenue in Los Angeles, and DeMille visited her constantly with flowers and presents. To his great sadness he was not with her when she slipped quietly away in the early hours of the morning.

On November 6, Jesse signed an agreement with DeMille in which DeMille would resume his duties as director-general of the corporation, and would make a new picture, *Triumph*, immediately after *The Ten Commandments* was released. DeMille, swallowing his pride, issued an uplifting memorandum to the press: "Years of close personal and business friendship between Adolph Zukor, Jesse Lasky and myself have brought unbreakable ties which we are now perpetuating in a new contract." But privately he told Barrett Kiesling he blamed Lasky for not taking his part sufficiently strongly in the negotiations which almost destroyed *The Ten Commandments*.

When the cutting of *The Ten Commandments* was finished at last in November, DeMille firmly refused Zukor's demand for a public preview and held one privately at Laughlin Park. He had the Ritz-Carlton orchestra perform in the small hallway while the executives, headed by Zukor and Lasky, crowded into the study, where the picture was shown. In the midst of the most enthralling passages, a loud snoring was heard. DeMille glanced around, feeling agonized. Suppose it should be one of the executives? Then he noticed that everyone else was glancing round for the source of the snoring too. At last he located it—right under his feet. To his red-faced fury, he discovered it was his favorite bulldog, Angie. He gave it a well-aimed kick and it flew out of the room, causing everyone in the room to roar with laughter and the whole mood of the picture to be broken.

The Ten Commandments opened at the George M. Cohan Theatre, New York, on December 21, 1923, before a celebrity audience. Reviews were favorable more for the sheer size of the prologue than for the overlong and rambling modern story. The *New York Times* critic had some mordant things to say: "If an old mother reads her Bible it is no reason why a motion picture director should have her carrying around a volume that weighs two hundred weight." The anonymous critic of the *New York World* summed it all up when he wrote: "In its earlier episodes the film has moments of grandeur in setting and majesty in movement which are exciting and beautiful. When the story hurdles the centuries and settles into a present day symbolization of what has gone before it is ordinary movie melodrama of the commonest type, heavy-footed, unimaginative and ponderous." But the public adored the picture: audiences both at the George M. Cohan and the Egyptian Theatre in Hollywood cheered the film to the echo.

David Belasco cabled DeMille on December 24: I CONGRATULATE YOU DEAR CECIL ON YOUR WONDERFUL ACHIEVEMENT IN THE TEN COMMANDMENTS / I'M PROUD OF THE LITTLE BOY WHO USED TO BRING CANDY TO ME AT ECHO LAKE WHOSE FATHER WAS ONE OF THE MOST BRILLIANT MEN THAT EVER LIVED AND THE SWEETNESS OF WHOSE MOTHER I SHALL NEVER FORGET / THE DEMILLE FAMILY ARE ALL TUCKED AWAY IN MY HEART / A MERRY CHRISTMAS TO YOU AND YOUR DEAR ONES / DAVID BELASCO.

The Ten Commandments was an immediate and extraordinary success. Even Zukor felt compelled to cable from New York: MAY THE FIRST PERFORMANCE OF THE TEN COMMANDMENTS TUESDAY NIGHT BEFORE THE PUBLIC MEET IN EVERY WAY YOUR HEARTFELT DESIRES / I AM NOT UNMINDFUL OF THE TERRIFIC TASK SO MAGNIFICENTLY DONE BY YOU IN THE MAKING OF THIS EPOCHAL PRODUCTION / MY SINCERE GOOD WISHES / ADOLPH ZUKOR. Clara Beranger, James Quirk of *Photoplay*, Walter Wanger, Mrs. Billy Sunday, Edward F. Magnin, and dozens of others sent shoals of letters and telegrams.

The Ten Commandments and a new contract firmly under his belt, DeMille faced 1924 with nothing very interesting on hand. Excited by the great success of the premiere, it seemed only appropriate that he should make *Triumph*, but it was a not very exciting work, based on a *Saturday Evening Post* story by May Edginton. He cast Rod La Rocque and Leatrice Joy in the leading roles. He also cast a sturdy newcomer, Victor Varconi, a Hungarian who had just come from several years of success with the National Theatre in Budapest and in films with Pola Negri. On January 7, after a period of closure, the Lasky Studio in Hollywood reopened with George Melford's production of *The Dawn of Tomorrow*, starring Jacqueline Logan.

Triumph was the story of two brothers, played by La Rocque and Varconi, who fight for the hand of the girl, played by Miss Joy, with a characteristic flashback to the story of Romeo and Juliet. It added little to DeMille's reputation and came as little more than a trivial footnote to the story of fraternal rivalry told in *The Ten Commandments*. Certainly it gave no hint of the fantastic weirdness of DeMille's next picture, self-indulgently entitled *Feet of Clay*.

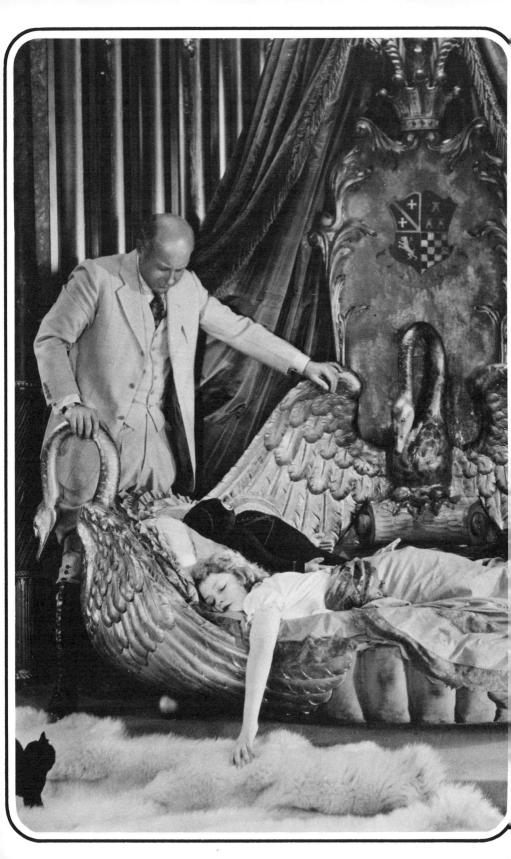

6

Oddities

Arguably the most peculiar film DeMille ever made, *Feet of Clay*, which he began in the first months of 1924, was drawn from a variety of sources. The original novel, serialized in the *Ladies Home Journal*, was by a wealthy woman, Margaretta Tuttle, who simply wrote a straightforward story about a soldier who comes home after losing the toes of one foot in World War I. No doubt DeMille's obsession with feet drew him to the title. He decided to add to the story an element of the supernatural, following upon the current craze for spiritualism and the great success of plays dealing with the world after death, most notably Sutton Vane's celebrated

DeMille, Lillian Rich: The Golden Bed.

Outward Bound, about a group of passengers crossing over to the "other side."

At first, DeMille decided to have Lasky buy Sutton Vane's play and combine it with Beulah Marie Dix's novel and play *Across the Border,* which Lasky had bought in 1915. Lasky cabled him on February 18, 1924, that *Outward Bound* would never make mass entertainment, but DeMille argued him out of that position. Then Lasky cabled DeMille on March 7, 1924: WE ARE HELPLESS TRYING TO BUY OUTWARD BOUND IN TIME FOR YOU / ADVISE YOU STRONGLY YOU DO COMBINATION OF FEET OF CLAY AND ACROSS THE BORDER SO THAT WE DO NOT GET INTO TROUBLE LATER BECAUSE OF ANY SIMILARITY TO OUTWARD BOUND.

Beulah Marie Dix's *Across the Border* had been produced by Holbrook Blinn at the Princess Theatre, New York, in November 1914, when DeMille originally saw it; later it was published in novel form (Henry Holt Company, 1915). The story concerned a young officer who is killed by German snipers on the Western Front. His soul leaves his body and rushes blindly along the road to another world where he meets a figure called The Master of the House. Gradually, the young man realizes he is among the dead. He is taken to a place of punishment, but begs to be given the task of righting certain wrongs on earth. This, he says, will involve preaching against violence. The Master of the House gives him the chance, and he becomes a pacifist, living out the full span of his life.

Aided by her intimate friend, the writer Bertram Millhauser, Beulah Marie Dix finished the screenplay in May. She also drew material from O. Henry's story "The Furnished Room." The new version involved a radical departure from both sources: Kerry Harlan is a handsome but hard-up young athlete who falls in love with a beautiful socialite, Amy Loring. He rescues her from drowning in a motorboat race off Catalina when her boat blows up (DeMille used the incident of the sinking of the *Cecilia* as a basis of this accident). During the rescue, his left toes are bitten off by a shark. They marry, she works as a fashion model, but Amy's sister Bertha tries to capture the handsome youth for herself. Spying on the pair, Bertha falls to her death from a window ledge, a scandal eventuates, and Amy and Kerry make a suicide pact. But they are found in time and brought back to life. In the interim they travel to the next world, where The Keeper of the Books gives them a second chance.

While Beulah Marie Dix was working on the script, DeMille sent a representative to Margaretta Tuttle's home and offered to buy the rights for twenty-five hundred dollars. She asked ten times that much, saying that she had been offered twenty-five thousand dollars by other studios. Much to his chagrin, DeMille fell into the trap. Once she had wrung the figure of twenty-five thousand from him, Miss Tuttle bombarded him with letters on purple notepaper, typed with a mauve ribbon. An excerpt from a typical example (April 14, 1924) ran as follows: "You who know Love, know its Feet of Clay, set upon good Earth, the golden light upon its forehead that is the light from the lamp carried by the one who loves.

"Love begins with clay; molding it as a child molds clay. Then Love grows with its effort to mold its clay, and the clay is not enough. It must have living tissues to mold.

"So it breathes the light upon its forehead into the fibres of its clay body and the cells of its earth-brain. . . ." She wrote characteristically to Zukor: "I believe Aladdin had two genii who obeyed him, but Mr. DeMille is not now using the genii of the ring, but of the lamp . . . a light-bearing genii."

When shooting started that summer, with Rod La Rocque as Kerry Harlan and Vera Reynolds as Amy Loring, DeMille made the serious mistake of asking Miss Tuttle to Hollywood to watch the shooting. She proved to be an unmitigated nuisance. Asked by reporters when she stepped off the train in Los Angeles on June 3 what she thought of the project, she said: "It is only the feet that interest him."

Rod La Rocque was among the welcomers. He told her:

"Why in the name of sanity didn't you make this hero hurt his hand and not his foot? I shall be crippled for life hobbling around ten hours a day for ninety days." "Well at least I only used shrapnel," Miss Tuttle replied. "It took Cecil B. DeMille to think of a shark."

The authoress was whisked off to San Pedro to be taken to Catalina by boat. She was astounded when La Rocque told her that DeMille was using five yachts in the picture "which was only natural, since you wrote a story about millionaires."

"The story," she replied weakly, "is set in Springfield, Ohio, and everyone is poor." When she reached Catalina, looking around at the powerboats driven by handsome young men in white flannels, the wharf strung with flags of pink and yellow and red, the blue sea and sky, she said to La Rocque, "I should have written the book about all this. It would have been much more fun to do."

DeMille had turned Catalina into an authentic millionaire's Paradise for the film. The beach, originally stony, was converted into a lovely crescent of white imported sand, brought from Hawaii at great expense. Brilliantly vivid tents, striped green and mauve and scarlet, dotted the foreshores. Each day, the cast was served by white-coated servants, off tables loaded with solid gold, Spode, and Wedgwood plate. They ate rainbow trout in aspic, truffles, pâté de foie gras, and pyramids of crystalized fruit. Later, Miss Tuttle recalled her first introduction to the director-general:

"Good morning, Miss Tuttle. I'm glad you could come. Will you dine with me tonight—on the yacht at seven?"

" 'Automatically I said, 'Thank you.' "

"The director looked back in the camera. 'More light on that castle,' he said.

"I turned, rather desperately, to someone beside me. 'What do you wear for dinner on a yacht?' I asked.

" 'White flannel trousers,' was the reply."

The altercations between her and DeMille were frequent and bitter. On one occasion, during the scene in which Rod La

Rocque is recovering from the shark-biting incident on a yacht, DeMille stopped shooting and said sharply to her, "You would-be authors come forward and sweat a little blood."

Everyone turned to look at her. DeMille was frowning and biting his right forefinger: sure sign of trouble. She said brightly: "That lets me out. I am no *would-be* author."

Everyone froze. DeMille's voice was like a knife blade. "I *mean* you!" he shouted.

She managed to improvise a line. DeMille approved it with a curt nod, but her next one was greeted with, "I could do as well by waving my arms about my head." She barely spoke to him after that.

DeMille not only had constant quarrels with Margaretta Tuttle, he differed strongly with Paul Iribe on the designs, and replaced him early in the shooting with Norman Bel Geddes. Bel Geddes, famous in the theater, found it as hard as Wilfred Buckland to adapt to the demands of motion pictures. He was annoyed by DeMille's insistence on extravagant display, and complained that a ballroom scene was going to be an absurdity if DeMille had his way. But DeMille forced him to create the set of a mansion with extraordinary baroque grandeur, fill its surrounding gardens with strutting peacocks, and dress every woman at the ball in real jewels. Margaretta Tuttle and Norman Bel Geddes stood on the sidelines, commenting unfavorably on everything, until DeMille ordered them removed.

DeMille had another severe problem with the boat race in which the hero's left foot is maimed. The boat race itself was fine, with scores of lovely girls standing on rainbow-striped aquaplanes, drawn along by fleets of powerboats. In one hand they held spears, fluttering with scarlet and gold ribbons, and plunged these weapons into passing fish. The problem lay with the sharks. DeMille wanted a shot of one in a glass tank lowered below the water rushing at Rod La Rocque. But weather caused endless delays, and each day a shark, put in the tank, beat itself to death against the glass. No less than fifteen

With Gladys Rosson.

The Candy Ball from The Golden Bed.

sharks died in this manner before the scene was successfully completed.

DeMille finished *Feet of Clay* on July 7, 1924, and left at once on the *Seaward* for a two-week trip around Catalina on his yacht while Anne Bauchens prepared a rough cut.

The picture was released in the fall—and at once ran into a storm of censorship. To DeMille's horror, not only did various state boards reject the film, but individual exhibitors began dropping reels out of it which they found offensive, beginning with the manager of the Strand Theatre, Omaha, Nebraska. The Pennsylvania State Board of Censors was so finicky it insisted on changing a title which read PASSION DIES WITH THE DEAD BODY to LOVE DIES WITH THE DEAD BODY. DeMille saw the advantages in a publicity campaign against such alterations at once, sending a telegram to his press agent Barrett Kiesling (October 10, 1924): THIS IS TOO GOOD TO LOSE / IT COULD BE EDITORIALLY COMMENTED ON ALL OVER. He bombarded Will Hays with telegrams demanding something be done about Pennsylvania, and other censorious states, and at last succeeded in getting PASSION put back in place of LOVE.

As soon as the film was previewed in London, Sutton Vane contrived to see it. He stormed out of the screening and immediately instructed his solicitors, Field, Roscoe and Company, to sue DeMille for plagiarism. What upset him was the final reel, dealing with the journey of the young couple to the life hereafter. Just as in his own play, the lovers gassed themselves, and were allowed another chance at life; their pet dog is permitted to awake them.

Neil McCarthy and Gladys Rosson (who in addition to being DeMille's secretary was a Notary Public) took depositions from Beulah Marie Dix, Bertram Millhauser, and DeMille himself. Skilfully worded, these gave the complex history of the work in question. DeMille, in further prepared statements for the New York Superior Court and the Court of Chancery in London, neatly evaded the charges, but the case was finally settled out of court in Vane's favor.

It was an uncomfortable business, which DeMille always resolutely refused to discuss in later years. And right on top of it, he faced another plagiarism suit: Mrs. Mattie Thomas Thornton, an Atlanta, Georgia, housewife, claimed that she had written the original story of *The Ten Commandments* in 1918, had submitted it to Famous Players-Lasky and had not received it back from the company. In the Atlanta court she produced a carbon of the synopsis, which was identical with Jeanie's plot line, including the Egyptian prologue. She appeared at screenings of the film both in Georgia and in her native state of Alabama, welcoming arrivals to see "her" film.

Neil McCarthy called DeMille to his office and together they spent hours poring over a copy of the carbon material. Finally, DeMille got up and began pacing excitedly around the room. "I've got it!" he said. He had noticed some infinitesimal errors in the plot which, he suddenly realized, had been those originally committed by Hallett Abend, film critic of the *Los Angeles Times.* Abend had written a very long and detailed account of the plot before the film was released. Quite obviously, Mrs. Thornton had copied the plot from Abend's review, reprinted in theater programs in the Deep South.

McCarthy at once called the *Times.* The editorial office told him that Abend was on a hunting trip in the High Sierras. Luckily, DeMille knew the area like the back of his hand, and immediately instructed a pilot on the most likely trail areas. The pilot located Abend's camp, dropped a leaflet with a long DeMillean memorandum on it, and Abend at once made his way back across the mountains, arriving looking distinctly flustered in McCarthy's office a few days later.

He left at once for Atlanta, but the judge threw out his evidence, pointing out that he might easily have based his synopsis on Mrs. Thornton's original synopsis. Meanwhile, however, Neil McCarthy had arrived in Georgia, and he and Barrett Kiesling engaged specialists to examine the carbon copies of the manuscript. They announced definitively that the paper upon which the material was typed had not been available in 1918. It was as a result of this action that, in the future, no studio in Hollywood ever read an unsolicited or an unagented manuscript.

In the summer of 1924, DeMille was back at work on a new picture, *The Golden Bed*, based by Jeanie—who had been on leave flying seaplanes to and from Catalina—on the novel *Tomorrow's Bread*, by Wallace Irwin.

It was the story of the rise and fall of an old Southern family: Lillian Rich was the daughter of the house who had been born in an immense golden bed, Vera Reynolds played her noble and dedicated sister. Lillian Rich's husband was Theodore Kosloff, whom she drives to commit suicide in the Swiss Alps. Later, she returns to find the plantation in ruins, with La Rocque as its owner. She ruthlessly seduces him into marriage, then systematically wrecks his life, forcing him to give a giant Candy Ball, the final extravaganza which finishes him financially. In an extraordinary last scene, the great house is shown turned into a bordello, with nothing in its crumbling ruins except the bed, now the scene of wanton and meaningless lust.

A sermon, like so many of his films, on the dangers of money, *The Golden Bed* has a compulsive power which still can affect an audience. Jeanie MacPherson's script has a superb, driving logic, and the last sequence of the bed is a master stroke of theater not equaled by DeMille and his writer since *Joan the Woman* and in many ways the equal of a Tennessee Williams' work of the 1950s. Lillian Rich was extraordinary as the destructive, ultimately self-destroying gold digger.

Shooting in Hollywood, on Paul Iribe's inspired sets, was reasonably straightforward, and DeMille got along famously with Lillian Rich, Vera Reynolds, and Rod La Rocque. But when he went to Mount Rainier in August to shoot the scenes of the death of Theodore Kosloff in the Swiss Alps, he ran into serious trouble. Filming the sequence on a glacier, the company was warned by a guide to be off by three o'clock. DeMille grandly ignored the warning. At four twenty-four, a blizzard swept over the glacier; the party, numbering twelve, was forced to divide into three separate guided groups making their way with immense difficulty back to the inn. Lillian Rich, Jeanie, and Claire West had to be carried by the male members of the team in the final stages, and DeMille had to run for his life, leaving a tent and twenty thousand dollars worth of equipment behind. His journey back across treacherous ice made good telling when he got home at the end of the month. He kept his family up late at night describing how camera tripods and platforms, tent pegs and film boxes, had to be chopped and burned to provide warmth in the bitter wind. And of his extraordinary journey back across a slippery cliff edge to the encampment where he heard that the tents had been blown away and snow and debris were scattered over the place where they stood.

Other tales of the adventures at Mount Rainier were on DeMille's lips for months after that. In a scene in which Robert Cain and Theodore Kosloff fought on the edge of a chasm over Lillian Rich, they slipped into a crevass and were badly bruised. Cain was confronted with a huge grizzly while on an evening walk, and pack rats swarmed into DeMille's room at the old Mount Rainier Inn, making off with his socks, jumping on the dresser, and crawling into his clothes.

Aside from the scene on the glacier, *The Golden Bed* offered the ultimate in DeMille extravagance: the Candy Ball, designed to show the ruinous self-indulgence of the central figure played by Rod La Rocque. In the center of a sumptuous ornamental garden, a huge open candy box showered immense chocolates made of brown satin. Gigantic candy canes stood everywhere, and massive baskets of real candies flanked the trees. In this garden, DeMille showed a slave market with a slave master whose hair was made of lollypops and his beard of stick candy. And he even had young men licking the chocolate from living female candy bars.

7

At Mount Vernon

A t the end of shooting *The Golden Bed*, DeMille was deep in complex negotiations for the rights to Marie Corelli's famous novel *The Sorrows of Satan*. To his great disappointment, these could only be procured on the author's specific proviso that DeMille not direct the movie version of the book. She detested his films. News of the proviso did little to improve the already disintegrating confidence of Zukor, who had been more and more displeased with DeMille's work since *The Ten Commandments*. Relations between the two became so strained that once again Lasky, fearing his own position, felt compelled to desert his old friend and side with Zukor. By the time *The Sorrows of Satan* became available following the

141

*The gala opening of "Mt. Vernon"—the Ince Studio—
as the C. B. DeMille Studio (1927).*

author's death in 1924, it was too late to patch up the quarrel.

Meanwhile, DeMille was searching for his own independent studio, and for a complete break with Famous Players. He discussed his ambition with Constance at Laughlin Park, with McCarthy in offices downtown, with Jeanie at the studio, and with Julia in their still continuing weekends together at Paradise or on the *Seaward*. Everyone agreed he must make a move, and he instructed John Fisher to find him something.

On December 8, 1924, Fisher learned from several officials of Thomas Ince's studio at Culver City—including Carpenter, the general manager—that the studio was up for sale or rent following Ince's sudden death on his yacht some three weeks earlier. The studio had been making pictures mainly for First National, at two hundred thousand dollars each, with an average profit of between fifty thousand dollars and sixty-five thousand dollars a picture. The studio had under contract Florence Vidor, Jacqueline Logan, Barbara Bedford, Mary Astor, Clive Brook, and Warner Baxter. Directors on the payroll included Roy William Neill, Lambert Hillyer, and George Archainbaud. The replacement value of the studio was put at five hundred thousand dollars and there were fifteen acres of real estate valued at two hundred thousand dollars, bringing the total cost to almost three quarters of a million.

While he weighed the facts which Fisher put before him, DeMille fretted miserably over a series of stern memoranda from Zukor in New York. These severely restricted DeMille's power, demanding that he cease forthwith to engage stars under contract and that he trim his budgets still further. To add insult to injury, the memoranda were not sent direct, but filtered through—and endorsed by—Jesse. Sidney R. Kent, sales executive of the studio, and a powerful supporter of Zukor against DeMille, also sent stern warnings.

One ray of light came at Christmas when DeMille learned that Lasky had finally persuaded Zukor to permit a DeMille version of *The Sorrows of Satan*. Impulsively, against the advice of John Fisher, who begged him to stay and make arrangements to take over the Ince Studio, he shelved all discussions on the matter and packed for a trip to London. There he planned to make a location survey for *The Sorrows.*

Early in January, DeMille started out on the trip with Peverell Marley, Mitchell Leisen, Constance, Jeanie, Julia, and two friends, Mrs. Claire O'Neill and Mrs. Louise Covell, for London and Paris. They never sailed. On January 8, Zukor advised DeMille he had changed his mind yet again and decided not to let him direct *The Sorrows of Satan* after all. DeMille strode from Zukor's office white with rage. He resigned the next day, despite Lasky's desperate efforts to dissuade him over lunch at the Waldorf, and immediately cabled Fisher in Hollywood to proceed with the obtaining of the Ince Studio at a price of two hundred thousand dollars below the one asked. That evening, he managed to persuade the fabulously wealthy banker and railroad man Jeremiah Milbank to back him financially in the purchase, thus aiding him in making a life of Christ. It was a shrewd move, because Milbank was deeply religious, and by sundown the promise had been made.

Aided by friends on Wall Street, DeMille spent the next few days energetically organizing his new company. With his own money, he bought a 50 per cent share in the ailing Producers' Distributing Corporation, through which, in future, all of his pictures would be released. Simultaneously, he incorporated the Cinema Corporation of America, a holding company which would own all of the shares of stock in PDC and the whole of the stock of Cecil B. DeMille Pictures Corporation. The Cinema Corporation of America was owned 50 per cent by Milbank and 50 per cent by DeMille. In PDC, DeMille was allied with an old friend, John Flinn, who, together with F. C. Munroe, Raymond Pawley, and Paul C. Mooney, succeeded in reactivating the company from the dead bones of the old W. W. Hodkinson Corporation.

Back in Los Angeles in February, DeMille made a complete survey of the Ince Studios, which he bought on behalf of his backers for a bargain five hundred thousand dollars. The main administration building was already one of the most famous landmarks in Hollywood. A complete replica of George Washington's home, Mount Vernon, Virginia, symbolizing Ince's magnificent vaingloriousness, ninety-six feet long and thirty feet deep, it boasted a pillared piazza, a large entrance hall with liveried butlers and flunkeys, a sweeping staircase leading to an upper landing flanked by portraits of presidents, business chiefs, movie stars, and episodes in the saga of independence. Sumptuous scarlet curtains, looped and tasseled, framed tall windows looking down over rolling groomed lawns dotted with oaks, elders, and pine trees. DeMille immediately went a step further than Ince. He redecorated his study as an exact copy of George Washington's, even to the inkwells.

On March 2, 1925, the great studio was reopened, and DeMille proudly took up residence. Much as he disliked leaving his great office at Vine Street and Selma Avenue, where he had enjoyed more than a decade of power, he was intensely happy at the grand prospect which seemed to be opening up. His eyes misted with pleasure at the welcoming ceremony arranged by the Los Angeles Chamber of Commerce. Harry Culver, founder of Culver City, declared an official holiday, encouraging two thousand citizens to turn out upon the rolling lawns of Mount Vernon. In golden sunlight, a band struck up DeMille's favorite airs, flowers tossed in newly planted beds, Los Angeles Mayor C. V. Loop extended an official welcome, and Louis B. Mayer, Joseph Schenck, and Al Christie on behalf of the producers wished DeMille well. After a speech in which he promised to do his utmost for the present prestige and future glory of Culver City, DeMille led two hundred stars, feature players, directors, technicians, and members of the public into Mount Vernon for champagne and caviar.

As soon as he was installed in Washingtonian glory at Mount Vernon, DeMille began negotiations to attract as many stars as possible away from the Lasky organization to his own. In most cases, he shrewdly invited them to Laughlin Park on Sundays, in the case of the ladies for a discreet late morning cup of coffee, in the case of the men for cocktails, or dinner followed by brandy and cigars.

He felt the need to build up a body of contract stars. Just as in the teens of the country, he would be in complete charge of all productions as well as his own. At last, he felt, he would be free of interference from New York: Zukor, that painful thorn in his side, had at long last been removed. It was an exhilarating feeling. He confronted the rest of 1925 with overpowering confidence.

His flair for publicity stood him in good stead that spring. He arranged a wedding in the sky for the female star of a new aviation picture. He arranged for a ring-tailed monkey to escape from the studio and make its way into the nearby Meralta Theatre, causing consternation as it crawled over the audience's legs. After a wild chase during which most of the women in the audience fled in terror, a studio employee brought it down in a flying tackle. Needless to say, the beast had a large sign around its neck which left nobody in the slightest doubt it was working for DeMille. There were many such stunts in the months that followed.

At the outset of 1925, DeMille settled on the policy of his corporation: forty pictures to cost not less than four and a half million dollars, and not more than five million, DeMille to direct one big picture which would cost not less than eight hundred thousand dollars and not more than one million; and a complete list of pictures to be drawn up.

He also instituted a procedure which he maintained to the end of his life. Before each picture, DeMille had the entire crew and company, as well as every single featured contract player and member of the staff, sit in his immense Washingtonian office in semi-circles while he told them the entire story of the film, scene by scene, line of dialogue by line of dialogue, an exhausting ritual sometimes lasting several hours. Members of the press, with pride of place given to *Photoplay*'s editor James R. Quirk, were always present. At the end of the preparations,

DeMille would reach for a glass of water, then stride around the room asking for any criticisms. Once these were given, by the press or by others, he would have Gladys Rosson make a detailed note of them. They were seldom heeded.

Among the first stars whom he brought over from Lasky Studio was Jetta Goudal, a distinguished French actress who had enjoyed a stage career before coming to Hollywood. As a vehicle for her, for Vera Reynolds, and for Joseph Schildkraut (whom he saw as a rival to Valentino) he bought Beulah Marie Dix's and Evelyn Greenleaf Sutherland's play *The Road to Yesterday*, which he had originally enjoyed at the Herald Square Theatre in New York on December 31, 1906, and had deeply admired. He had attempted to buy it for Famous Players-Lasky in 1915, but had not succeeded; it had been tied up for many years in a lawsuit over possible plagiarism. He engaged Beulah Marie Dix to work with Jeanie on adapting it for the screen. The rest of his team, John Fisher, Paul Iribe, Peverell Marley, Claire West, Mitchell Leisen, Anne Bauchens, Gladys Rosson, Mrs. Elizabeth McGaffey, and Barrett Kiesling among others, had come with him en masse and worked far more happily now that they were free of New York grumblings.

DeMille was attracted to *The Road to Yesterday* because it involved the theme of reincarnation, then enjoying a vogue as extreme as the fashion for spiritualism which had inspired *Feet of Clay*. His use of scenes present and past, interwoven into the narrative, had, if truth be told, always reflected a deep private interest in the subject. What was implied would now be clearly stated. The picture of past life would not simply be triggered off by any ingenious Macpherson plot device. It would be part of the warp and woof of the drama.

The story concerned Kenneth Paulton (Joseph Schildkraut) whose lovely wife, Malena (Jetta Goudal), rejects him sexually. She is obsessed with the idea that in a previous incarnation he had injured her physically and spiritually. With two friends, Jack Moreland (William Boyd) and Beth Tyrrel (Vera Reynolds), the unhappy couple take off on a train journey through

On location at the Grand Canyon: The Road to Yesterday.

Jetta Goudal in The Road to Yesterday.

Peverell Marley and C. B. on location: The Volga Boatman.

William Boyd in The Volga Boatman.

the West. They are involved in a disastrous train wreck, which makes them revert to their former lives in England in the Middle Ages: we see Paulton as a gallant knight and Malena as a gypsy whose death he causes at the stake. Reverting to today, the characters are able to see the errors of their ways.

That spring of 1925, in addition to supervising two features not of his own making, DeMille was chiefly concerned with the Dix-Macpherson screenplay: re-creating the medieval world of England, and devising the most spectacular train wreck ever filmed in Hollywood. Paul Iribe and Mitchell Leisen together built a tremendous castle with accompanying towers each of which was over one hundred feet high.

To light the set for one hour, more electricity was consumed than was used for the street lights of Los Angeles. For a scene of a village feast, DeMille supplied two whole oxen, seven roast suckling pigs, and twenty-six giant hogsheads of liquor. He bought a tremendous new generator, three hundred-kilowatts strong, and placed on a special trailer fifteen sun arcs and fifty spotlights for the many night-by-night scenes.

For the train crash scene, DeMille had his staff build an exact replica of his favorite K-4 passenger engine, eighty feet long, which used to pull the old Broadway Limited between New York and Chicago. The scene of the crash was shot at night in the Union Pacific freight yards in downtown Los Angeles. Two Pullman coaches were completely demolished for the scene.

The camera was fixed up at the end of a Pullman and the front of the great engine was seen crashing toward the camera, twisting the steel frame and crushing the seats. DeMille built a special device, which swung the entire carriage around in a circle, hurling the passengers from their seats to the roof of the compartments and finally depositing them on top of a shattered window. He also arranged to build one of the Pullmans in lead instead of steel, so that it would crumple effectively and melt under the force of the fire that swept through the carriages.

DeMille told the stars that since nothing could be faked, they would be in the gravest danger during the scene. He told Jetta Goudal: "When I give a signal, you are simply to fall on the cow catcher on the front of the engine. If you are a moment late or early you will not only kill yourself, you will endanger the lives of everyone else." He wanted her to lie on the cow catcher, apparently unconscious, and be moved forward several feet until the engine was almost on top of Schildkraut, who must sit absolutely motionless until the engine was just one inch from his body. Vera Reynolds would be shown an inch from the engine also, but a stand-in was used for her who could be catapulted to the top of the overturned carriage. William Boyd would have to bear the weight of a heap of splintered wood and tortured metal on his back.

Despite anguished protests from Milbank and his associates in New York, DeMille insisted on proceeding with a scene which, had there been one mistake, could have killed all of his stars. The scene could be done only once, and could not be rehearsed. For hours, the four players, Iribe, Leisen, and Marley sat around working out the precise dictates of the sequence, poring over blueprints. Then, one night, the sequence went off without a hitch—except for the fact that Joseph Schildkraut was badly scalded by steam as they made their way from the red-hot engine through a fire that had already been started by DeMille's assistants.

DeMille and Anne Bauchens cut the picture with great speed, and it was released in the fall. Unfortunately, it proved too complicated and diffuse for audiences, and to DeMille's bitter disappointment it collapsed at the box office. This was an inauspicious start for his new studio, and the New York backers, excepting the loyal Milbank, proved restive. Seeking scapegoats for his own error, DeMille began attacking projectionists across the country. A typical cable went to Hal Horne, manager of the Figueroa Theatre on Santa Barbara and Figueroa streets in Los Angeles. Dated November 27, 1925, it read: PROJECTION OF ROAD TO YESTERDAY AT FIGUEROA THEATRE ON FIRST EIGHT REELS IS SO BAD THAT IT DEFINITELY INJURES THE

PICTURE / THERE IS FAR TOO MUCH LIGHT FORCED THROUGH THE
FILM WHICH IS COMPLETELY DESTROYING ALL THE BEAUTY OF
THE PHOTOGRAPHY AND COLOR / IN CHANGING FROM ONE
MACHINE TO ANOTHER THE OPERATORS ARE CUTTING OUT FROM
ONE TO THREE SCENES / FOR SOME REASON CANNOT EXPLAIN THE
PROJECTION OF THE LAST TWO REELS IS GOOD WHICH SHOWS IT IS
NO BASIC FAULT OF YOUR PROJECTION BUT THE RESULT PROBABLY
OF EITHER A CRIMINALLY CARELESS OPERATOR OR AN EQUALLY
CRIMINALLY IGNORANT ONE / WHATEVER THE CAUSE I WISH YOU
TO TAKE IMMEDIATE STEPS TO CORRECT THE PROJECTION AS WE
SPEND MANY THOUSANDS OF DOLLARS TO GET THESE EFFECTS ON
ACCOUNT OF THE PSYCHOLOGY THAT IT CREATES IN AN AUDIENCE
WATCHING A PICTURE OF THIS TYPE AND TO HAVE IT CALMLY
DESTROYED IS BOTH BAD BUSINESS AND BAD ART.

On the *Seaward* on a recuperative cruise after the sad failure
of *The Road to Yesterday*, DeMille told Julia he was at his wits'
end to know what to do next. He was too distraught to attempt
The King of Kings, the "story of the Christ" which he had
promised Milbank would be his main purpose in creating the
new studio. She advised him to concentrate on making the
DeMille Studio at Mount Vernon the most powerful film
organization in Hollywood, a rival of Lasky's and Mayer's
outfits, and of Carl Laemmle's Universal. The idea went to his
head completely. He brought William deMille over from
Famous Players to direct for him. He merged with several small
studios, the combined operation placed under the management
of an administrator, William Sistrom. The Producers' Distributing Company obtained a new chain of theaters, and the Cinema
Corporation of America merged with the Keith chain, which
meant that Edward F. Albee, chief of the Keith chain, and his
assistant, J. J. Murdock, were also on the board of Cinema in
New York.

Unfortunately, by agreeing to these expansions, DeMille not
only swallowed a whale, but a pack of sharks as well. From the
very beginning, J. J. Murdock proved as dangerous to him as
Zukor and Elek Ludvigh had been before. A constant flow of

irritable telegrams passed to and fro between the two men, cramming the files in the DeMille office. His every move was questioned, and had it not been for Milbank's friendship and absolute trust, he might well have been dislodged from supreme office that difficult fall of 1925.

In October, despite some opposition from Murdock, DeMille went obstinately ahead with a new production, *The Volga Boatman*, based by Lenore J. Coffee on the novel by Konrad Bercovici. The subject attracted DeMille because Russian friends, especially Theodore Kosloff, had been urging him for some time to attempt a Russian subject. When Kosloff lent him the book, he bought it at once.

He was drawn to the film also by some portents: in a New York shop window on a visit that fall, he had seen a group of Russian figures crouched around a Mazda bulb in a shop window advertisement, had heard the "Volga Boat Song" sung by Chaliapin on the radio, and had attended the Chauve Souris Ballet, which danced mainly Russian works that season. Visiting the Metropolitan Museum, he became fascinated by a painting of men dragging a barge along the Volga.

The film was the story of Princess Vera, who is attracted to Feodor, a Volga boatman; during the Russian revolution, he is the leader of the revolutionary group which ransacks her house. He spares her life, enters into an affair with her, and pretends to his fellow revolutionaries that she is his wife. When, during a counterattack, the imperial forces seize her and Feodor, she is humiliated, but manages to save Feodor's life. When the revolution triumphs, she is at last free to enter a genuine marriage with him.

DeMille had originally asked Jetta Goudal to play Princess Vera, but she felt the part was too "slapstick" and DeMille released her from the obligation. He signed instead a little-known actress named Elinor Fair, who resembled her. He cast William Boyd as Feodor, Victor Varconi as her aristocratic lover Prince Dmitri, and the once troublesome Robert Edeson of *Call of the North* as her father, Prince Nikita.

Forbidden absolutely by Murdock and his clique to make the film in Russia, DeMille shot it instead, in November 1925, on the Sacramento River of California, in dismal weather conditions which all too realistically matched those of a late Russian autumn.

Fog was so heavy in the Sacramento Basin that in one break of only twenty hours of weak sunshine, DeMille had to shoot sixteen scenes. MAYBE I'LL HAVE TO VISIT THE VOLGA AFTER ALL, he cabled Gladys Rosson on November 12. The wind was bitterly cold. On November 16 he cabled her: TERRIBLE WEATHER / LESS THAN THIRTY FIVE MINUTES OF LIGHT FOR SHOOTING AND BITTERLY COLD WIND LIKE GUADALUPE AND AGAIN I AM WORKING MEN VERY SCANTILY CLAD / POSSIBLY SATURDAY BEFORE RETURN / IF NECESSARY WILL SEND FOR YOU. Elinor Fair, from the moment she arrived at the location, proved uncongenial from his point of view. LOOKS LIKE I'M ON THE VOLGA FOR LIFE, he cabled Gladys on November 21. The rain kept up a constant tattoo, and at night, unable to sleep, he sat up working on a new story, *For Alimony Only*, which had been sent to him by the studio.

In addition to the weather problem, another was that panchromatic film had begun to replace orthochromatic film in Hollywood. For night shots, which demanded the use of red filters, Peverell Marley's associate, the young and brilliant Arthur Miller, developed some special makeup to conceal the fact that panchromatic film made faces look unnaturally white against the darkness. DeMille asked Miller to make some tests, and he did: of an old man escaping from the Imperial troops in a hay wagon. He showed the wagon silhouetted against a hill, and the sky emerged very black, with the face not glaring white but soft with moonlight. Miller told DeMille he would have to switch film from orthochromatic to panchromatic film within a shot, but when the time came to do this, the delay was so extreme in the middle of a dramatic scene that DeMille found it impossible to keep the actors in the right mood. He screamed at Miller: "First you want ortho, then you want panchro, what do you want?" "You just told me I could switch films, you bastard!" Miller yelled.

When the rushes came in, DeMille showed them in a small theater in the Sacramento Valley, but he could not make out the images on the screen. Each three A.M. after shooting he dragged everyone—cast, crew, assistants—all the way to a bigger theater one hundred miles up river to see them. Only his loyalest devotees forgave him for that.

DeMille was depressed by the long work on location, and consoled only by the sets, begun by Anton Grot and Max Parker and developed by Mitchell Leisen, of a prince's house with glittering black floors, and of a Russian village, furnished to the last detail, with solid walls which could be rolled up and down to admit the cameras. None of the performances pleased him, and he was desolate when the New York office proved cold toward the finished work.

The film was selected to open the Carthay Circle Theatre in Los Angeles. Hundreds of spectators gathered outside to cheer the arrival of the stars, who stepped out of their limousines to Harold Roberts' Collegiate Band playing ragtime and Russian tunes. The doorman was dressed in Russian uniform and the ushers were made up as Cossacks. The Carli Elenor Orchestra began the performance with a swinging overture based on themes from the film and Kosloff and a team of Russian dancers performed expertly. When DeMille entered the theater just before the curtain rose, he received a standing ovation. The opening in New York was equally spectacular.

It opened there on April 13, 1926, to a tremendous audience at the Times Square Theatre, with the thirty-six-piece orchestra under Hugo Riesenfeld conducting Russian music, and among the first-night crowd Gloria Swanson, bedecked in diamonds, Feodor Chaliapin, Major Bowes, Jules Brulatour the Kodak king, Fannie Hurst, Anita Loos and her husband John Emerson, the Selwyns, and Walter Wanger. DeMille himself was there, mingling happily with the fashionable crowd and joining them for a magnificent party afterwards. While in New York,

DeMille completed plans in consultation with the banks for a staggering total of forty-one DeMille productions in 1926–1927, of which he would direct three features and produce all of the rest.

DeMille received very good reviews. He was given particular praise for a scene which had given Will Hays some pause: Elinor Fair is being stripped by Imperial officers, and their lustful observation of her lovely body is recorded on their faces. The reviews, however, failed to help the film at the box office. DeMille was only half-surprised when he heard the news that it was failing. "I guess I shouldn't have listened to you," he told Theodore Kosloff over dinner one Wednesday night at Laughlin Park. "The American public just isn't very interested in Russia, is it?"

8

The
King of Kings

At first in the spring of 1926, DeMille planned to make a film entitled *The Deluge*, about the Biblical Flood. But he was forced to abandon this plan when he learned that the Warner Brothers were planning the story of Noah's Ark. Instead, he busied himself supervising the transference of his brother William to the new studio, and the preparation of a number of pictures, including *Corporal Kate*, to be directed by Paul Sloane, *The Cruise of the Jasper B*, and *Yankee Clipper*, for which he bought the old and leaking clipper ships the *Bohemia* and the *Indiana*. William deMille worked on *Nobody's Widow*, for which Leatrice Joy had been lured from Lasky, and plans were drawn up for *Rubber Tires*, about auto camps.

159

Most of the new plans were severely attacked by Murdock and others, and Milbank felt constant pressure to dislodge DeMille. Finally, he made it clear that DeMille must avoid his express promise no more; he must gird his loins, rescue his reputation, and at once make *The King of Kings*, despite the fact that Murdock was opposed to a religious subject.

In mid-June 1926, DeMille summoned Jeanie to his office and told her gravely that he was about to give her the most important assignment of her life. He handed her a text: the small, worn family Bible, dated 1874, which his father had used as a lay reader at the Episcopal Church in New Jersey, and which had been the inspiration of DeMille's own childhood. He instructed her to follow the great drama to the letter, impatiently dismissing her suggestion that she should use a modern story as a counterbalance.

As at the time of *The Ten Commandments* he sent copies of the Bible to every member of his staff, ordering them to memorize every word of the Gospels, and called them in every day for a Bible lesson. At weekends on board the *Seaward*, Jeanie was forced to be gracious to Julia as the two women worked with DeMille's researcher Mrs. Elizabeth McGaffey on the basic preparation. When a wind blew pages of notes in the ocean, DeMille, fit and bronzed in a swimming costume, dove overboard and fetched them back. At night, Jeanie fumed in her cabin while Julia was entertained in the captain's cabin. Day after day this curious little *ménage* worked on the most ambitious film of the silent period.

When the story was finally licked—it had to be cut and recut to meet the requirement of two hours of film—DeMille returned to Hollywood and began supervising Mrs. McGaffey and her research staff of twelve in two months of brutally hard work. Her team explored twenty-five hundred volumes and fifty thousand feet of documentary film, boiling the material down to some ten packed, typed volumes for Jeanie and her own assistants to examine.

A typical note to DeMille from Mrs. McGaffey (July 27,

1926) reads: "According to the Catholic Encyclopedia Vol. 4 and Kitto's Encyclopedia Volume 1 the Crown of Thorns was a branch of the bush Zizyphus Spina Christi which is noted for its long thorns. Mr. Wright, the florist, obtained two branches which I am now giving to you. He obtained it from a bush growing on a vacant lot on the corner of Broadway and Sapphire Street, Redondo Beach . . . Would suggest that we go down and steal this bush at once."

DeMille spent weeks running films to make a selection of the cast. For every horse-mounted soldier in the picture, he chose an experienced cowboy, and he had every horse's hoof covered in rubber. He chose three thousand extras and fifteen hundred assorted animals and reptiles himself. No sooner was this task completed than he had to supervise, with the aid of linguists, the foreign version of the script, with titles in twenty-seven languages. After that, he arranged for the installation of a ten-stop organ to be installed in the studio, to provide inspirational music for the cast.

DeMille instructed the cameraman Peverell Marley to study hundreds of biblical paintings, examining precisely with what effects of light the old masters achieved their work. Two hundred and ninety eight paintings were fully reproduced in the film. Marley used seventy-five lenses as against his usual four, and seven different kinds of film stock, as well as special stock for the Technicolor sequences. For the crucifixion scene, based partly on DeMille's beloved Gustave Doré, partly on Rubens, he employed the most powerful sun arcs used up to that time, and two hundred fifty special lights set up around the hill of Calvary, fixed by a team of one hundred seventy-seven specialists, and giving out a strength of twenty-seven thousand amperes.

His biggest problem was in lighting the Crucifixion scene. After the death of Jesus, DeMille planned a tremendous earthquake, dust swirled high by fierce winds and the atmosphere impregnated with dust. Marley wrote for the *New York Herald* later (May 30, 1927): "How could you photograph it?

Light reflects from dust; in fact, you never see a 'ray' of light unless there is something in the atmosphere. But here we must give the impression of swirling dust without light streaks. In other words, we must give the illusion of a storm—dank, gloomy lightness—and still use enough light to permit its translation to the celluloid. . . ."

DeMille worked with Marley for a whole day just on one shot. They moved huge arcs again and again, sometimes only a few inches, improvising shades of every kind to prevent "streaks." Even when they had managed to set up the shot they had to make a special strip of film and examine it as a test.

They worked for days on the grading of grays. The tragic scenes of Judas from the betrayal to the suicide began with pale dove grays, then gradually darkened to the sinister blackness of the shadow cast by the suicidal gibbet. In the Raising of Lazarus the reverse procedure was used: the scene began in pitch darkness, the screen filled with a brooding, funereal black, then gradually brightened to gray, and finally showed the screen flooded in light, bathed in rich golds as the color system emerged and Lazarus saw the Saviour. For the scenes of the purging of the temple, DeMille and Marley used unusually brilliant high-key lighting, enhanced still further when the Devil shows Christ the temptations of the material world. But in the sequences in the Via Dolorosa, the Street of Sorrows, the shots were done through funeral veils, seemingly casting the images under the shadows of moving thunder clouds.

In June also, Paul Iribe excitedly began the great task of planning nothing less than a complete physical re-creation of Christ's era. But DeMille grew daily more dissatisfied with his sets, finding them too plain, too severe, too dull. When Iribe protested that he had drawn from the most scrupulously observed historical records, DeMille reminded him that he did not want accuracy so much as a painterly richness of imagination. Struck by the contradiction, Iribe reminded DeMille of his first address to the staff, in which he had spoken of adhering to the very letter of the text. DeMille retorted angrily that nobody knew exactly what Palestinian buildings of that time looked like anyway.

They quarreled again when Iribe proposed shooting the crucifixion scene on a mountain. "How the hell do you get a storm on cue?" DeMille yelled at him. The final rift came over the scourging scene. Iribe decided on a set made of rough-hewn stone, and DeMille tossed the designs on the floor. "Is this your final design?" he snarled. "Yes," Iribe replied. "You're God-damn right it's your final design!" DeMille shouted. "Now get the hell out of here and don't let me ever see you again." Turning to Mitchell Leisen, who was standing nearby, DeMille said: "Take over the picture now." Immediately Iribe, white and shaking, went to his office, cleared out his desk and drove home. He never spoke to DeMille again.

Secretly, DeMille was grieved at the loss of his old friend, but the picture came first. Leisen redesigned the scene of the scourging in rich woods and draperies, then began preparing the crucifixion scene. Iribe's cyclorama of a ragged sky with drifting cumulus clouds was not to DeMille's liking, but he did not dare to scrap it; instead, Leisen had instructions to do his very best with it. Leisen arranged ten sixty-inch arcs revolving on wheels, giving an impression, through the shadows cast on the cyclorama, that the clouds were moving. He told DeMille it would cost seventy thousand dollars to build steel rafters to support the lights. DeMille became speechless with rage and sank into a chair. But he finally saw the wisdom of Leisen's choice.

The Jewish library set was particularly striking, with exact replicas of antique parchments, their titles printed on yellow and blue tickets, and fantastic tablets, aged as exact copies of the original.

The set of Mary Magdalene's house was an extraordinary masterpiece of design. It was not a simple prostitute's house, but a positive palace, with pools of water in the reception room, real swans floating among giant lily pads. The fluted columns were covered in real gold leaf attached in small squares; one

The King of Kings: *the Crucifixion scene.*

side of each column fluttered free in a specially wind-machined breeze, making the walls appear to shiver like melting gold.

For the huge set of the Praetorium of Jerusalem, the judgment seat of Pontius Pilate, one whole wall of sound stage was removed. Around it spread the entire governmental district of Jerusalem, miraculously re-created. Corinthian columns, perfect in every detail, led to the entrance, which was guarded by real bronze gates eighty feet high. The throne, of real marble, stood in front of a bronze Eagle of Rome thirty-seven feet high.

Architect Pridgeon Smith designed the set of the Temple of Jehovah, the Nicanor Gate to the Holy of Holies, the streets of Nazareth and Jerusalem, and the Mount of Olives. The Temple of Jehovah was one thousand feet square, the Nicanor Gate one hundred sixty-nine feet high, the doorway to the Holy of Holies forty feet wide and sixty feet high. Two hundred fifty carpenters, working in three eight-hour shifts, worked day and night for over a month on the Holy of Holies dome. Four hundred thousand board feet of lumber were used, while fifty thousand square yards of lath, and a corresponding surface of tar paper and plaster were used in completing the Temple of Jehovah. Ten thousand pounds of spikes and one hundred eighty kegs of smaller nails held the set together.

While the great sets were being constructed, DeMille engaged technical advisers: the Rev. Dr. George Reid Andrews, Chairman of the Film and Drama Committee of the Federated Churches of Christ in America, and Bruce Barton, author of the life of Jesus *The Man Nobody Knows*. In addition, Father Daniel A. Lord of the Society of Jesus lent a hand. DeMille seldom agreed with Lord on points of detail, and on one occasion told that learned Jesuit to "go to Hell." "I'm afraid that won't be possible," Father Lord replied politely. "I already have a reservation elsewhere."

As Jesus, DeMille cast the gentle and fragile H. B. Warner, whom he had produced in *The Ghost Breakers* some twelve years earlier. Other members of the cast formed an international group: Dorothy Cumming (the Virgin Mary) was an Australian, Rudolph Schildkraut (Caiaphas) an Austrian born in Turkey, his son Joseph (Judas) another Austrian, Ernest Terrence as Peter was Scottish, Victor Varconi as Pilate was Hungarian, and of other members of the cast, Theodore Kosloff was, of course, Russian, Sam DeGrasse was Canadian, Sohin was Japanese, and Otto Lederer Czech.

DeMille had a well-publicized search for an actress to play Mary Magdalene: Gertrude Lawrence, Vilma Banky, Seena Owen, Gloria Swanson, and Raquel Meller were among those considered. Finally, he offered the role to Gloria Swanson but, after keeping him waiting several weeks, she turned it down. Jacqueline Logan obtained the role finally, after she told DeMille: "I don't want to play her as a bad woman, but as a woman who doesn't know the difference between right and wrong."

On the second day of shooting, DeMille assembled a throng of religious figures, led by members of every denomination in America. He insisted on unraveling for seven hours the entire story of the Four Gospels to distinguished clerics who were scarcely unfamiliar with it. He even forced them to stand in semi-circles while he addressed them from a pulpit on the meaning of the New Testament, and chose unhappily the set of Mary Magdalene's prostitute's palace to do it in. After the sixth hour, a faint cry was heard. "Who was that?" DeMille cried out through his megaphone. "It is I," said Judas Iscariot, Joseph Schildkraut. "Can't I let Jesus sit down? I've been propping him up for the past hour."

From the beginning of shooting, H. B. Warner was driven to the set in a closed car with the blinds down, wore a black veil as he left the car for the set, and when on location ate alone in his tent. Unfortunately, the problems of playing the role sparked off an old drinking problem, kept secret by DeMille's and the publicist Barrett Kiesling's most resolute efforts.

The Virgin Mary also presented some problems. DeMille's contract with Dorothy Cumming specified that she should bind herself absolutely to him to "regulate her personal life that no possible blemish of character may eventuate." She was not to attract scandal, not even to divorce her husband, a fact that became crucial when she defied him by beginning divorce proceedings against her husband Frank Elliott Dakin, an English actor and founder of the Sixty Club in Hollywood.

The press exploited these scandals, much to DeMille's chagrin and much to the delight of his enemies led by J. J. Murdock in New York. A characteristically satirical *Brooklyn Eagle* reporter visited the set one day and wrote: "Verily there was light and a thousand 'extras' did flock to the scene as a thousand moths eager to singe their wings upon the flames of the Klieg lamps. And there arose before them the graven image of DeMille and they bowed down their heads to him and there was heard in Hollywood a terrible din."

Other visitors saw something resembling a circus: a man training one hundred white doves to fly across the stage in formation, Mary Magdalene's leopard pacing about a golden cage, a brilliantly plumaged Bird of Paradise sunning itself behind a wire netting under a giant arc light. Scenes by the Sea of Galilee were held at Catalina, where Father Lord conducted a Field Mass to mark commencement of shooting. In order to shoot on the island, DeMille had to ship seventy-five tons of props in fifteen trucks to the docks at San Pedro, where an entire passenger steamer waited to take cast, staff, and props across the water.

A curious episode took place during the shooting of the Crucifixion scene. D. W. Griffith visited the set, and DeMille conferred with him briefly. Suddenly, he handed him the megaphone and said, "You shoot this bit." And Griffith directed a tiny sequence of a group of persecutors gathered around the foot of the Cross.

As shooting proceeded through fall and into winter, the Murdock group began once more to talk of throwing DeMille into the street. In October, DeMille dispatched Neil McCarthy to New York to try and patch up the deterioriating situation.

The box office results on *The Volga Boatman* had proved as disastrous as those for *The Road to Yesterday*. Murdock told McCarthy point blank that he felt DeMille without the controlling force of Lasky and Zukor was "a dead duck at the box office." McCarthy was by now in a position of literally having to save his friend's professional life.

Milbank and Murdock begged McCarthy to make DeMille accede to a merger with Pathé, which had over four million dollars worth of assets, and to change the policy of DeMille productions to that of making cheap pictures, under two hundred thousand dollars in most instances.

DeMille was absolutely opposed to this move from the outset. He cabled McCarthy on November 8: I CANNOT SEE THAT PATHE WOULD BRING ANYTHING OF VALUE TO THE MERGER EXCEPTING A NAME WHICH STANDS FOR CHEAP PICTURES AND SEVEN HUNDRED THOUSAND CASH. He was desperate at this stage, suggesting that the entire company be taken over by Famous, First National, Metro, or Joseph Schenck. He also weighed Walter Wanger's suggestion that Famous Players might take over *The King of Kings* if the board of Cinema decided to offload it. He turned to Goldwyn as well.

On November 11, McCarthy cabled DeMille from the Hotel Ambassador: FILM DAILY REPORT THIS MORNING YOU OPPOSED TO MERGER AND WILL PROBABLY BLOCK SAME / THIS DETRIMENTAL TO SITUATION AND IN ORDER TO OVERCOME SAME I AS REPRESENTATIVE ISSUED STATEMENT MERELY DENYING THAT YOU ARE OPPOSED TO MERGER.

Even while the daily work on *The King of Kings* grew heavier and heavier, DeMille was in the appalling position of having to try some way to make someone take the picture off the hands of his own corporation, and the wires to McCarthy grew more and more frantic, some of these running to as much as eight pages. On November 8, he cabled McCarthy a desperate plea to arrange a deal with Lasky whereby Lasky and Zukor would take over the picture and reimburse its backers, giving DeMille a percentage of the gross. The worst thing was, and it caused him endless insomniac nights, that he could not easily speak to McCarthy in person due to the poor quality of long distance telephone and that he could not be in New York while the complicated negotiations went on.

The DeMille company threatened to collapse as costs on *The King of Kings* soared to almost two million dollars. McCarthy, faced in New York with the fact that the company had been inadequately financed from the outset, was trying to find ways to raise the necessary amount of capital. He wired DeMille on November 23 that the company needed within ten days four hundred thousand dollars to meet maturities to capital, four hundred thousand dollars to meet present bills and running expenses in New York, three hundred thousand dollars for the studio. One million six hundred thousand would have to be paid to the banks, and one million five hundred thousand dollars worth of notes matured within eight months.

Finally the bankers, led by Jeremiah Milbank, again demanded that the company merge with Pathé, which would issue debentures and lend it five million dollars, the distribution of all DeMille pictures being given to Pathé in order to secure one million dollars. By November 27, after a series of late night conferences, McCarthy cabled that the situation had worsened in New York. The Capital company which was supplying the money to make *The King of Kings* had withdrawn its support, and a harassed Jeremiah Milbank was keeping it going single-handed, despite extreme pressure to withdraw and force *The King of Kings* to close down. It looked as though DeMille would have to come to New York, to try and sort out the appallingly complicated situation which had developed. As it was, he was forced to shoot virtually around the clock to keep the budget under two and a half million.

DeMille put in a final plea: PATHE HAS STOOD FOR THE CHEAPEST BRAND OF MOTION PICTURES FOR SO LONG AND THE NAME DEMILLE HAS STOOD FOR THE BEST BRAND IT WOULD BE A LITTLE LIKE COMBINING TIFFANY AND WOOLWORTH / POSSIBLE DEMILLE METROPOLITAN PATHE MIGHT BE BETTER NAME /

Jacqueline Logan: The King of Kings.

DeMille, Jeanie, Sid Grauman.

METROPOLITAN IS A GOOD AND DIGNIFIED NAME AND STANDS MORE OR LESS AS A BUFFER BETWEEN DEMILLE AND PATHE. But the deal went ahead that December.

On Christmas Eve, DeMille flung an open-house party for reporters—to see the sequence of Christ being tied to a pillar and lashed by a whip. The visitors crossed the great lawn outside Mount Vernon, rapped the brass knocker with its wreath of holly and ivy, were greeted by the doorman in blue presidential livery, entered the great colonial hall with its antique portraits, fire crackling in the grate, and winding, mahogany-railed staircase, and passed in brilliant sunshine to the ten-acre lot at the back. There they saw a spotlight focused on a tall, thin man tied to a pillar, Judas shrinking at every blow of the whip, the soldiers laughing and jeering. A reporter for the *Boston Globe* described the scene (December 26, 1926): " 'Throw that whip higher,' I heard a megaphoned voice direct. 'Keep his arms extended. Don't let them drop!' Peering through the dimness, I saw what might have passed for a throne. On it was perched a high chair, roughly constructed of wood, with broad arms and two steps. In the chair, sat a man, wearing tweeds, with knickers, a soft felt hat and leather puttees. Monotone glasses hid his eyes, the megaphone covered his mouth . . . It was Cecil B. DeMille."

When *The King of Kings* was finished, it consisted of one million five hundred thousand feet or three hundred miles of negative—enough to stretch from Los Angeles to San Diego with a couple of mountain tours thrown in.

Under pressure from Murdock and the Producers' Distributing Corporation's John Flinn, DeMille reluctantly cut the picture to fourteen hundred feet. He wanted to cut the first Mary Magdalene sequence, but Flinn absolutely opposed this, calling instead for cuts in the scenes on the shore of Galilee, Mary Magdalene at the tomb, and the sequence of the mad boy cured by Christ. The Gaiety Theatre in New York—a possession of the all-powerful Abraham Erlanger—was secured for

the Easter release of the picture. Flinn demanded that Barrett
Kiesling be removed from publicity for the picture, because he
had released a statement that *"The King of Kings* had certainly
done something to encourage the enmity of the leaders of the
many denominational faiths." DeMille called Kiesling in and
carpeted him. Kiesling was horrified, and examining the piece
of paper in his hand stammered that the word "enmity" should
have been "comity." He asked DeMille to accept his resignation at once; he had, he said, failed to read the proofs of the
release correctly. "Your resignation won't correct the error,"
DeMille said coldly as he showed him the door and dictated a
cable to Flinn explaining the horrible mistake.

In February DeMille began shipping reels of *The King of
Kings* to the composer Hugo Riesenfeld in New York. Accord-
ing to Riesenfeld's suggestion, he cut some sequences and put
back footage in order to expand some others. He forbade
Riesenfeld to show the picture to anyone else. On March 8, two
and one half reels of the temple sequence were shipped, on
March 25 several more, including the reel covering the storm
and earthquake. On March 28, he cabled in response to
Riesenfeld's beseeching him to make the Via Dolorosa and
Crucifixion sequences longer: CANNOT MAKE VIA DOLOROSA OR
CRUCIFIXION LONGER AS I FOUND AUDIENCE CANNOT STAND IT.
The film had to be constantly adjusted from sequence to
sequence to allow for Riesenfeld's requirements. Finally Ries-
enfeld was finished. His score was largely made up of hymns:
when the blind girl was healed he used "Lead Kindly Light,"
when Christ picked up the lamb "The Lord Is My Shepherd,"
the Last Supper "Abide with Me," and the death of Jesus
"Nearer My God to Thee." He cabled DeMille on March 29:
THE KING OF KINGS IS THE MOST MARVELOUS ACCOMPLISHMENT A
SHOWMANS BRAIN EVER CONCEIVED / I ONLY HOPE I WILL BE
ABLE TO DO JUSTICE TO IT WITH MY MUSIC / THOUGHT YOU
WOULD BE INTERESTED THAT AT A FORMAL LUNCHEON TODAY AT
WHICH ALL THE NEWSPAPER PEOPLE WERE PRESENT WILL HAYS

USED THE OPPORTUNITY TO TALK ABOUT YOUR PICTURE AND SAID
THAT YOU HAVE GIVEN SOMETHING MONUMENTAL AND
UNFORGETTABLE TO HUMANITY.

On March 10, 1927, the dreaded merger finally took place, bringing together Keith Albee, the Orpheum Circuit (West Coast theaters), The Pathé Exchange, Inc., and the Producers' Distributing Corporation. But even after the merger was completed, DeMille quarreled bitterly with J. J. Murdock and other members of the combine. It had become obvious to him that without autonomy—an autonomy which had lasted barely two years—even the splendors of living in Thomas Ince's shoes and occupying a replica of Mount Vernon were wearing very thin. He was reduced to a cog in a wheel in an immense organization in which his was only one voice in many. What was worse, apart from Jeremiah Milbank, he had no keen supporters on the joint board. Almost as soon as the merger took place, his fretfulness at being linked with Pathé also reached a peak of intensity. He had, he felt, to get out, and he began looking for an escape—to First National and United Artists at first and then, when they shook their heads over his box office record and the fact that he had no interest in *The King of Kings*, to Metro-Goldwyn-Mayer. His depression was increased by two fires at the studio which destroyed three hundred fifty thousand dollars worth of material and a set for *The Wreck of the Hesperus* as well as several sound stages. Ten fire departments took two hours to put out the flames and seventy-five police were called in to hold the crowds at bay.

As if all this were not enough, a sudden economy wave following a tense meeting of the Motion Picture Producers' Association resulted in the cutting of every single star's and employee's salary as well as DeMille's own. There was talk of widespread shutdowns, and that the DeMille studios might even cease to exist.

To DeMille's overwhelming relief in this dark hour, the New York opening of *The King of Kings* on April 21 was an immense sensation. The first-night and first-matinee tickets were sold out hours before the performance. The Riesenfeld accompaniment for thirty-six musicians and a chorus of forty voices brought the audience to its feet. Although the picture ran in two parts, from 8:30 to 10 o'clock, a seven-minute intermission, then from 10:07 to 11:15, the audience was completely enthralled from first shot to last. Finn cabled Sid Grauman in Hollywood exultantly, telling him to expect a sellout for the opening (at twenty-two dollars a seat) in Hollywood.

The Hollywood premiere was to open the splendid new Grauman's Chinese Theatre on Hollywood Boulevard. It was a fabulously gaudy structure: the millionaire C. E. Toberman who had sold DeMille Laughlin Park had wanted it to include a complete replica of a Chinese gate one hundred eighty feet high, and a Chinese village complete with peasants; but the Chamber of Commerce decided it would be a hazard to traffic. A triumph of kitsch, the Chinese Theatre with its minarets of burnished copper, solid façade of masonry forty feet high, surrounded by four ornate obelisks, and forecourt of palms and cocoanut trees, was still sufficiently vulgar to satisfy anyone. The bronze, square-cut pagoda roof, aged to the exact color of green jade, was underlaid by two immense octagonal piers of coral red. Underneath the roof and set between the piers was a giant stone dragon modeled in relief on a slab twenty feet square.

The theater opened on May 19. For four days and nights, beforehand, DeMille worked with Sid Grauman, director of festivities Fred Niblo, and the compeer and master of ceremonies, D. W. Griffith, on the arrangements for the premiere; Mary Pickford's finger was chosen to "touch the button that would change stone and celluloid into screen history"—in other words, release the curtain. Over twenty-two hundred invitations were sent out, and every single star and feature player in Hollywood was asked. Each member of DeMille's staff and list of contract players was of course included. Mayor Cryer, Fire Chief Ralph Scott, and Chief of Police Davis even went to the extreme of dressing up in Chinese clothes to greet DeMille at the door. It seemed appropriate, in view of DeMille's fetish, that he should suggest to Grauman the idea of immortalizing the feet of the famous in the soft clay of the forecourt, beginning with Mary Pickford, Douglas Fairbanks, and Norma and Constance Talmadge.

From one end to another, Hollywood was hung with multicolored bunting, flags, and flowers, and two dozen search-lights ranged over the night sky. One hundred thousand people packed Hollywood Boulevard for the event, kept more or less under control by five hundred police and one thousand members of the One Hundred Sixtieth Infantry.

As soon as the audience was settled in its seats, a Chinese gong reverberated and a voice announced D. W. Griffith. He spoke briefly about the agency of films in world peace. He introduced DeMille, who dedicated his film to the public. Will Hays praised the genius of DeMille and of Sid Grauman, and Griffith introduced Mary Pickford who told the audience that movies were for them. The great orchestra under Constantin Bakaleinikoff began to play Dr. Hugo Riesenfeld's medley of the classics.

Sid Grauman's live Prologue was undoubtedly the most extravagantly opulent creation ever shown in Hollywood. At last the curtain rose on "The Glories of the Scriptures," a scene of a market place crowded with one hundred figures representa-tive of the time of Jesus. "Twilight" fell—the lighting was very ingenious—and people sank to their knees to pray under a violet sky. An ebony slave danced, palms swayed in an artificial breeze, a row of Israelite High Priests chanted in Harvard English, a series of tableaux followed like the Bible-in-pictures, and a boy soprano sang "The Holy City" accompanied by the wordless singing of the chorus in a composition by Dr. Riesenfeld. The tableaux represented Joseph and His Brethren, Daniel in the Lions' Den (the lions were drugged for the occasion), the Star of Bethlehem, the Nativity, the Flight into Egypt, and the Spirit of Faith.

After all this, the film began at 10:30 P.M. Then disaster

struck. The distinguished audience, worn out by two and a half hours of Prologue, began coughing, shuffling, and moving in its seats. DeMille twice yelled for "Silence!" to be greeted by groans from people who did not recognize the owner of the voice. When the intermission was announced around one o'clock, all except 2 per cent of the audience—the DeMille and Grauman staff, Will Hays and Griffith—walked out in one body, delivering such remarks as "H. B. Warner's beard seemed moth-eaten." "Horrible Mary Magdalene." "Maybe Christ was having an affair with his mother." At two A.M. Will Hays turned to DeMille as he stalked off followed by the grim-faced members of his personal entourage and family and said, "Well, Cecil, there's only one thing left now. And that is to get run over on the way home."

9

Talkies!

Despite an extremely mixed press—many critics found the film the aesthetic equivalent of the Bible in pictures—*The King of Kings* enjoyed an excellent public reception, particularly in Europe in foreign versions, where in some countries it ran for more than two years. Although DeMille's heart rejoiced at the gradually accelerating, then engulfing, wave of public acclaim, he was still deeply troubled during the spring and summer of 1927.

His chief worry was local censorship. A number of states insisted on specific sequences being removed, particularly those implying a more than tentative personal relationship between Jesus and Mary Magdalene. Jewish organizations, led by the

179

*Photographer Peverell Marley and DeMille
filming the staircase scene of* The Godless Girl.

B'nai B'rith, specifically requested their members not to see the film, claiming that it treated Jewish authorities of the time of Christ with hatred and contempt. The film narrowly escaped being banned in England, where several cities (including London) had special ordinances forbidding the display of Christ's face in public. It was only through the most urgent intercession of Neil McCarthy, who had powerful legal contacts in London, that this disaster was avoided.

On July 27, 1927, DeMille made his radio debut, talking from the Los Angeles Express Radio Station KNX in the Studebaker Building about *The King of Kings*. On September 30, he was presented with an elaborately wrought Roman gold tablet embossed with the signatures of many stars to celebrate the two hundredth "jubilee" performance of *The King of Kings* at Grauman's Chinese Theatre. Whenever business fell off, Grauman arranged for immense crowds of school children, boy scouts, and religious bodies to see the film at special prices.

Grauman's stunts were endless: on September 7, he began exhibiting a pin with the Lord's Prayer engraved on the top by Charles Baker, a former official of the United States Bureau of Engraving in Washington. Charity groups and even invalids were shunted in, clergymen flown from New York, incense sprinkled all over the theater (until several people with sinus trouble complained).

Then came a bombshell. On September 8, Valeska Suratt, a screen vamp who had retired to become a nurse in 1925, filed a one million dollar suit in the County Clerk's office in New York against Cecil B. DeMille, Jeanie Macpherson, and Producers' Distributing Corporation, Keith-Albee vaudeville exchange, and Cecil B. DeMille Picture Corporation charging plagiarism. She said that she was the sole owner of a scenario entitled *Mary Magdalen*, written by Mirza Ahmad Schrab, that in 1925 she had submitted it to Will Hays, who had referred her to DeMille. She claimed that DeMille had entered into a contract with her, using "essential features and portions" of the material without payment. Only two weeks before, a Mrs. Joan Armstrong

Alquist charged that in May 1924 she had submitted her book *The Wooing of Mary of Magdalene* to DeMille, and that it had been plagiarized. The sum of money demanded by Mrs. Alquist was a million dollars also. Ignoring Mrs. Alquist's claim, which was subsequently dropped, DeMille issued a statement to the press on Miss Suratt, which read, "I have always been under the impression that Matthew, Mark, Luke and John were the first to write the story of Jesus Christ," he said. "If Mirza Ahmad Schrab was its author, and pre-dates them, the record will have to be changed." The case was thrown out of court.

This victory, and the success of *The King of Kings*, gave DeMille a temporary stay of execution at Mount Vernon. Even J. J. Murdock was quietened in his demands for DeMille's removal. But unfortunately the ground was still far from secure under DeMille's feet. The films made under his imprint, but in fact not directed or, after 1926, even properly supervised by him, failed one after the other. Even with *The King of Kings*, a commercial and inspirational triumph, the complex company was on the edge of bankruptcy by August.

Meanwhile, that summer, DeMille had begun plans for a picture which would be the precise antithesis of *The King of Kings*: entitled *Atheist*, then *The Fiery Furnace*, it was to be the story of a girl in a reform school who absolutely rejected God. This change of pace was a certain way of attracting national publicity and a sure way also of exciting new interest in the director's moral views. To DeMille's great delight, the American Association for the Advancement of Atheism wired him a lengthy cable of protest at his plans; Barrett Kiesling immediately released the cable to every wire service in the world. In October, DeMille was exciting more publicity by indicating that the entire cast would consist of "persons of high-school age." In the meantime, his research machinery was going into high gear once more. In September, he had detailed diagrams made of the gingham dresses worn by the girls in the Florence Crittenton Home in New York. Precise floor plans of the home were drawn up, and minute particulars sent of the staffing, routine, and formal discipline. Lawler and Degnan, attorneys of Los Angeles, sent in an exhaustive breakdown of juvenile law. Charles Beahan of PDC in New York sent breakdowns on dozens of reformatory schools. Reform boys and girls were interviewed in sixteen states. Elizabeth McGaffey prepared a file of information: the size of desks in a variety of schools, the precise routine of incarceration in every state, the particulars of atheistic pamphlets found in desks of such places as the Hollywood High School, a detailed report on an outbreak of girls in a mutiny at Whittier. The American Legion sent facts about communism in schools, and young girls on his staff arranged to be disguised as criminals to observe conditions from the inside. Each day, more affidavits, photographs, and diagrammed floor plans poured in, filling two drawers in DeMille's office files.

Shooting of the film, finally entitled *The Godless Girl* in Jeanie's script, began on November 21, when a special technical director, George Ellis, started shooting at the State Training School for Girls in Gainesville, Texas. A week before, after much anguished consideration, DeMille finally settled on an old friend and former Follies girl, Lina Basquette, recently widowed by the death of Sam Warner, for the role. He had admired her in *Serenade* opposite Adolphe Menjou, and ran the film *The Noose* as well as twenty-five special tests prepared by Frank Gordon. Ernest Pascal worked with Jeanie Macpherson on the screenplay. It was decided, despite the enormous current success of *The Jazz Singer*, to shoot the film silent. DeMille's own first word on the subject appeared in a press release dated November 1, in which he said, "the picture will expose an insidious propaganda that is secretly distributed among students in high schools and which tends to subvert American ideals."

On November 28, DeMille cast George Duryea, star of *Abie's Irish Rose* on Broadway, opposite Lina Basquette. Duryea had traveled from New York especially and simply demanded he be given a screen test. DeMille gave in after Duryea had spent three days cooling his heels in the lobby of Mount Vernon. Though not conventionally handsome, Duryea had extraordinary sex appeal in the tests. Eddie Quillan, once a Sennett comedian, was also cast. High school girls by the hundred arrived at the studio, only to be turned down cold. The last important cast member chosen was Marie Prevost, already in the grip of the drug habit which finally brought about her downfall.

The production began on January 12, 1928. A *New York Sun* reporter visiting the elaborate reform school set built by Mitchell Leisen noted that, after all these years, DeMille still had a four-piece orchestra playing an overture when he arrived to direct a scene, still insisted nobody talk above a whisper, still demanded that building on other sets cease the moment he arrived and not resume until the moment he left, still was followed by an assistant with a chair, and still sat on an elevated throne to direct the simplest sequence. Visitors noticed that the sets were startlingly, grimly realistic: a high, electrically wired fence separated the boys' from the girls' quarters, a guard stood at attention in a tower, holding a rifle, even when not required in a shot, and a "mud horse" was operated for several days. This was a hand barrow which the boys in the prison filled with rocks, then refilled every time the rocks were dumped. DeMille showed that stocks were still being used in America, that children were fastened together in squads with iron rings, and locked to their beds at night. Barrett Kiesling went overboard on describing in releases what horrors the film would expose: flogging (still lawful in fifteen states), solitary confinement, stringing up by the thumbs, piercing under the fingernails, shackles, water cures, ice-packed blankets, semi-starvation, dirt and exposure in semi-hygenic conditions, and in four states tracking by bloodhound if the unfortunate victim of all this torture should manage to escape.

As usual, Peverell Marley worked with great ingenuity on the picture. He shot it entirely with one camera—unheard of for DeMille—using a movable carriage which could be elevated to the top floor of the reform school or lowered to the first, or could be moved forward or backward at any moment into medium, long, or close-up shots. This was accomplished through the use of an overhead tram system, the car hanging from the monorail being equipped with a power unit which could make an elevator out of the camera carriage. The controls were operated from the camera carriage, which carried Marley, Leisen, DeMille, and the camera operator all at once. Marley's most astonishing shot was achieved in the last reel. He had to show subjectively the dizzying fall of an inmate down the stairwell of the reformatory, giving the spectator the feeling of a vertiginous and perhaps fatal plunge onto hard stone. Marley was strapped in a special swing seat with a camera in his lap, with DeMille on another narrow seat above him. The camera was started, and the swing dropped through the stairwell by means of the mechanism of the overhead tram car. It was a revolutionary effect in motion pictures.

Whereas DeMille directed Lina Basquette, George Duryea and Marie Prevost to the last flicker of an eyelash, he sensibly allowed Eddie Quillan, with the actor's superb Sennett training, to improvise his scenes. Sometimes he accepted a decision of Quillan's over his own: virtually unheard of before or after that production. In a scene in which Quillan is attracted to Marie Prevost across a barbed wire fence separating the male and female wings of the reformatory, he wanted Quillan to take a peach can out of his garbage hand-cart and say to the girl, "You're a peach." Quillan felt that this would be a mistake, as it was unlikely a peach can would be in something about to be fed to pigs. "What would you do?" DeMille asked. "I'd raise my cap to her, and of course I'd drop the cart and spill its contents," Quillan said. DeMille instantly accepted the idea.

He sometimes had quarrels with other members of the cast. During a scene in the reformatory wash room, George Duryea said he was unable to hear the director because of the running of the taps. DeMille whispered an instruction to an assistant. Shooting stopped completely for several minutes while Duryea

Marie Prevost and Lina Basquette: The Godless Girl.

DeMille with Jeanie on the set of The Godless Girl.

Jeanie, Louella Parsons, and Cecil on the set of The Godless Girl.

The prison set: The Godless Girl (*1928*).

paced about, feeling nervous. Finally, with a loud creaking sound, the great reformatory doors opened and an assistant arrived with a megaphone fifteen feet long in a wheelbarrow. DeMille had a step ladder set up, climbed right to the top of it, and addressed Duryea in a voice which would have wakened the dead, "Can you hear me now?"

He was even more merciless with the crew. An electrician, walking around in the flies, let a pair of pliers fall to the floor in the middle of a scene. *"Who was that?"* DeMille shouted. *"It just slipped out!"* the man yelled back. *"You* can slip out, you're through," DeMille said. "I have one hundred kids in this picture, and any one of them could have been hit. Good afternoon, and pick up your paycheck as you go out!"

As usual, during the shooting of *The Godless Girl*, special visits by authorities on the subject were arranged. A group of women specialists in penal reform arrived on February 20 to be greeted by the extraordinary sight of DeMille, immaculate in gray, directing Lina Basquette in a scene in which she was surrounded by forty squealing pigs, cleaning out an extremely filthy trough. Asked by a reporter (for the *Boston Globe*) what she was playing, Miss Basquette, dripping ordure from her blue homespun, pulling a battered black felt hat over her eyes to protect them from the sun, said: "I am the Joan of Arc of atheism." The reporter asked DeMille if the picture was to be "a sermon, like *King of Kings.*" "*King of Kings* was *not* a sermon," DeMille snapped. "It was the fount from which all sermons come." Then, conducted by Kiesling, the reporter and the lady reformists went on a long and daunting walk through long tiers of rough wooden bunks, rows of battle-scarred bureaus ornamented only by tin cups, the four flights of steps down which an inmate plunged to her death, and the set which was to catch fire in the last scene. A few days later, Adolphe Ochs, publisher of the *New York Times*, also visited the set and marveled at its realism.

For the whole week until March 19, the great reformatory fire scene was staged. Mitchell Leisen helped prepare a special solution which prevented the girls from being burned. But the scene was still extremely dangerous to shoot. After four hours of rehearsal, DeMille declared himself ready. The building was actually set on fire, the carefully trained girls clambering up to the roof and down the other side of the building through a smoke-filled attic to a flame-free stairway, followed all the time by Peverell Marley's camera in an astonishing single take from a movable platform mounted on a scaffolding. Two girls on the roof were late leaving, and were badly singed. A moment later, exactly on cue, one complete wing of the set completely collapsed, pulled by special wires. Two girls perched on the edge of a narrow roof had a miraculous escape. They had to slide down a pole to the ground but flames prevented their exit. Showing great presence of mind they clambered up a slippery gable and slid down the other side, fighting through a smoke-filled attic to a safe stairway. A riot scene almost got out of hand as the girls threw vegetables, eggs, oranges, and other missiles with so much energy that DeMille received an undignified half-melon in his face. Scenes of the escape of Lina Basquette and George Duryea to an abandoned farm were shot at the Los Turas Ranch, forty-five miles out of Los Angeles, the guards who followed them equipped with real bullets.

In the midst of making the picture, the already shaky company began to break apart. Pathé, that constant thorn in DeMille's side, was on the edge of bankruptcy, even Milbank began cutting his investment, and the Capital Corporation was restive. Despite its success, the two-million-dollar *King of Kings* was still very far from netting anything like a substantial profit. Even while he was working on the biggest scenes in *The Godless Girl*, DeMille saw his dream of an independent studio disintegrate: the prominent director James Cruze left him suddenly, Donald Crisp followed, Phyllis Haver was loaned to D. W. Griffith for *The Battle of the Sexes*, Paul Sloane walked out, and Rod La Rocque, Victor Varconi, Rupert Julian, Vera Reynolds, and other stalwarts either drifted away completely or were sent for indefinite periods to other studios.

After the completion of *The Godless Girl*, DeMille faced a number of harrowing problems that summer. A new series of fires in the studio caused extensive damage and brought charges from Murdock in New York that DeMille had provided inadequate fire prevention devices. By disagreeable coincidence, shortly afterward, on June 21, a fire swept through the *Seaward*, rendering her unseaworthy for several months.

On the night of July 4, after the family at Laughlin Park had retired to the sleep-out porch following the Independence Day celebrations, Fred Rowland, watchman of the DeMille estate, was making his rounds when he noticed a mysterious package on a window ledge. As he reached it, a gun was pressed in his back and he was marched several blocks to a waiting automobile, then flung into some grass. The thieves had made off with thousands of dollars worth of jewels, stolen from Constance's room while she slept.

On July 7, the Julian Petroleum Corporation was indicted for overissuing stock in the corporation, and for pool manipulations. DeMille himself was charged with usury, in a special complaint filed by E. J. Hickey, the city prosecutor, who charged that DeMille had received a twelve-thousand-dollar bonus on a sixty-thousand-dollar loan to the oil company which had recently collapsed. Threatened with arrest only eight days after the *Seaward* burned, he was threatened also with permanent damage to his image of saintly rectitude. Fortunately, further investigation cleared him of the complaint in the usury suit, but he never entirely escaped the suspicion of many in Hollywood, and Murdock was delighted by the scandal.

DeMille's only consolation, apart from the satisfactory completion of *The Godless Girl*, was the throwing out of court of the Suratt suit for plagiarism of *The King of Kings*. Otherwise, his only moments of real happiness were, as always, with Julia on the *Seaward* or at Paradise—which he began to populate with buffalo and kangaroo—and in seeing Cecilia and Katherine grow up into beautiful young women at home. His sons John and Richard in many ways proved a disappointment to him: John was restless, shifting from one school to another, talking of running away to sea; Richard was taut and introspective, clever and scholarly but far from DeMille's ideal of a golden young athlete. Between the disappointments of Mount Vernon, that disintegrating dream, and the disappointment of his boys, DeMille was a desperate man that fall. Another problem was his collision with Murdock and the Pathé executives over the use of sound sequences in *The Godless Girl*.

The success of *The Jazz Singer*, which he had felt to be only temporary, had proved so immense that every studio was rushing into production of talking films. DeMille obstinately insisted that they were foolish, and that *The Godless Girl* would be a huge success as an entirely silent work. The arguments over this became so extreme that he finally decided to resign from his association with the company. When Joseph Kennedy of the Film Booking Office took over the collapsing Pathé side of the business, DeMille decided that he could not face yet another series of quarrels; he knew that Kennedy had very mixed feelings about his administration of the company. In July, DeMille had lunch with Louis B. Mayer at Metro-Goldwyn-Mayer, and a series of private discussions at Laughlin Park. The result was that early in August 1928 he signed an agreement to make three pictures at M-G-M, and with his personal staff, headed by Mitchell Leisen, he moved lock, stock, and barrel out of Mount Vernon on August 8.

After DeMille left Mount Vernon, the tide of sound became absolutely engulfing. That October, Murdock and the bosses of Pathé—which had gradually assumed dominance of the complex combine—decided that some talking sequences would have to be added to improve *The Godless Girl*'s somewhat limping career at the box office. In what was virtually a dip-in-the-barrel, an energetic German actor, Fritz Feld, was engaged to direct the talking sequences. DeMille—faced with the uncomfortable choice of staying where he was and having someone else direct a scene in a DeMille picture, or suffering the humiliation of returning to the Pathé fold—settled on the former choice.

Feld, who had directed nothing before, worked with great skill in settling the various problems of the new medium. He had to produce the sound of a rapidly beating heart after the reform girl falls down the stairwell, punctuating an otherwise silent image. He had another girl, specially engaged for the occasion, lie bare to the waist in a room from which all save a skeleton crew was excluded, then made her jump up, skip with a rope, and fall back on a table, where he recorded her with a complicated electrical apparatus. He even cut frames out of the film itself to give an illusion of accelerated sound. When he played the track he was distressed to find that the heartbeat resembled a locomotive going at sixty miles an hour. He managed to damp it down for a realistic effect. Sounds of fire were suggested by rumpled paper. He had a serious problem with Lina Basquette, who had never "talked" before. Trapped in the fire, this atheist is supposed to recite the Lord's Prayer in her state of terror. Unfortunately, she quite forgot her lines; it was impossible for her, despite several takes, to remember the prayer or to speak it with the slightest degree of conviction. Finally, Feld slapped her hard across the face; she burst into tears, remembered the prayer, and spoke it, convincingly afraid, through her sobbing.

The part-talkies scenes, the crackling of flames during the reformatory fire, the use of recorded music under the direction of Hugo Riesenfeld—these were sensations of the New York and Los Angeles openings of *The Godless Girl*. At M-G-M, DeMille could only regard the reception of these effects with wry amusement. He had already begun to realize that he was wrong about film talk.

10

An Interlude
at Metro

DeMille settled comfortably into a temporary suite of offices in the middle of the M-G-M lot in September, while Louis B. Mayer prepared for him a special bungalow, equipped with private offices for his staff, which included Jeanie (who spent part of the time at Culver City finishing work on a couple of left-over DeMille productions), Peverell Marley, who had now married Lina Basquette after a romance conducted on the set of *The Godless Girl*, Mitchell Leisen, who was virtually a full-time assistant by now as well as art director, Russel Treacy, head bookkeeper, the indispensable Gladys Rosson, Barrett Kiesling, Anne Bauchens, and a new and charming addition from the Metro stenographic pool,

Paradise.

Florence Cole. There, early in 1929, he began work on a new film, *Dynamite*, designed to launch him in the sound era. He had been enjoying breakfast about two months earlier when he had spotted an item in a newspaper which made him set down his coffee cup and begin making urgent notations. He cut out a small article with his pocket penknife. An hour later, he gave it to Jeanie at the office. She looked at him and nodded. The item, datelined Trenton, New Jersey (July 18, 1928), was headlined: MAN MARRIES WOMAN TWO HOURS BEFORE HE IS HANGED FOR MURDER. A few days later, DeMille found another item, about a woman who paid a sum of money to a wife with which to buy the husband. Jeanie spent a month combining the two stories. DeMille was delighted. Then, immediately, DeMille started casting. Charles Bickford was hired out of a Broadway play called *Gods of the Lightning*. He was the ideal choice to play the powerful coal miner in the film (a rich woman marries him in a death cell on a bet). Tyler Brooke was hired from the *No, No Nanette* company, and DeMille found the female star, the English Kay Johnson, acting with beautiful sensitivity in a Los Angeles production of *The Silver Cord*. Julia was ideal as Marcia Towns, a society woman who tries to sell her husband for twenty-five thousand dollars down and seventy-five thousand dollars on delivery.

DeMille and Jeanie felt the story lacked a strong "last act." This came from yet another news story, a mine explosion at Parnassus, Pennsylvania, in which forty men were trapped. DeMille sent a wire five minutes after the extras were published demanding that every detail of the rescue be made available to him, and he and Mitchell Leisen painstakingly copied from sketches the details of the mine.

Hedging his bets, DeMille decided to make silent and sound versions of *Dynamite.* The sound version presented him with innumerable problems. He had been shrewd in picking Bickford and Johnson, both of whom had beautiful stage voices. But Julia was a problem: she had a rather awkward, nasal voice, and he had to work immensely hard with her. Moreover, the problems of shooting the film were considerable. Because the early microphones picked up the slightest external sound, they had to be carefully placed away from street noises, and the doors of the sound stages religiously closed at all times. The heat and lack of air were insufferable. Microphones had to be placed in lamps, bowls of flowers, outsized cigarette lighters, and other accessories, and if a player moved away from the microphone his voice would become too faint to be heard.

There were all kinds of unexpected problems during the shooting. Kay Johnson, absolutely at ease in the sound version, became terrified in the silent version, hated to do dumb show, and in a kitchen scene dropped a whole box of eggs on the floor. Later, she was stricken with appendicitis and had to be rushed to the Cedars of Lebanon hospital, slowing up production for days. She wrenched a knee during an automobile race scene; DeMille, for much of the rest of the shooting, had to "borrow" Kay Johnson's legs for the close-ups of Julia's. In one scene, Kay Johnson had to attack Charles Bickford with a perfume bottle. She picked up the wrong bottle and knocked him out cold.

In the finale, Conrad Nagel, Kay Johnson, and Charles Bickford were trapped in a coal mine with fifteen minutes of air left. The roof caved in—the timing was immensely difficult—shutting off the players in a wall of coal. As the cameras stopped grinding, DeMille heard some chuckling from the crew. He looked around to see Kay Johnson peeping out above the coal in blackface as a result of the dust, miserably dabbing her sad face with powder.

During the shooting of the same scene, a special machine had to blast dust at the players to make them look sufficiently soiled and bedraggled. Due to a miscalculation, the machine blew directly at DeMille and Peverell Marley, making them emerge in blackface, gesticulating helplessly.

When the film was finally cut together, DeMille had good reason to be pleased with it. Handsomely made, it showed an extraordinary command of the resources of sound. In his finest scene, DeMille showed Charles Bickford in jail while Russ Columbo, then at the height of his popularity, sang a sad Dorothy Parker lyric, "How Are We To Know?" Daringly, DeMille added a guitar accompaniment, using two sound tracks in defiance of studio instructions. He became excited by the sound track at once. All the way from fearing it a year before, he became intoxicated by its possibilities, and the film was as superb aurally as it was visually.

After a year of work, on September 16, 1929, DeMille's bungalow office was at last ready for occupancy. Wallace Reid's armor from *Joan the Woman* hung by an ornate fireplace. The Grail used in the Last Supper of *The King of Kings* was placed in a special cabinet. Huge spears from *The Ten Commandments* adorned a doorway leading to a garden patio. A Burmese silver dispatch case from *The Cheat* lay on a table, and ancient Aztec ornaments from *The Woman God Forgot* lay everywhere. There was a large collection of firearms: dueling pistols from many European nations, including a gold-mounted set made by the armorer of Louis XIV of France; one flintlock bore an Arabian transcription promising death to unbelievers; another, from a sect of Chinese Christians, had the story of Christ on silver relief on the barrel. In one enormous cabinet was a large collection of precious stones, carved jade, and ivory. An Eskimo's letter to his family was inscribed on two elephant tusks. An oyster shell contained a pearl in the form of a small fish.

DeMille had barely settled in the bungalow when disturbing news came from the East. Julia Faye telephoned him long distance from her home in New York to say that Arthur Brisbane, William Randolph Hearst's right-hand man, had told her there was going to be a stockmarket crash. Immediately, DeMille instructed Gladys Rosson to sell all of the stocks he held. She had a strict rule at all times only to sell at half a point above the market. But when an offer was made to accept them at half value, she refused. As a result, DeMille lost one million dollars when the bottom of the market fell out. Gladys burst into tears of self-recrimination as she brought him the news. Happily, the shock was cushioned by the fact that DeMille still had immense holdings in real estate.

That winter Cecilia had fallen in love with a man DeMille deeply admired, Francis (known to his intimates as Frank) Calvin, son of Eugene Calvin, former president of the Union Pacific Railroad. On January 7, 1930, the engagement was officially announced at a luncheon at Laughlin Park. On February 22, the wedding took place in drenching rain at St. Paul's Pro-Cathedral on 8th and Figueroa Streets, followed by a wedding reception at Laughlin Park. Cecilia looked lovely in white satin, with her bouquet of lilies and gardenias, surrounded by her bridesmaids in orchid satin. The DeMilles' wedding present to the couple was a charming house just over the hill from Laughlin Park, set in superb plantings of fir and pine.

Shortly after the completion of *Dynamite*, Peverell Marley left DeMille, announcing that he and his wife Lina Basquette would be going on, of all things, to a career on the vaudeville stage. When Miss Basquette had failed to obtain a suitable dancing partner for her vaudeville act in New York, she had asked Marley to fill in. An excellent dancer, he had been a great success. DeMille was so amused by the whole idea he neglected to express his usual fury at the desertion of a colleague.

He decided, following a request of Louis B. Mayer's, to follow *Dynamite* with a musical, keeping within the current vogue for musical productions with spectacular climactic scenes. He engaged Herbert Stothart, Clifford Grey, Elsie Janis, and Jack King to prepare a score for a feature to be entitled *Madame Satan*, including "Meet Madame," "Dance Moderne," "The Cat Walk," "The Madam Satan Waltz" and "Forgive, Forget and Love Me," and "The Girl Auction." As a dance director, he engaged the brilliant LeRoy Prinz, who devised a magnificent *ballet méchanique*, to take place in a Zeppelin which would be shown breaking loose from its moorings in a storm near New York. Jeanie prepared the story—about a dull wife, played by Kay Johnson, who tries to capture her husband's interest by disguising herself as a sultry French vamp. The title, like *Dynamite*, was drawn from a film being made at the time DeMille first came out to Hollywodd: it had stuck with him ever since.

During an intermission in the shooting of the Zeppelin dance, the bit player Natalie Visart, Katherine's childhood friend, who later became DeMille's chief costume designer, almost lost her life. She was standing near an open box of electrical wires when her elaborate dress—made of layers of taffeta—caught on the wires and the heat ignited it. A moment later, she was on fire. Fortunately, she had the presence of mind to stand absolutely still; if she had run, the breeze would have increased the flames. But nobody came to her rescue, until finally LeRoy Prinz, just as the fire reached the final layer of skirt and would have burned her to death, rushed forward and doused the flames.

DeMille was not on the set during this incident, which took place during a break for lunch. But he was present shooting part of the ballet when a girl on a high perch in the Zeppelin threatened to faint with exhaustion after standing for several hours. LeRoy Prinz called an immediate halt to the shooting. DeMille screamed with rage at what he had done, brushing aside Prinz's remark that the girl might easily have fallen to her death if she had slipped.

DeMille's genius was vividly expressed in these final scenes. Mitchell Leisen's set of the Zeppelin's interior was masterly, and Theodore Kosloff, still flawlessly handsome as the Spirit of Electricity, brilliantly led the troupe in LeRoy Prinz's fantastic dance routines. The parachuting of the throng out of the stricken Zeppelin was an astonishment, one girl dressed as a many-armed Burmese goddess descending on a group of drunks in a park, and another—played by Lillian Roth—dressed as a golden pheasant swinging from a weather vane on a church steeple. Roland Young, playing an aging roué to the manner born, arrived in a lion pit, clinging to a tree at feeding time.

C. B., Julia Faye, and a set visitor,
Dr. Jogesh Misrow, noted Brahmin: Dynamite *(1929).*

Kay Johnson and Charles Bickford in Dynamite.

Zeppelin disaster: Madam Satan.

Unfortunately, the film, aside from this sequence, was extremely slow, dull, and unfunny, and it was not a success. *Dynamite* had done fairly well, but this new flop confirmed the views of DeMille's enemies at Metro that the Murdock interests had done right to dislodge him from Pathé. Louis B. Mayer had the unpleasant duty of calling DeMille into his office and telling him that once his three-picture contract had expired, it would not be renewed.

In desperation, DeMille decided to rush through a final picture to complete his M-G-M contract, yet another version of *The Squaw Man*. Even though his former co-director, Oscar Apfel, who was now a celebrated character actor, offered to appear in the film and congratulated him upon making it, "Squaw Man III," as DeMille later described it, was not exciting as a prospect. He went depressingly through the motions as Mayer signed up the rights to Edwin Milton Royle's work from Zukor and Lasky. He moodily accepted the fact that current conventions forced him to cast non-Indians in the roles formerly taken by Indian actors. He even cast a *Follies* star, Lupe Velez, as the lovely girl once played in happier times by Red Wing. He cast Warner Baxter as the Squaw Man and Eleanor Boardman as Lady Diana, scarcely bothering to instruct her in the manners of an English lady of position.

In October, DeMille underwent an excruciatingly painful operation on his weak heels, which had splintered in an accident at his house. From his hospital bed, he instructed Gladys Unger and Elsie Janis in writing the screenplay of Squaw Man III, Jeanie having point-blank refused to be involved in so dismal a project. Finally, at Christmas, the script was more or less ready, and DeMille desultorily took his cast of seventy-three to Hot Springs Junction, Arizona, to shoot the picture; by a supreme irony, it was near the location he had rejected for the first version in December 1913.

For some weeks, Mitchell Leisen had been building the set of the old Western ranch house and several barns. Lupe Velez was a continuing problem on location, temperamental, foul-mouthed, and uncooperative. DeMille felt so bereft of inspiration during the first days of shooting that he asked Gladys Rosson to send a print of *Squaw Man I* down from Los Angeles to inspire him, but it emerged that it had been destroyed in a fire at the Lubin Laboratories in Philadelphia.* He picked up slightly when Winifred Kingston popped up on location and played a bit role. But he didn't mean it when he told a visiting reporter from the *Baltimore Sun*: "I love this story so much that as long as I live I will make it every ten years."

After the dreary shooting, DeMille left at once for the newly refitted *Seaward*, which was showing few marks of the fire. During the past few years he had developed a passion for deep-sea diving, and while Anne Bauchens cut the rambling feature to tolerable length, he forgot everything in the green depths off Catalina. He told the *New York Times*: "When you stand on the bed of the ocean forty or fifty feet below the surface you're in absolutely a new world, with new sensations. It's like exploring some prehistoric Cambrian fen, with the waving movement of the water and the sun filtering through, furnishing unique effects. None of the inhabitants of the water is afraid of you at that depth, and the first time a shark brushes up against you you're not going to forget the experience. The water pressure is pretty severe and when you come up after half an hour you feel you've done a good day's work." He did not use the standard diving apparatus, but bathing trunks, leaving most of his body bare, and a watertight eighty-pound steel helmet with a plate glass front and an oxygen tube which Captain Ed McNeary of the *Seaward* or DeMille's trusted valet, Arthur, always controlled.

These were the happiest days, with Ed McNeary and Arthur on the *Seaward*, or, as always, at Paradise. Julia never ceased, even after all these years, to be an enchanting light-hearted companion. She had much trouble in relaxing DeMille during those months.** He longed to escape from movie making

---

* Another print was located in 1932, after Squaw Man III was in circulation.
** At times, in the past few years, he had enjoyed the favors of Gladys Rosson also, a frequent bone of contention between the two women.

altogether, speaking to her of taking the *Seaward* and sailing to some quiet cove in the South Seas, to laze and dream away the rest of his days.

In this period of uncertainty, moments of escape, and intermittent depression, DeMille sought the formation of an organization known as the Directors' Guild, not to be confused with the Screen Directors' Guild, which brought together a group of four, the other members being Lewis Milestone, King Vidor, and Frank Borzage, dedicated to the principles of fresher, freer, and more creative management in Hollywood. The hope which he and his colleagues held high was that the director, in the future, would be able to choose his own subjects, that he would not be governed by rule of committee. The idea seems to have been borne out of pique that M-G-M had wanted him to remake *The Squaw Man*, since in fact he had agreed to make both *Dynamite* and *Madame Satan*, and Mayer had given him an unusual degree of freedom in the use of his personal staff and assistant crew. The idea of the Directors' Guild made him extremely unpopular with Mayer, who was already under pressure from his superior, Nicholas Schenck, to have DeMille removed from office (Schenck had attempted to cancel *The Squaw Man* even before it was produced, despite— or perhaps because of—the fact that Mayer, with whom he was having executive differences, had set the production in motion).

The Squaw Man, like *Madame Satan* before it, was a disaster at the box office. DeMille felt an agony of depression as the first figures came in, and decided at once to cancel all of his plans, dismiss most of his staff, and leave for an extended vacation in Europe with Constance, the vacation he had planned at the time of the rift with Lasky.

To make matters worse, he was again charged with usury.* Richard L. North and J. G. Kelley, receivers for the Elmer Oil Company, charged usury against the Cecil B. DeMille Com-

* These charges were dismissed in 1932.

pany, in making four loans to Elmer: seventy-five thousand dollars on January 23, 1930, for ninety days; fifty thousand dollars on July 30, 1930, for ninety days, fifty thousand dollars on August 13 for ninety days; and the same amount for the same period on November 6. North and Kelley charged that DeMille's corporation was given in return for these loans a royalty in certain wells, each totaling fifteen thousand dollars, and that fifty-three thousand seven hundred fifty dollars was paid to him as an usurorship interest.

Cecilia's beloved chestnut saddle mare, Love Lee Dare, died in a fire at the Oakland horse show, and DeMille had to check in for yet another operation on his heels. Robert Edeson died of a heart ailment in March. Then, as if he had not enough to contend with, the Cinema Corporation of America sued him for having stolen the rights to *The Volga Boatman* as his own, even though in fact they still belonged to that organization. He was forced to settle out of court.

Weighed down with all these matters, DeMille attended an ironically jovial farewell dinner preceding his trip to Europe at the Ambassador Hotel in Hollywood, with Louis B. Mayer as a genial host. Another thorn in his side, Samuel Goldfish (now Goldwyn), was among the guests. On his way to New York, he had the pleasant experience of stopping at Ashfield, his birthplace, to see some old childhood friends, and at the Pennsylvania Military College, which awarded him an honorary degree as Doctor of Letters.

A visit to Pompton Lake was particularly enjoyable. Henry G. Hershfield, a school chum who was now a prominent local businessman, gave the party at the Hotel St. Moritz, calling upon close childhood friends to give speeches of reminiscence. Mayor Stephen H. B. Jacobs welcomed DeMille back to his old borough, and Dr. William Colefax, who had been the DeMille family doctor, told amusing stories. DeMille's speech of acknowledgment came from the bottom of his heart. He spoke of the "old paths [he] could picture, the old homes and the old lanes over which he used to run as a boy." Next day, he

DeMille's Spanish-style office at M-G-M, 1929.

Talking to Soviet cinema men in Moscow, 1931.

*Theodore Kosloff, DeMille, and Mrs. DeMille
while visiting a Russian prison (1931).*

In Egypt, 1931.

explored those paths, glowing with happy reminiscences in the warm June sunshine. His only real sadness was that his school did not exist any more; the MacDavitt estate where it stood was now occupied by the imposing bulk of the Adam Sanitorium.

Pamlico, however, still stood, looking gorgeous in the glow of the sun. He wandered over the house, now owned by Mr. and Mrs. Dobbs, and saw a beech tree he had planted as a boy; he even found his favorite pony trail, across the nearby meadow and through the lovely trees which had been saplings in his youth. It was a wonderful, unforgettable day.

The trip to Europe that June had been scrupulously planned in Hollywood by Gladys Rosson working with American Express and Intourist (for the Russian portion). DeMille left with Constance for England on board the *Ile de France* on June 24, after he had obtained an option on the rights to the play *The Sign of the Cross*, by Wilson Barrett, now owned by Mary Pickford's company. It was the story of the love of Marcus Superbus, a Roman soldier, for a lovely Christian slave girl, with Nero and his Empress Poppaea figuring in the action, and unlimited opportunities for orgies, Christian sacrifices, lions, and vestal virgins, a kind of sequel to *The King of Kings*.

The crossing on the *Ile de France* was smooth and comfortable, a far cry from the ghastly crossing on the *Berengaria* ten years before. The DeMilles luxuriated in the great ship, the beloved "Boulevard of the Atlantic," with its gilded main dining room, its statues by Baudry and Dejean, its sumptuous bas-reliefs and paintings, and, above all, its lovely chapel, with the Stations of the Cross sculptured in wood. A great fascination on the crossing was seeing a pilot and radioman climb into a Loire and Oliver biplane and hurtle off the decks with a deafening roar—a pleasing novelty introduced by the shipping line just over two years before.

The DeMilles adored London, and spent every night seeing plays; during the day, DeMille visited various studios, but attempts to arrange for him to make British films collapsed: word was out that he had a series of flops, and nobody was prepared to go ahead without a guarantee of distribution from an American company.

The DeMilles traveled to Belgium and the Netherlands, where they saw the church in which Anthony DeMil had been married in 1653, and then proceeded via Berlin to the major goal of the trip: Russia, with Theodore Kosloff joining them in Germany as translator-guide.

In Russia, DeMille kept a careful diary from day to day, written in violet ink, blue ink, and pencil in a cramped scrawl on a tear-off calendar. A typical entry reads: "WEDNESDAY, September 2: The funerals, one old horse pulling a wagon with four white posts on the corners. The coffin tied to the body with rope. First five or six followers walking bareheaded in street, and white coffin. One follower a woman."

Everywhere he translated his experiences into images. He found Kosloff's sister selling matches in the street, noticed a broken window plastered up with pictures of Jesus and the Saints, attended Gorky's *Bread* at the Moscow Art Theatre, and was fascinated by Maxim Gorky on stage after the performance carrying a little satin skull cap. On September 3 DeMille wrote: "The flow of people on the street gives the feel of a mighty river which nothing can stop. Two experiments started about the same time. Prohibition has failed and socialism succeeded. The magnificent Opera House. The strange costumes of the audience. The mediocre dancing. The propaganda at the end of opera ballet, RED POPPY." He saw *Storm over Asia*, visited a women's prison where he noted the same plot as *Bread* now made real—a woman sentenced to two years for hiding her wheat. He was thrilled by the great parade of Russian youth in the Red Square and was deeply impressed by a play, Kataev's *Squaring the Circle*, to which he bought the film rights. He summed up the play's qualities on September 8: "The gypsy orchestra. The room of the dead like Pompeii, peopled with the spirit of the past. The gypsy singers and dancers in their gay colors playing to the gorgeous great empty room."

Jugglers in the street, the people's court, the Kremlin ("the old woman . . . arranging the wealth of the Czars without emotion"), the faces of the poor ("Russia has perhaps one face in every ten marked by smallpox"). The journey to Leningrad was bitterly cold, with no dining car on the train, and only a porter with a samovar to make tea. Leningrad offered drenching rain, a freezing ride in a droshky; and the trip to the Volga was almost as uncomfortable. Nizhgi Novgorod was even colder than Leningrad, but the Volga was a great thrill, although DeMille wrote to Gladys Rosson that the Volga Boatman in his picture was "more reel" [sic] than the one in the movie. Once again, his images were those of a pure picture maker, as he traveled on the Volga boat: "The woman pulling the inside of the fish and eating it. The tea made out of apples. The drunken boy who thought he was put off the boat. The bales of goat skins cut in small pieces."

He described every stage of his journey up the Volga in the diary, his eye constantly lighting on telling details. Stalingrad was miserable, the hotel dirty, the dusty, wretched streets a hazard to traffic. The train journey across the Steppes was fascinating, but the DeMilles were feeling the strain of eight days without proper rest or a bath. They traveled across Georgia to Tiflis, which they loved, visited monasteries and churches, and adored Batum, with the snow-capped Caucasus Mountains in the distance. The journey over and around the Black Sea took several days, and DeMille paused for a reflection: "Russia is a land of no liberty—of much paper money—of terrible filth—of great determination—of high ideals—of almost hopeless poverty."

In October, the couple proceeded to Istanbul, Greece (he sat in the chair of Marcus Aurelius in the Theatre of Bacchus), the Greek Archipelago ("The sea is heavenly calm and blue"), Alexandria ("I set foot on African soil for the first time"), the Continental Hotel at Cairo, the Pyramids at Gizeh ("The view of the Nile from the Citadel. One sees seven thousand years of history spread before them and the endless Lybian desert beyond that.").

It was a fascination to visit the scenes he had re-created at Guadalupe in *The Ten Commandments.* With eleven camels, two donkeys, and one horse he and Kosloff and Constance set out boldly into the desert. They rode to Memphis. DeMille was mesmerized by "the water pumps drawing water by a blind-folded ox or two men operating two jars on weighted poles exactly as in Pharaoh's time, and making mud bricks with straw." Typically he was reminded of his favorite artist: "A body in an open coffin is being carried on the heads of a group of men to a waiting boat to be borne to the old Mohammedan cemetery on the other side of the Nile. It is like Doré's painting of Charon waiting to ferry the departed souls across the River Styx."

It was as well that the trip was so fascinating because the brief letters DeMille received from home could not have been less encouraging. The film industry, after the initial fillip of the talkies, was sinking into a period of recession. Neil McCarthy, acting on DeMille's behalf, was forced to arrange the mortgage of Laughlin Park, and to borrow extensively on all properties. By the time De Mille returned to New York on the *Augustus* on November 24, he realized that, strictly speaking, the great expense of the trip had not been justified and that he was virtually broke. All he had to show for the outlay was a vast collection of photographs of his travels and the rights to *Squaring the Circle,* which he ultimately never made into a film.

The outset of 1932 brought a new host of problems. The income tax authorities in Washington followed an earlier charge in January 1931 by charging him with five hundred twenty-five thousand eight hundred and seventeen dollars back taxes plus sixty-nine thousand two hundred and eighty-three dollars personal taxes. He challenged the ruling, but at the moment prospects of escaping the charges were very slim.

11

The Return
to Lasky

Back in Hollywood, DeMille decided to proceed with plans for making *The Sign of the Cross.* After urgent consultation with Neil McCarthy he came to the conclusion that the only hope of making it lay in an appeal to Lasky and a return, humbly hat-in-hand, to his old studio (now known as Paramount). At first, Zukor proved adamant: DeMille could never work for the organization again. But Lasky prevailed, aided by Ben P. Schulberg, head of production on the West Coast.

DeMille was forced into a position of making strict guarantees on the new production. Zukor abruptly reminded him in a series of brief and coldly worded notes that he had scarcely left

Karl Struss (left), Claudette Colbert, Fredric March, and C. B. on set: The Sign of the Cross.

the Lasky organization on favorable terms, that he had had a
very poor record at his own studio, and that his M-G-M period
had been nothing short of disaster. In the jovial parlance of the
film industry, he was "box-office poison." Only the absolute
faith of Lasky and Schulberg would make tolerable DeMille's
name on a Paramount picture, but in return he must make his
film for the lowest possible figure. DeMille, his back against the
wall, smarting with the horrible indignity of his situation,
simply promised that he would make the spectacle for a mere
six hundred fifty thousand dollars, half of which would be
borrowed money invested by his own company. He himself
would draw only four hundred fifty dollars a week as director.
No sooner had Zukor reluctantly bent to this arrangement,
than DeMille's partisan Ben Schulberg was forced out of office
in a power struggle, to be replaced by Emmanuel ("Manny")
Cohen who disliked and mistrusted DeMille as cordially as J. J.
Murdock had.

Matters worsened in April, when DeMille received the
shocking news of Jesse's dismissal from the company he had
helped build from its foundation. A continuing clash between
Sam Katz, head of the Paramount subsidiary, the Publix
Theatre Chain, and Sidney Kent, the brilliant head of sales, had
caused a severe rift in the company, and Lasky had been caught
in the middle. Katz brought powerful allies including John
Hertz, the Yellow Cab and rent-a-car millionaire, and Albert
Lasker, the advertising tycoon, into the company, forcing Kent
out, and Lasky with him. Even Zukor was endangered, and was
later forced out as president of the company, permitted to stay
on in a largely nominal capacity as the Katz factions virtually
took over.

It was an impossible situation. With both Lasky and
Schulberg out of office, DeMille's whole *raison d'être* at
Paramount seemed to disappear. Katz, Hertz, and Lasker were
far from happy with DeMille on the scene, as they associated
him with the collapsing regime. Sleepless, tense, and irritable,
and afraid that there might be a repercussion of his former

struggles with Murdock, DeMille steeled himself to go forward and reassembled his personal staff, disbanded upon his departure for Europe in the summer of 1931: Mitchell Leisen, who had been earning a pittance as a dress extra, came back at one hundred twenty-five dollars instead of six hundred dollars a week, Anne Bauchens came back at fifty dollars a week, and, also at greatly reduced salaries, he hired back other trusted employees (Gladys Rosson and Florence Cole had been kept on the payroll and had worked up at the house during his absence). He gave Leisen strict instructions on keeping the sets—and the costumes—at an absolute minimum figure, which involved some rather desperate improvisation. Nero's palace—though not announced as much in publicity—was largely a miniature set, with special flights of stairs and ramps for people to walk along, with nothing around them outside of the film frame line. When the crowd entered the palace, he had to make shots directly onto them, as the slightest off-center movement would disclose that there were nothing but blank spaces around. To suggest that vast crowds were assembled the cameraman, Karl Struss (who had done much the same thing on *Ben-Hur*), employed a prism lens which effectively doubled the size of the crowd.

DeMille's largest problem, once the agreement with Paramount had been signed, was casting the epic. Two weeks off production on June 18, 1932, he still had not been able to locate the correct star for the role of Empress Poppaea, the wife of Nero. Pola Negri and Norma Talmadge were seriously considered—followed by Elissa Landi, who was finally borrowed from Fox to play the Christian girl Mercia instead. Then one day he noticed the beautiful Paramount star Claudette Colbert walking by the office. "Claudette, how would you like to play the wickedest woman in the world?" he cried through the window. "I'd *love it!*" she exclaimed, and he hired her on the spot.

Earlier, Charles Laughton had been cast as Nero (DeMille had seen him in London playing in C. S. Forester's *Payment Deferred*), and Fredric March as the handsome hero Marcus

Superbus. Theodore Kosloff was hired to help LeRoy Prinz stage the fantastic dances; they had met in Rome during the European trip and conferred on the details. Another old friend, John Flinn, returned from another assignment to handle the publicity for the production. The film would open at Grauman's Chinese, which had been closed for remodeling for several months.

Before shooting began, DeMille told a reporter from the *New York American* (June 15, 1932) in a strike-out at the Department of Internal Revenue: "Do you realize the close analogy between conditions today in the United States and the Roman Empire prior to the fall? Multitudes in Rome were then oppressed by distressing laws, overtaxed and ruled by a chosen few. Unless America returns to the pure ideals of our legendary forbears, it will pass into oblivion as Rome did." Asked his interpretation of Nero by the *New York Evening Journal*, Charles Laughton said, "Nero was nuts. I play him straight."

Mitchell Leisen worked brilliantly to execute DeMille's miniature Rome, a structure built by four hundred workers on the Paramount ranch over a four-month period. This entire miniature city was burned while Nero plucked at a harp; at a given sign, a workman turned a gas valve, sending smoke and flame leaping into the sky. Four thousand men, women, and children rushed into the streets on cue, screaming with terror, their anguish recorded by twelve cameras under the cinematographer Karl Struss. DeMille ordered Poppaea's bath, filled with actual milk, copied from blueprints and charts of baths found in recent excavations. Unfortunately, after Claudette Colbert had been bathing in it for two days it began to turn to cheese, and the smell was appalling. The most elaborate set was the Roman Circus, an ampitheater seating seventy-five hundred people, and a ninety-thousand-square-foot arena. Lions, tigers, bears, and elephants were requisitioned from eleven zoos and trained with incredible precision. DeMille engaged giantesses and dwarfs from fun fairs to fight with each other, and General Ivan Ikonikoff and Captain Clifford (brother of Victor) Mc-

DeMille on set: The Sign of the Cross.
Charles Laughton extreme right.

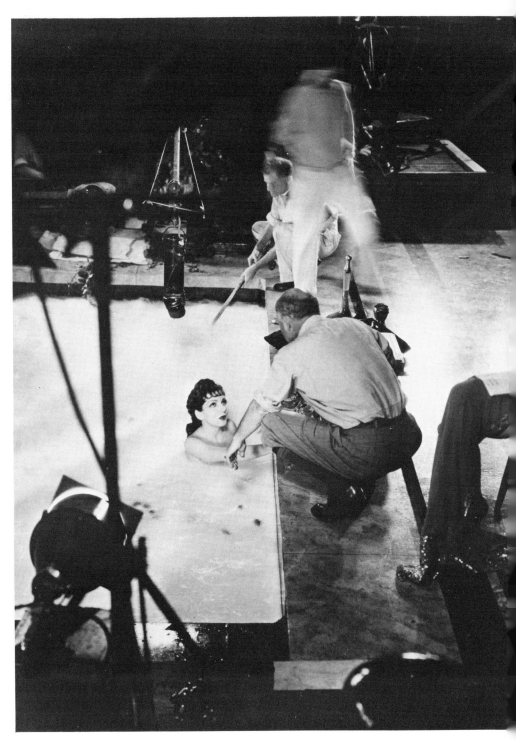

Claudette Colbert and C. B.—
the bath scene: The Sign of the Cross.

Claudette Colbert in The Sign of the Cross.

Laglen to train the gladiators in the precise rules of ancient combat. Daringly, he shot the entire picture through red gauze, to give an impression of time remembered, and all of the night scenes were illuminated only by torches, because he wanted to save money on the arcs.

His method of directing the extras had not changed since *Joan the Woman.* He still divided up the crowds into ten, with an assistant director in charge of each. This enabled him to isolate tiny details in the crowd of the arena: one man has lost his seat check and quarrels frantically with the ushers; another is trying to soothe his wife, who is upset about the location of their seats.

Aside from the cheese bath, a major problem was that the lions hired to maul the Christians were reluctant to perform their duty. Leisen arranged for the carcasses of lambs to be wrapped in the simple clothes of the Christian sect, and chained them to the ground to prevent the lions revealing the truth by pulling the clothes off too far. The lions proved entirely uninterested. Finally, they just stood in a line quietly lapping up the blood. Nothing happened even when the trainers used chairs and whips, and finally DeMille was forced to fake almost every shot.

On the last day of shooting, at three o'clock in the afternoon, the assistant director, Roy Burns, suddenly arrived on the scene in the arena and whispered in DeMille's ear, "We've just used up the budget." DeMille wheeled around, looked him in the eye, and yelled "Cut!" in the very middle of a take. Not one more shot was made, and Anne Bauchens was instructed to have a complete rough-cut ready within one week.

On October 6, 1932, DeMille wrote a memorandum to the board of directors of Cecil B. DeMille productions, indicating that he had completed "this enormous production in eight weeks at a cost of six hundred fifty thousand dollars."

Lasky and even Zukor were deeply impressed by the film, which combined sadism, religious elements, and an agreeably sophisticated distortion of history with immense flair. There was much to give the censor pause—an erotic dance in which the ballerina Joyzelle Joyner appeared as the Bride of the Moon, a resplendent orgy, a naked male slave seen to accompany Nero and implying that the emperor was a homosexual, a lesbian handmaiden for Cleopatra, and numerous sexual images, of hands, lips, thighs, feet (especially), and a mouth spouting milk to fill the empress' bath.

But DeMille refused to alter a single shot, the publicity department exploited the film's erotic elements to the hilt, and the public flocked to see the film.

Just before Christmas 1932, DeMille traveled to Philadelphia for the opening of *The Sign of the Cross* at the Aldine Theatre. He delighted reporters at a dawn railroad station press conference by telling them of a theater he had visited in Asia Minor. It boasted three screens: in the middle the Hollywood film with special titles printed underneath in case anyone in the audience was deaf, on the right a smaller screen carrying the dialog in Arabic, and on the left another carrying the dialog in French. He also kept the reporters happy with such specialized tidbits as the statement that Rudolph Kopp, composer of music for *The Sign of the Cross*, had to go back to Gregorian chant to find music "not anachronistic to 64 A.D."—whatever that meant. In New York, he attended the opening at the Rialto and told reporters there, when asked what he thought of Claudette Colbert "really," that "she is like a beautiful, poisonous cobra."

The enormous success of *The Sign of the Cross* reinstated DeMille as a major force in the industry, and even made Zukor's heart glow. By casting "art" to the winds, DeMille had at last achieved an ambition that had burned in him for two years: to provide an adequate retort to the hated J. J. Murdock and to his subsequent enemies at Metro. From now on, he would completely cease to have the artistic aspirations which had driven him as a young man. He would simply set out to be a supremely successful film maker in the years to come.

As so often before, he followed a great spectacle, which taxed his powers to the limit, with a potboiler: *This Day and Age*, a story about delinquent youth, similar to *The Godless Girl*, but without the frenetic energy and technical panache of that film. He simply rushed it out, as he had rushed out *Triumph* after *The Ten Commandments*, "to keep the presses busy."

On February 20, 1933, a luncheon was held at Twentieth Century-Fox honoring Jesse L. Lasky's twenty years in pictures (he was a prominent producer there). DeMille's tribute was impassioned, though he flinched slightly when Lasky recalled that the first *Squaw Man* had been budgeted at twenty-five thousand dollars and had cost forty-three thousand dollars which was "all we had." But a pall of gloom was cast over the luncheon: the realization that Hollywood was in the severest financial difficulties since its inception.

For eight weeks, the industry's leaders agreed, from March 9, every single star and featured player would take a 50 per cent salary cut. Louis B. Mayer took an 85 per cent cut in his salary saying that he had done this "to save my studio."

On July 7, DeMille and Constance celebrated their twentieth anniversary in motion pictures by cutting a cake at the Paramount barn, now converted into a gymnasium. Soon after that, he transferred his headquarters to the *Seaward* for the rest of the summer. Among the books he took along was an entertaining novel, *Four Frightened People*, by the British writer E. Arnot Robertson. It was the story of a group of people who escape a ship stricken with bubonic plague and make their way to the mainland of Malaya, where they enjoy various bizarre adventures in the jungle. DeMille saw the possibility of what could virtually be a remake of *Male and Female*—without the butler. He loved the idea of showing immensely civilized and sophisticated people reduced to rags and filth in a setting of primitive squalor, and at once arranged to make the production his next. He selected Claudette Colbert (who would be rendered prim and proper in severe tailoring and thick spectacles), Herbert Marshall, Leo Carrillo, Mary Boland, and William Gargan for the production, and Roland Anderson began designing a magnificent studio jungle. But a sudden studio strike forced DeMille to change his plans overnight. Suddenly he announced that the entire production would be made on location in the Hawaiian Islands, and, after arranging for the cast to follow, he left without a finished script or prepared material on the Matson ship *Malolo* bound for Honolulu on September 9, 1933.

The crossing was comfortable, and DeMille spent much of the time walking around the deck with the art director Roland Anderson, discussing minute details of the scenes. Other conferences, either in his stateroom or over meals, were held with his cameramen (again, the reliable Karl Struss), his writer Bartlett Cormack (Jeanie had been on leave during the preparation for the production), and Roy Burns. The arrival of the little group was greeted with immense enthusiasm, dozens of beautiful girls rushing up the gangway and festooning DeMille and his colleagues with leis. The instant the party was checked into the Royal Hawaiian Hotel, they began looking for suitable location sites. At Waialula they found a marvelous jungle region, as dense as any in the Malay Archipelago, and there were equally suitable locations at Keauohano.

Back at the hotel next morning, DeMille received a Western Union cable at his breakfast table. It contained alarming news. Claudette Colbert wired that she had been stricken with appendicitis on the very eve of her departure on the *Lurline*. DeMille absolutely refused to delay production and at once sent cables to Elissa Landi and Gloria Swanson offering them the roles. They were both "thrilled" to receive the invitation but wired back that they were committed to other pictures. DeMille was so desperate he even began combing the local Hawaiian agencies for a white woman who might be able to act. He spent morning after morning in his suite of rooms at the Royal Hawaiian Hotel poring over lists of hundreds of names: the afternoons were spent with Wayne Stuart, of the Royal Hawaiian Transport Company, flying to the other islands looking for more locations. Finally, he received word from

Claudette that she would be able to come to Hawaii after two weeks, spending the third week of recuperation aboard ship.

When the bulk of the cast arrived on the *Lurline* followed by Claudette on the *Matsonia*, DeMille made a final selection of the locations, mainly on the big island of Hawaii. As he traveled from island to island he was greeted by crowds carrying leis and heralded by brass bands and committees of the various island chambers of commerce. Leo Carrillo and Mary Boland took part in a tree planting ceremony on the new Banyan Tree Drive, and William Gargan walked his feet off inspecting new buildings.

For the sequences shot in the jungles and on the slopes of the extinct volcano Mt. Mauna Loa, sixty-five tractors were needed to haul the sound machines, light generators, and equipment. DeMille had fifty thousand tons of sawdust laid down on the rough lava beds over which the equipment was skidded behind the tractors. An idol had to be built in the jungle: the molds were brought from Hollywood and the plaster had to be mixed and set on the spot. The inhabitants of a nearby mental sanitarium were allowed to walk about in the jungle; when they saw the idol and reported it to the Japanese sanitarium doctor, he told them it was obviously a hallucination. When they finally persuaded him to come to the spot, the idol had been moved to a new location.

Shooting the picture was full of hazards. The water where the fugitives were supposed to struggle ashore was infested with sharks. To prove to the company that he did not shirk any danger himself, DeMille stripped and dove off the crew barge swimming half a mile to the shore. When he returned, he told the company, "Now who's afraid of sharks?" "I am," said Claudette. "You have nothing to fear," he told her. "Sharks don't like dark meat, and you've gotten a marvelous tan." "Yes, but suppose one of the sharks is color blind?" she asked.

Mary Boland kept the crew constantly amused with her wit. After crawling through wet underbrush for hours with Herbert Marshall, who was severely handicapped by his artificial leg, she said: "Tell me, Bart, do you think the old-fashioned waltz is coming back?" And, referring to DeMille she would keep saying to anyone who cared to listen, "I wonder when that hilo-monster will let us finish the scene?"

Giant spiders crawled everywhere, frequently dropping on the heads of the cast. In many scenes, the players had to wade through swamp water and crawl through prickly bushes for eight or nine takes.

One important sequence showed Claudette Colbert bathing in a waterfall. DeMille spent weeks looking for the ideal falls; when he finally located it on the island of Hawaii, he spent hours walking under it, drenched to the skin, climbing up on rocks to examine it from many different angles, observing the way the spray fell. He decided to improve it: he used boulders to form a dam at the top which would make the water fall like a bridal veil, turned part of the cliffside into a natural arch, and arranged some rocks at the foot to make a framework for the star's attractive movements. He also obtained mosses and hung them on an immense banyan tree which had a five-hundred-forty-foot outer circumference and was ninety-four feet around the base. When it began to pour with rain during the sequence, he simply made the cast move under the tree and used it as an ideal natural umbrella. After bathing in the pool, Claudette came down with severe intestinal influenza, then made her way to a grueling location where cars had to be drawn by steel cable and lowered over a mountainside to a swamp by gasoline winches. Weak with exhaustion, she was barely able to walk and had to be lowered to the location by a special kind of pulley and chute. Scorpions and centipedes scuttled through undergrowth, which had to be carved away with knives inch by inch.

The evenings were desultory: while DeMille sat in his tent as had been his wont for twenty years brooding over the script by the light of a hurricane lamp, the other players lay exhausted but unable to sleep, watching spiders as large as hands crawling on the walls, or listening to the sound of the construction crew hewing the next day's paths out of solid lava.

In addition to these visual and aural endurances, they also had to put up with the loathsome, sickly-sweet smell of sugar cane pulp, which was put down to prevent the cameras and equipment sinking in mud a foot thick. The only bearable evenings were spent around Claudette Colbert's portable phonograph in rare spots where there were electrical connections, listening to her favorite singers as she wound up the machine.

The endurance test dragged on for weeks; everyone except DeMille had attacks of dysentery, fever, and severe headaches brought on by the humidity. He rejoiced in the ordeal; wakened in the mornings by an army bugle, he would walk naked from his bed and out into the jungle, defying a snake or poisonous reptile to sting him to death. Then he would dive into an available stream and swim as far as he could.

The shooting finally dragged to a conclusion, and everyone packed up and went home on the *Lurline* on November 14, most of them to give extremely unflattering interviews about DeMille's ruthless driving of them on location. The odd, sophisticated humor of the production left the Paramount executives cold; although Lasky found the film irresistibly amusing, Zukor felt it was like a parody of *Male and Female* and barely sat out the screening in New York.

The public was similarly left cold by the production, and to DeMille's bitter disappointment, it failed at the box office. "Better do another historical epic, Cecil, with plenty of sex," Zukor told him. "Or do something entirely different."

Bored by the first possibility, DeMille cast about for a complete change of subject that winter. He bought the rights to the novel *When Worlds Collide*, by Philip Wylie and Edwin Belmer, an exciting science-fiction story about an unidentified planet which astronomers determine is heading directly for the earth. Dr. R. Langer, of the physics department of Caltech, worked with DeMille for several weeks at the studio, but finally the film was canceled. The reason was that old bugbear, Warner's *Noah's Ark*, which had killed his previous flood story

*DeMille with John, Constance, Katherine, and Richard
about to depart for Hawaii, 1934.*

The Sign of the Cross.

Cleopatra.

planned for 1928: *Noah's Ark* was reissued with a sound track, making his own film redundant.

Almost despairingly, he turned to "an epic with sex," *Cleopatra*, originally filmed with Theda Bara in 1918. It seemed an assured success, and he engaged Jeanie, Bartlett Cormack, and Manuel Komroff for the script. Claudette Colbert, whose Poppaea had pleased all but the most severe critics, would obviously be ideal as the queen. He began telling the press that the man he wanted to play Julius Caesar would be "like a great St. Bernard dog, with a chest an army could camp on." ("How about King Kong?" Associated Press correspondent Hubbard Keavy wrote in his column.)

While Jeanie and a team of writers prepared the groundwork for the script in December, DeMille learned that the government's long-planned action against him for repayment of back taxes had at last been put into effect. On December 3, with Constance, DeMille traveled to Washington by Pennsylvania Railroad to testify before the Board of Tax Appeals. The charge made by the Bureau of Internal Revenue was that DeMille Productions, Inc. had retained earnings in an accumulated surplus to avoid paying surtaxes on their distribution to stockholders. J. Edgar Goodrich, member of the appeal board, listened enthralled to DeMille's recitation of his career, and even asked him the secret of the parting of the Red Sea in *The Ten Commandments*; DeMille told him (over the protests of the government attorney, Mason B. Leming) that the matter was irrelevant. DeMille's counsel, A. Calder McKay acting for Neil McCarthy, pointed out that DeMille's overheads and losses had been immense during the transition from Lasky to the DeMille Studio at Culver City to M-G-M.

J. Edgar Goodrich, who secretly admired DeMille, informed him that he would consider the case in April, and that it might be necessary for DeMille to reappear at that time. Back in Hollywood, DeMille tried to drown the worry of the case by plunging into immensely detailed research with Jeanie and her team. They ensured that even Cleopatra's hairpins were museum copies, Egyptian water clocks and Roman calendars perfect replicas of the originals. A staff of twelve under Jeanie answered notes of DeMille's of this kind: "Let us take that room of Cleopatra's palace at Alexandria, with Julius Caesar seated in an Egyptian chair. What models of instruments of war would he be playing with? What sort of room was it and how was it furnished? How was his hair cut? I want to see it all."

Typically, DeMille spent weeks checking on details such as the correct pronunciation of the name *Cleopatra*, and on her makeup. He announced that she would wear black paint for the eyelids and brows, made from moistened powder ground from antimony, manganese of oxide, and lead. She also used a concoction of lampblack of burned almonds and manganese. She used a tinted cold cream and hennaed the palms of her hands and the soles of her feet. She wore green face powder in the evenings.

Claudette Colbert was the only possible choice as Cleopatra. But the quest for Mark Antony was a severe problem: DeMille interviewed dozens of leading men in the Christmas period of 1933, felt their legs and biceps, watched them in Roman tunics, and decided that the entire motion picture colony was peopled with weak sisters, homosexuals, and flabby middle-aged men. Unfortunately, Fredric March, so powerful as Marcus Superbus in *The Sign of the Cross*, was making another picture that winter. It seemed that somebody entirely new would have to be found, but all of the beginners DeMille looked at were hopelessly clumsy and inept, and had no idea how to handle a broadsword.

Then he had a remarkable stroke of luck. On January 6, 1934, he was waiting to be admitted to a room where he could run some tests of young athletes and some New York and foreign actors, when he heard a marvelous deep voice reverberating from some test footage being run in an adjoining cubicle. He walked in unannounced, and saw that it was test footage for a film about horses, *Shoe the Wild Mare*, to be made by Benjamin Glazer. He took one look at the owner of the voice—a superbly handsome, virile and beautiful British actor —and drove over at once to Emmanuel Cohen's house, demanding that the new player be handed over to him at once. Cohen grumblingly agreed.

The young man's name was Henry Wilcoxon, destined to become one of DeMille's best friends in the years to come. Born in the West Indies, Wilcoxon had distinguished himself on the English stage as Robert Browning in *The Barretts of Wimpole Street.* He had also appeared in several English films, and at the time of his signing by Glazer he was starring in *Eight Bells* in the West End. Paramount's entire publicity department worked on exploiting the details of Wilcoxon's arrival: his missing the plane from London, his getting a piece of metal in his eye during a stopover caused by violent storms in Salt Lake City, his saying after meeting Mel Schauer, personnel executive at the studio, "I hope he won't be a cold Schauer." Twenty-eight, six feet tall, and magnificently built, Wilcoxon proved the finest romantic hero DeMille had engaged up to that time.

Their first meeting was rather strained. DeMille addressed Wilcoxon in his usual dignified manner on the subject of Mark Antony: "He was a man who thought in terms of nations not of individuals. He did and thought things on a grand scale. The world was his canvas." Wilcoxon absorbed these words carefully and said, "Why don't you play the part?"

Despite this exchange the two hit it off at once: both uncomplicatedly masculine, straight-backed and fearless, contemptuous of weakness in themselves and others, they were utterly drawn to each other. As Caesar, DeMille finally cast Warren William, after ruling out Charles Laughton as too weak and soft for the role. At the last minute, Katherine's old friend Natalie Visart, who worked on the costumes with Travis Benton and Mitchell Leisen, came up with some interesting facts: that Cleopatra was a pure Greek, and always dressed in the Egyptian style, and that her disastrous historical image had been the result of a propaganda campaign intended to damage the reputation of Julius Caesar.

During the first days of shooting, an odd mishap took place. The Paramount property department prepared a catapult for use in one scene. It was loaded with walnuts instead of rocks. DeMille examined it, and then walked down to the set to look at it through his viewfinder. Claudette Colbert had a look at the catapult, reached out, and touched a cord. It was the trigger, and a shower of walnuts hit DeMille and several members of his crew squarely on their heads.

Muriel Babcock of the *Los Angeles Examiner* described a visit to the set on April 8, 1934: "It was a hot, a blistering hot day. On a raised platform high above his mob of some five hundred people was Director DeMille giving his commands into a loudspeaker which broadcast them over several blocks at Paramount. DeMille, last of the early directors to affect this picturesque garb, was in riding breeches and boots and a lavender shirt.

"On the steps of the Roman Forum—huge steps that are replicas of that famous building which stood in the reign of Caesar—was a huddle of Roman senators in their togas, gray flannel effects with red trim. . . .

"There were men in leather pants laced up the sides, and in sandals—and nothing else. There were some ladies of the street in flimsy Roman rags that I doubt would be permitted on Main Street today without arrest. There was a mammoth colored gentleman who admitted to two hundred seventy-five pounds, wearing bright purple pants and a bit of armor who said he was Cleo's chief executioner. In sharp contrast to this sweltering, half-naked mob there were other actors and actresses in velvet capes and handsomely embroidered gold and silver costumes. Horses with leopard skin saddles, peacocks fanning huge white tails in the sun were about. The whole scene was colorful, spectacular. Somewhere in the distance I heard the muffled roar of a lion."

DeMille also had immense pleasure with the scene on Cleopatra's barge, in which Cleopatra stages a feast for Mark Antony to help conquer him when she learns that he has been sent to bring her back to Rome in chains. A slave girl danced almost nude on the golden bull, and eight mermaids chained to the side of the barge with solid gold chains brought up a huge net of clamshells filled with jewels. For the scene, DeMille had Colbert dressed by Travis Benton in a stunning costume with a set of flat gold chips strung together in layers and fitted round her throat. Bracelets of gold, floating draperies under which she was completely naked, and a headdress of small gold beads forming a bandeau with solid gold wings over the ears created an altogether captivating picture.

There were various mishaps during shooting. Two hair-dressers and a script girl fainted when Mark Antony kissed Cleopatra for the first time. Worse, during a scene in which Antony stood on a fifty-foot wall surrounding the set of Alexandria, Wilcoxon slipped on some gravel and began to fall. He just managed to cling to the parapet, ripping out one side of a leg in the process; if he had fallen, he would have been severely injured, and perhaps killed.

During a duel scene between Mark Antony and a Roman soldier under a gnarled tree, based on a sketch of Doré's, Wilcoxon was supposed to catch the swing of the extra's sword on his own, breaking the weapon of the Roman warrior. The Roman was supposed to step back and throw his broken sword at the face of Mark Antony, who would then stop it with his shield. DeMille rehearsed this passage over and over again, to avoid the slightest slip; then, as the camera rolled, the two fighters clashed. It was a rousing duel with real weapons, the only difference from a normal duel being that the extra's sword had been cut halfway down the blade so that it would break over Wilcoxon's sword.

The scene emerged exactly as it had been rehearsed. The extra's sword broke realistically and he stepped back to throw the broken blade and stop Wilcoxon in his advance for the death thrust. At that crucial moment, Wilcoxon tripped and dropped his shield. His face was exposed; the extra knew that if he continued the swing he might kill the star. He couldn't stop the swing, but he changed his aim, his jagged blade cutting deeply into Wilcoxon's thigh, sending him to the hospital for several days.

To make matters worse, Colbert was ill during most of the production. She had never gotten over her attack of appendicitis before going on location for *Four Frightened People*, or the ravages to her system caused by posing under the icy waterfall in Hawaii or trudging through jungle paths. Her stand-in, Gladys Jeans, had to rehearse the scenes, speaking actual lines, as the star was too ill to do more than stand for a few seconds while the shots were made. She collapsed several times on the set, and had to spend several days in bed while DeMille, frantic with worry in case she would not be able to finish the picture, shot around her. When she was visited by a fan magazine reporter (Don Calhoun, of *Movie Classics*) she told him, sweat running down her brow, "So you know what the temperature on this set is? Eighty-six! It can't be one degree cooler or these purple ostrich feathers will moult! I look as though I have almost nothing on, don't I? This veil weighs seventy-seven pounds, with the jewels!"

In the famous death scene, Cleopatra had, of course, to be stung to death by an asp. Miss Colbert told DeMille from the outset she would not touch a snake, and that a stand-in's hand would have to be shown in a basket. He was adamant. She still refused. Finally, he walked onto the set with a huge snake coiled around him. She shrieked and ran for cover, telling him she would not touch it. Then he brought out the tiny snake which was an exact copy of an Egyptian asp. "Oh! That little thing! Give it to me!" she said eagerly, and played the scene without a murmur.

Cleopatra proved to be a great success, confirming DeMille yet again in his belief that the public really wanted not the shrewd social commentary of a *Four Frightened People* but handsome men, pretty women, and as much sex as the traffic would bear.

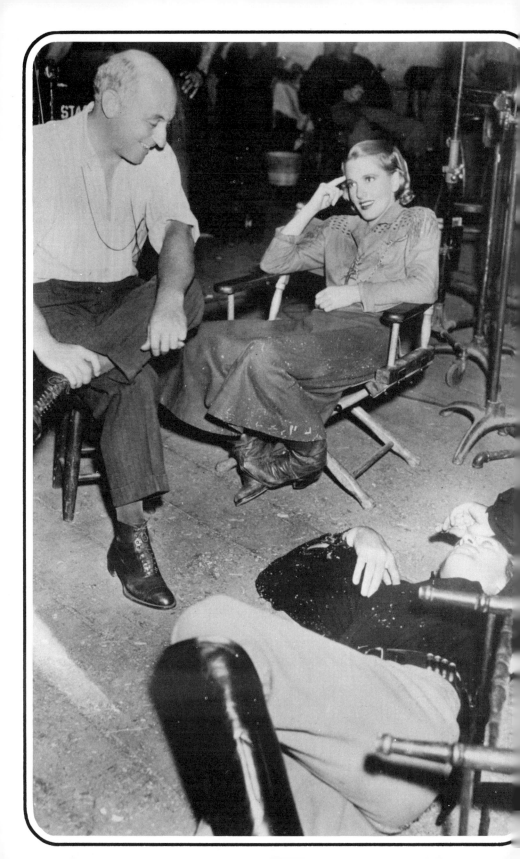

12

New Epics, New Adventures

Now that Zukor's position at Paramount was so severely weakened, DeMille softened in his attitude toward him, and for the first time in their lives, the two men actually became friends. DeMille invited Zukor on April 23, 1934, to be his guest on the *Seaward*, along with Emmanuel Cohen. When Zukor expertly landed a thirty-five-pound white sea bass, DeMille arranged for him to receive a silver button and life membership in the Catalina Light Tackle Club. Zukor was also entertained splendidly at the Tuna Club, his speech about the glories of fishing greeted with rousing cheers by the members.

That May a son was born to Cecilia and to Francis Calvin. In

237

*C. B. with Jean Arthur and
Gary Cooper:* The Plainsman.

September John, who had now, after a shaky career which never seemed to settle, joined the Bank of America, married Louise Antoinette Denker. The wedding was a lavish affair, held at the Church of the Good Shepherd in Beverly Hills, and Katherine made a lovely bridesmaid. She had begun a career as an actress following a tiny role in the Zeppelin sequence of *Madame Satan.* Her dark-haired beauty had already made her a popular figure at Hollywood parties, and her grace and charm captivated everyone. She, almost as much as Cecilia, had become the apple of DeMille's eye. He was seldom more excited than when he saw her play beautifully a featured role in *Belle of the Nineties*, with Mae West, that year.

Also that year, DeMille reconsolidated his happy platonic relationship with Constance and seldom saw Julia Faye, who had drifted away and in fact had become an annoyance because of constant requests for money in letters sometimes written under an assumed name. Jeanie was, of course, in constant attendance, although she, too, had proved recklessly spendthrift, causing him constant heartache with her requests for cash. She had grown hard and dry with the years; it is doubtful whether, after the collapse of their sexual relationship in the late teens of the century, any other man had entered her boudoir. She burned a sacred flame which was never extinguished until her death.

Now that the family circle was more fully consolidated than it had been, DeMille developed a custom—an event which took place weekly at Laughlin Park: the Family Forum. At dinner—with DeMille at the head of the table flanked by Constance, Katherine, John, and Richard—someone would make a statement of fact, and the others would immediately question it. Encyclopedias were dragged in to support these arguments, and often, during them, someone would come up with an idea for a new production.

In the spring of 1934, John DeMille, now working happily at the Bank of America, suggested a film based on the Crusades. DeMille had been thinking for some time of a picture entitled

The Buccaneer, based on the career of the pirate Henry Morgan. But the morning after he mentioned this casually at a Hollywood dinner party, eight producers announced the idea and he was forced to postpone it, settling on John's idea instead.

By now, the political situation at the studio had settled down, and Emmanuel Cohen was out of office—to DeMille's immense relief. He had been replaced by the great Ernst Lubitsch, a fan of DeMille's from the early 1920s, and in some ways an imitator of him both in his historical spectacles and in his social comedies written by the brilliant Hans Kräly. Lubitsch was captivated by the idea of the Crusades as a DeMille subject and promptly overruled the usual demurs from New York.

In the summer of 1934 DeMille announced the new epic, the screenplay to be written by an authority on the subject, Harold Lamb. Lamb, shy and retiring, obviously was not going to be able to handle the job singlehanded, so DeMille engaged the experienced scenarist Dudley Nichols to help him, working with them both on the *Seaward* off Catalina for several weeks, with some tarpon fishing thrown in.

In October, DeMille cast Henry Wilcoxon as Richard I, instructing him to spend the next two months learning how to train a falcon to sit on his wrist. Berengaria proved harder to cast. "She must," the director announced, "act like Helen Hayes, have the vivacity of Miriam Hopkins, the wistfulness of Helen Mack, the charm of Marion Davies. And as for looks, she must be a combination of all four of these actresses."

Stricken with a mysterious virus at the very end of October, DeMille continued production plans while laid up in a bed at Cedars of Lebanon Hospital, choosing costumes and set designs while the nurses hovered anxiously around him. After unsuccessfully trying to borrow Merle Oberon from Darryl F. Zanuck at Fox, he selected Loretta Young as Berengaria.

By December 12, his office at Paramount was crammed with thousands of wash-drawings of the Crusades and six feet of piled-up Byzantine armor, chain-mail, cuirasses, and vizors, "copied to the last rivet from originals at the Metropolitan Museum." Among the mountainous heaps of books were obscure works of Abulfeda and Matthew Paris, which DeMille pointed out to visitors with a broadsword of forged steel five feet long.

Wilcoxon, and Ian Keith as Saladin, worked grimly under DeMille's command to perfect their swordsmanship. Wilcoxon had to split a war-mace without the slightest jarring of his arm, while Keith had to perform an historically famous trick—tossing a cushion in the air that would fall on the point of his scimitar and be cut in two.

Each morning in January 1935, DeMille had his male principals out riding in Griffith Park in full armor, an astonishing sight for early equestrians. Castles and splendid medieval tents began to rise on the Paramount Ranch, and the prop department faced up to a daunting task: building an eleven-ton catapult. Mounted on enormous iron-rimmed wheels, it was forty feet long, twenty feet wide, and twenty feet high, capable of hurling a half-ton rock or cauldron of burning pitch. It took two tractors and twelve men to guide it from the shops to the set.

Shooting at last began early in February, delayed partly through a sudden illness of Gladys Rosson and partly through the aggravation of reading ten thousand manuscripts submitted for a *Cleopatra and Her Times* essay contest in the *Los Angeles Times*. He became unusually short-tempered on the set: when the New York socialite Nan Pierson Brooks Macy, who had wheedled her way into a grand scene as an extra, appeared with a wig awry on her head, he bawled her out unmercifully in front of the cast and crew and she fled the set in tears. In one scene, three hundred crusaders were unleashed on two whole steers and four sheep, which had been specially barbecued for the occasion. George Brugerman, an athlete and bit player, seemed slow in tackling the meal. DeMille yelled through the megaphone, "I know it's at least four hours since you ate last. You don't even have to act. Why can't you look as though you enjoy it?" "Sorry sir," Brugerman yelled back. "Unfortunately, I'm a vegetarian."

While directing a battle scene in driving rain, with ten thousand extras in the same shot, DeMille was again taken ill—with influenza. But within three days he was directing scenes from a gilded litter, dressed in a blazing coral shirt, leggings, and a crimson tie. He particularly rejoiced in directing the scenes in a staggeringly authentic Windsor Castle; the floor was made up of huge flagstones, and the walls of giant chunks of granite, copied by experts in Europe. DeMille even added large chunks of moss, because Harold Lamb told him the castle was sufficiently aged by 1190 to have grown it.

The interior of the castle was a marvel. On February 16, 1935 Idwal Jones of the *New York Times* described it vividly: "The massive iron door clicked behind me. The day was shut out by the sunlight, and I found myself in the twilight of the Middle Ages. Three or four barons in chain mail were sauntering in a vast baronial hall hung with tapestry. Mastiffs were asleep on the hearth. In the shadows were lounging halberdiers, huntsmen, falconers, cupbearers and ladies-in-waiting."

DeMille was fascinated by the falcons: with the aid of the specialist Orin Cannon, he trained twenty of them, with hoods and bells, all captured by his assistants from cliffs since there were very few in captivity. He learned that they must be carried on the wrist daily for an hour, and given as much exercise as any dog. He told the *New York Times*: "Hunting with a gun seems very crude after you have once experienced the thrill of having your falcon make its first strike of a rabbit or a quail and wing back to your wrist to be praised."

During the shooting, Ernst Lubitsch was a constant visitor to the set. He stood for hours absolutely fascinated by what DeMille was doing. DeMille during a break in shooting said to the great master of comedy one day, "I liked *Trouble in Paradise* more than I can say. It's like a present from Cartier's with the tissue paper just removed. What on earth interests you so much in my poor efforts?" "I'm *hypnotized,*" Lubitsch replied. "There isn't a cocktail shaker or a tuxedo *in sight.*"

The film's most tremendous set piece was the Battle of Acre. The *Los Angeles Times* reporter described the scene on March 15: "Catapults and mangonels hurled rocks at the battlements. Crossbowmen sent a blizzard of arrows. Amid a rain of melted lead and tar, and a hard shower of javelins, Crusaders and Saracens thwacked each other with swords and battle hammers. Large numbers were skewered with arrows and lay collapsed in picturesque attitudes in gullies and under oaks. The fighting was done under asphyxiating clouds of yellow smoke, and with a din that created alarm in the furthest reaches of Hollywood. There are exactly 3,240 arrows in the Battle of Acre."

Harold Lamb was constantly present during the shooting of the siege, dodging arrows and narrowly avoiding being crushed by the siege tower. "Is that realistic enough, Mr. Lamb?" the director asked him at the end of the first exhausting rehearsal of the conflict. "Not nearly," Lamb replied, wiping his spectacles. "These soldiers seemed almost fond of each other. Medieval warriors were infinitely more sanguinary, let me assure you. What you need is a thousand battle axes red with blood." "That would make it a shambles," DeMille said. "Exactly. And also history," Lamb primly replied.

During the editing of *The Crusades*, Anne Bauchens suddenly slumped over with an agonizing pain in her chest. DeMille had her rushed to the hospital, where it was discovered she had a severe heart ailment. DeMille worked less happily with a replacement, Cordell Fray, wishing every night that Anne was beside him to hold his hand during the rushes.

The Crusades, unfortunately, was not the success at the box office that DeMille had hoped for. Nevertheless, during its shooting, he had received enormously cheering news: the authorities in Washington had cleared him of the charges of negligence in paying back taxes which had been leveled against

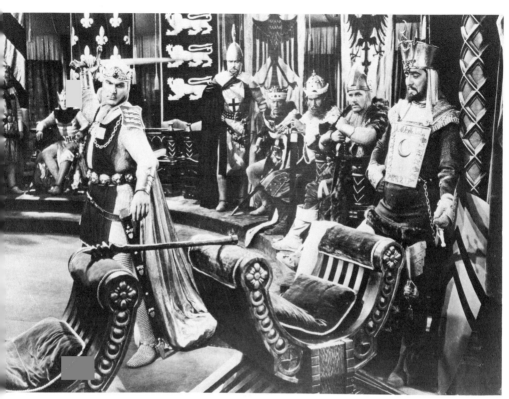

Henry Wilcoxon: The Crusades.

Ian Keith as Saladin, Sultan of Islam, in The Crusades.

Reap the Wild Wind.

him. This news, which removed the threat of bankruptcy, and the benign kindness and sweetness of nature of Lubitsch, gave him an immense feeling of encouragement that summer of 1935. He felt vigorous and in need of a change of pace.

Much as he had enjoyed making *The Crusades*, he felt that he had been too long away from American subjects, that he should once again breathe deeply the fresh air of the pioneers. For this reason, he made up his mind to have his next picture a Western. He settled on a classic American subject—Wild Bill Hickok and Calamity Jane—and simultaneously prepared a short, *Spirit of the Plains*, which drew on scenes not only from the film itself, but from *The Covered Wagon* and *Thundering Herd*, to be distributed by Bell and Howell purely for showing in schools and colleges.

Headed by Jeanie, a team consisting of Mrs. Ella King Adams, Joe De Yong, Dwight Franklin, Chief Thunder Bird, and Natalie Visart worked on preparing the production background of *The Plainsman*. DeMille took great pleasure in building, with Roland Anderson, three acres of sets in keeping with the 1865–1875 period. All of the Indian costumes and headdresses were made at the Rosebud Reservation in Montana from sketches by Joe De Yong. As usual, DeMille's insistences were academically recondite: deciding to include the phrase "Go West, Young Man," in the screenplay, he insisted the writers did not attribute the phrase to Horace Greeley, but attribute it correctly to John B. Soule, editor of the *Terra Haute Express*, who in an editorial had written, "Horace Greeley never gave better advice than, 'Go West Young Man.' " Greeley, of course, had never uttered those famous words at all.

Gary Cooper and Jean Arthur were ideally cast as Wild Bill and Calamity Jane, James Ellison made a convincing Buffalo Bill, John Miljan was a powerful Custer, and Frank McGlynn, Sr. cut a fine austere figure as Abe Lincoln. A young Mexican called Anthony Quinn also appeared in a tiny role of a Cheyenne Indian who gives a war cry to signal Custer's defeat.

All of the pistols in the picture came from DeMille's private collection—eighty-six of them.

For once, DeMille did not aim at strict historical accuracy in the story line: Wild Bill was inaccurately shown taking part in the Battle of the Arickaree, and he was shown falling in love with Calamity Jane in 1866 when she was a girl of fifteen still living at home with her mother in Alder Gulch, Montana. Jane was a coarse, vulgar virago, far removed from the spruce charmer so stylishly played by Jean Arthur. And worse, Wild Bill certainly never enjoyed a romance with her. But it did not matter: DeMille was aiming at a legendary abstraction of events, informed with the very spirit of the West. In this he triumphantly succeeded: the film had a blazing energy and drive, its skirmishes, battles, sieges of the wagon trains, and vigorous central romance showing the director at his best.

Shooting began excitingly, with DeMille using six acres of the Paramount lot for a magnificent re-creation of Fort Leaven-worth, Texas, in the 1870s, a Mississippi boat arriving, families crowding onto the wharf, the steam whistle blowing, and the pioneers looking with eyes shadowed by their hands into the hot dusty promise of the New World. DeMille rigged up a special telegraph office, an exact replica of one of the period, for the three hundred correspondents from all over the world to transmit their messages home.

Much of the picture was shot in Hollywood, but a unit was dispatched to the Tongue River country near Lame Deer, Montana, to film the massacre of Custer and the battle of Beecher's Island. Two thousand five hundred Cheyenne and Sioux Indians, together with several picked squads of the One Hundred Fifteenth Cavalry and the Wyoming National Guard, were sent along. DeMille directed many scenes by remote control, using a ten-foot model of Beecher's Island and of the other terrain to help him guide the assistant director Arthur Rosson by telephone from Hollywood. At one end of the ten-foot model was a circular barricade of boxes, trees, and covered wagons, where movable clay figures of pioneers and U.S. cavalrymen were "besieged" by toy Indians.

There was a sad footnote to the filming of *The Plainsman*. At eighteen, Helen Burgess, who had beautifully played the wife of Buffalo Bill, died suddenly of pneumonia in Hollywood following her elopement with a musician, Herbert Rutherford; the marriage had been instantly annulled on the grounds that he had not consummated the marriage. Her death was a severe shock to DeMille, who had cast her after seeing her in the studio commissary—the first time in his career that he had cast an actress in a leading role without previous experience.

Hitler's Germany banned *The Plainsman*, because Goebbels believed that DeMille was "consorting with Russia"—they had heard he had sent Christmas greetings to Boris Shumiatsky, then head of the Russian film industry, who had been liquidated by Stalin shortly afterward. Boringly, DeMille had to face another copyright suit: On June 2, John Hopper claimed that his book, *Blood over Kansas*, had been used as the basis for the script of *The Plainsman*.* And Waldemar Young, who wrote the admirable final draft script for the film, died, like Helen Burgess, of pneumonia, at the age of sixty, following the film's release.

As befitted a man in his fifties, DeMille's routine in the mid-1930s became firmly fixed. When he was on a picture, he rose at six, and at seven he was ready for the limousine to drive him to Paramount. When he was not on a picture, he rose at nine-thirty, took both a leisurely bath *and* a shower, and dried his towels personally in the sun over the back of a chair. He came down to breakfast at 11:30, and liked to have a particular breakfast almost every day: it consisted of fresh fruit *in season* (if it was out of season he would immediately return it to the kitchen), and rye bread, exactly one week old and stale, cut into the finest slices with a razor-sharp blade, and carefully baked in

* This case did not succeed.

the oven to resemble as nearly as possible the perfect quality of Melba toast. One cup of coffee accompanied this frugal meal, which was occasionally supplemented with bacon and eggs. At the studio, he always enjoyed a substantial luncheon right on top of breakfast with friends or important visitors, leaving in the limousine shortly after the noon hour. He would return at six, and enjoy a cocktail—almost invariably, a single scotch—and soda with cheese and graham crackers at seven. Promptly at eight, he and Constance would sit down to dinner at a small table in the living room. They usually liked to have prime rib of beef, cooked medium rare, a selection of cheeses, and coffee. Mrs. DeMille scrupulously planned the menu. In 1934 DeMille began to experiment with health foods: he liked Jerusalem artichokes, and saw to it that they were raised with the utmost care by the gardener, and cooked by Marie, his superb Finnish cook. She and she alone had the gift of cutting the bread and baking it to his exact specifications. After dinner, he would repair to his study, which adjoined his bedroom. There he would work solidly on research until exactly four A.M.

Scrupulously kind and generous always, he never for one moment rebuked his servants, reserving all of his spleen for the set. The domestic staff adored him: Frederick, still his butler, his valet Arthur, his launderers and chauffeurs. Needless to say, one evidence of dirt or disorder and the guilty servant would have been dismissed at once. But he had no fear of that: they were the finest household staff in Hollywood.

In 1936, Lever Brothers approached DeMille to launch a new radio program, the Lux Radio Theater, at a salary of two thousand dollars a week, featuring potted versions of film classics, and beginning with a condensed version of Joseph von Sternberg's *Morocco*, *The Legionnaire and the Lady*, with Marlene Dietrich and Gary Cooper. Beginning on June 1, the Monday night broadcasts became a fixture, adding to DeMille's already immense fame by literally making him a household word. His sign-off phrase, ringingly delivered, was one that millions of listeners would not miss short of a major family crisis: "This is Cecil B. DeMille saying goodnight to you from Hollywood."

The Plainsman was released on New Year's Day 1937, and became an immediate success. The plagiarism case against him quashed, and the Lux Radio Theater firmly launched, he felt a great surge of confidence as he approached his sixtieth year. He reverted to his earlier idea of making a life of Sir Henry Morgan; then gradually he changed his mind, feeling that Jean Lafitte would make a stronger subject: the privateer who allied himself with Andrew Jackson and held Louisiana against the British at the Battle of New Orleans. He was stimulated further in this notion by E. V. Richardson, head of a theater chain in the south, who invited him on a fishing trip which took them through Lafitte's ruined stronghold and along the bayou waterways where the privateer had hidden during intervals in his nefarious expeditions.

At the outset of 1937, he learned that Sam Goldwyn had bought a life of Lafitte, *The Pirate's Lady*, by John Larkin, and planned to make it, with Gary Cooper. Obviously, this plan must be forestalled at once. With a new special assistant, William Pine, and the writer Edwin Justus Mayer, William Herbert of the Paramount publicity department and Gladys Rosson, DeMille set off for the bayou and New Orleans for research, chartering a yacht to sail the party around the swamps. On the second day into the swamps a blanketing fog descended upon them, making movement difficult. Then a squall blew up, ruining most of their traveling equipment. In New Orleans, the group went on an extensive buying spree, piling up such items as guns, furniture, and letters of Zachary Taylor, Andrew Jackson, and Lafitte himself. Returning home, DeMille cast a temperamental Hungarian actress, Francisca Gaal, as the lover of Fredric March's Jean Lafitte. He tried to cast Ernst Lubitsch as Napoleon, but the plan fell through when Lubitsch proved camera-shy.

Alan LeMay wrote seventy-two treatments for the picture. He started work on the *Seaward* at eight A.M. He worked for two hours and had a twenty-minute swim, then DeMille would take off in his dory for a trip to Catalina. Jesse Lasky, Jr. would join LeMay after lunch and work some more and DeMille would return. The three men would argue the story until six P.M., when DeMille would serve a marvelous dinner, often with partridge or terrapin and champagne. Then they would return to work until midnight. Sometimes DeMille would get into a deep-sea diving suit and go down to the bottom of the ocean to think. Often he would return with a new idea which involved further work. When they finally returned to the studio for new preparations, a court stenographer would follow them everywhere, noting down every word.

During a story conference for the picture, DeMille had a pleasant interruption. Henry Wertz, of Teaneck, New Jersey, had a painting delivered to him of the house at Echo Lake. Fifty-five years fell away as he looked at it, and recognized the tadpole pond he fell into so often, and the site of the apple orchard, now full of a splendid planting of oak trees. He recalled the sound of woodpeckers as he looked at part of the picture, and gazed at the blurred window of his bedroom, remembering the simple desk table, the counterpane, the flowered wallpaper. He had tears in his eyes as he turned back to work with Jeanie and the others on the particular scene.

Once again, DeMille used his beloved Catalina for many of his locations. There he built the pirate fortress, which at the end of three weeks' shooting was completely destroyed by cannon fire.

Shooting of the picture began in July 1937. DeMille stayed in Hollywood supervising the direction of the second unit work in Louisiana, with Arthur Rosson in charge of the Louisiana shooting. Nine launches under Rosson's command, towing one hundred twenty-three pirogues occupied by two hundred swampers acting as extras, were nearing the location when a great wind struck and giant waves dashed over the sides of the small boat. Four pirogues were overturned and the launches were turned over in the waves. Moccasin snakes crawled out and over the cast, which had to swim, barely avoiding drowning, through rough wind-whipped waves to the shore.

Back in Hollywood, things were calmer; DeMille celebrated his fifty-ninth birthday with a gigantic Creole luncheon in the Paramount dining room on August 16. There were three hundred guests present to enjoy the gumbo soup, Jambalayah, salad, corn bread, yam pudding, and a magnificent birthday cake forwarded by Governor Richard W. Leche of Louisiana. Then several of the cast—full up and barely able to stand— made their way in a tremendous hurry to work on Stage 14 where Roland Anderson had built a superb set of Lafitte's bayou home, with cannon facing a painted ocean, loot from pirate ships constituting the furnishings, and Lafitte lolling on a green velvet hammock, smoking a cigar, and caressing a white cockatoo. That afternoon, DeMille between takes addressed the cast concerning a lovely T'ang Vase worth five thousand dollars. He told everyone what a priceless antique it was and that on no account must anybody break it. Then he turned around and walked away—only to brush it with his elbow and send it crashing to the earth where it broke into pieces.

Visiting a Catalina location for the film, the radio reporter Dorothy West on KPGK told her listeners about the colorful scene: "When I went ashore . . . I found myself in a primitive village, surrounded by four or five hundred of the most villainous looking men you ever saw outside of a story-book. Most of them wore beards, their faces were slashed with horrible scars, and many were tattooed on their arms and chests. Their clothes were ragged and soiled, they wore wide belts in which hung cutlasses and old-fashioned pistols . . . seventeen barge-loads of props and equipment were taken over to the island to build the village, and its thatched-reed huts certainly looked authentic. From the trees hung quantities of Spanish moss. I noticed a prop man unloading about twenty-five small barrels from a boat. I wasn't sure, but I thought I could read the word 'Gunpowder' on the barrels. Then I saw he was smoking a cigarette, very nonchalantly. So I nonchalantly began to stroll away."

The heat was overpowering that September of 1937. The players suffered agonies in their stiff and heavy brocaded costumes, and frequent faintings occurred. DeMille refused to work the company unless temperatures were kept below ninety degrees, and he had special wind machines installed to sweep across the set between takes. Often, despite the director's best efforts, the temperature was one hundred fifteen degrees on the set, and the cast had to be fed salt tablets to keep their energy up.

That fall, DeMille was concerned with a marriage and a divorce. Katherine DeMille, who played a role in *The Buccaneer*, had fallen in love with the young actor Anthony Quinn, and they were married on October 5. And also that fall Cecilia and Frank Calvin, who had been unhappy for some time, obtained their final divorce decree.

In March 1938 Paradise was flooded: heavy rains washed away three miles of road and took the pump house, fences and gates, and all of the bridges. The bridge between the guest house and the main ranch house was swept away, and the swimming pool was full of boulders that had to be dynamited out. DeMille wrote to Richard at Santa Barbara School on March 18: "Dear Big Boy . . . The Paradise road from the gate towards the ranch is something you simply wouldn't believe. It looks like the Niagara whirlpool rapids . . . for the next three months, we will have to reach Paradise by pack train."

After the completion of *The Buccaneer*, DeMille traveled on a promotional tour to New Orleans, where the picture first opened, Atlanta, Boston, and other cities. He was in Boston when he heard that the California State Republican Committee had endorsed him for senatorial nomination.

The news was startling, as he had been forced to indicate to the Republican forces on several occasions that his now fully

Marriage of Cecilia to Joseph Harper, Kansas City, 1938.

William Pine, Harold Lamb, Waldemar Young, C. B., Jeanie at a press conference for The Buccaneer.

On location: Union Pacific.

Prize catch on the Seaward, *1934.*

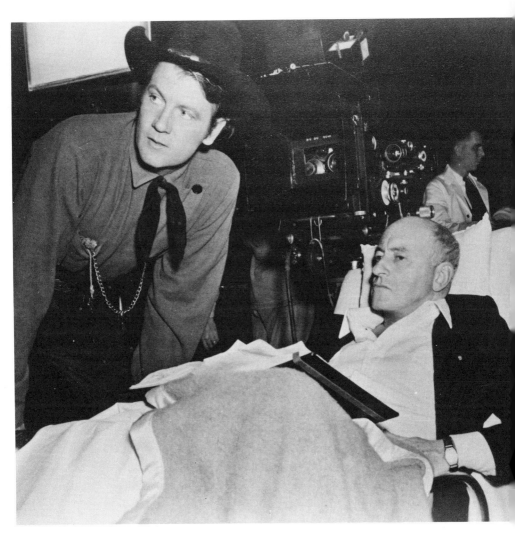

Directing from a stretcher
with Joel McCrea: Union Pacific.

consolidated career, free of tension and struggle for the first time in his life, did not permit political aspirations. The Republican Party had refused to take no for an answer, and had proceeded with their intentions in his absence. DeMille cabled at once that he would be unable to proceed with the nomination, and he conveyed his regrets in person to the appropriate officials when he returned to California.

One exceptionally agreeable aspect of the tour was that Cecilia, who had met and fallen in love with a prosperous young businessman, Joseph W. Harper, was able to arrange her marriage in Kansas City to coincide with an opening of *The Buccaneer* in that city. For many years, DeMille told against himself a joke connected with the event: just after the marriage took place, DeMille announced to the group of press men and women that he was delighted to present to them his new son-in-law, Frank Calvin. Fortunately, Joseph Harper had a quick wit. Bowing slightly, he said, to loud laughter: "Thank you very much, Mr. Goldwyn."

For a while, during 1938, DeMille contemplated doing an epic on flying, but he finally ruled it out because so much of the film would involve one or two characters and the shooting of empty space, which he believed would bore audiences. Since he had decided on transportation as his theme, he first thought about a ship story—possibly the *Titanic*—and a story about Hudson's Bay. Then, at the suggestion of Martin Quigley, he settled on a story about trains, tossing a gold coin to decide whether he should handle the story of the Santa Fé Railroad or the Union Pacific. The Union Pacific came up tails. From the outset, DeMille had the wholehearted cooperation of William M. Jeffers, president of the Union Pacific Railroad, who made available the railroad's files as well as splendid period trains and crack crews, including a track-laying squad.

DeMille sent Jeanie and a team of researchers to Omaha, Nebraska, where the Union Pacific Railroad began. They explored massive boxes and parcels of historical correspondence, stored away by Union Pacific and unexamined for more than seventy years. DeMille obtained four locomotives and thirty-seven passenger and box cars, brought a thousand Navajo Indians by bus round the rim of the Grand Canyon from Albuquerque, and hundreds of Cheyennes from Montana. Francis (Frank) Calvin and Waldo Twitchell prepared a one-hundred-fifty-eight-page book of research details, and every spare inch of DeMille's office was filled with model trains, sketches by the artist Dan Sayre Groesbeck, and tiny replicas of sets.

In Utah, DeMille supervised the construction of a complete reproduction of Cheyenne, Wyoming, furnished it inside and out, and peopled it with local citizens disguised as Westerners of the mid-nineteenth century.

His passion for detail made him include glass-ball fire extinguishers in the railroad carriages; he remembered them because he had been a touring actor aboard a train wrecked near Wheeling, West Virginia, when one of the glass balls fell and struck him unconscious. He would not tolerate imitation snow made out of cornflakes or gypsum and instead arranged for real snow to blow through the windows of an engine cab during a blizzard and melt on the firebox. Paramount sent a fleet of trucks between a downtown Los Angeles ice house and the set of the interior of the train, carrying barrelfuls of snow scraped from the refrigeration coils.

DeMille cast Joel McCrea and Barbara Stanwyck in the leading roles, together with a player new to the screen, Robert Preston, and Brian Donlevy as the villain who tried to stop the progress of the Union Pacific.

The stars performed their own stunts for the picture: DeMille was lost in admiration of Barbara Stanwyck, who leaped on and off railroad cars, allowed herself to be chased by stampeding buffalos, and exposed herself to danger constantly. In one scene she even lay flat on her back in a box car while sulphur and molasses spilt all over her.

During the shooting, DeMille collapsed with overwork and a temperamental prostate gland; doctors ordered him to bed for two weeks, and an emergency operation was performed at Laughlin Park. He proceeded to direct the rest of the production flat on his back on a stretcher, conveyed to different locations and parts of the Paramount studio in an ambulance.

For a reproduction of the episode in which a golden spike was driven home on May 10, 1869 to celebrate the completion of the Union Pacific Continental Railroad, Dr. Ray Lyman Wilbur, president of Stanford University, loaned the spike itself. It was removed in great secrecy from a vault at a branch of the Wells Fargo Bank in San Francisco and transported by train to Hollywood. DeMille re-created the scene superbly: two period trains, correct to the last detail, their engines running under their own power as their cowcatchers met; a troop of blue-clad infantry and a brass band striking up; Irish and Chinese track workers flinging their caps in the air; Indian onlookers silent and depressed, aware of what this decimation of their territory meant in terms of human suffering; horses rearing in the dust; political figures proud and somber in their gray suitings. The whole sequence was shot at Canoga Park, near Hollywood, while a second unit in Utah prepared many background shots with which the scene could be properly matched.

Unfortunately, someone was present to tell the press that the original drilling of the spike was not as colorful as DeMille made it seem. Robert V. Grewe II, who was the only survivor of that day in 1869, informed the reporters that there was only one train and a handful of people—not a vast crowd as DeMille characteristically showed.

Because of his illness, DeMille was compelled to have two other directors handle portions of the film: Arthur Rosson directed location scenes in Utah, and James Hogan action scenes shot in California. Anne Bauchens had a tremendous task cutting the sequences together so that the different directorial styles did not collide. She had to reduce the film from fourteen thousand to ten thousand feet, eliminating some of the finest action footage in the process.

Union Pacific—its credit titles boldly printed on rails that stretched to the horizon—proved to be a splendid adventure, given a tremendous ovation at its premiere in Omaha, Nebraska, scene of the commencement of the railroad. A three-day civic celebration was held and the entire city donned period clothing for the event. A costume Pioneer Ball was arranged at the enormous Ak-Sar-Ben Coliseum followed by a banquet for five thousand people, and DeMille and his entourage, headed by the stars of the film, arrived by the first transcontinental train itself in period clothes to join in the magnificent festivities.

Union Pacific cemented DeMille's relationship with Paramount absolutely and beyond question. For the first time in his career, he was virtually left alone, with an undivided executive staff behind him, and Zukor his complete ally at all times. The new head of the studio, Y. Frank Freeman, was an enlightened man who knew DeMille was on to a winning streak: he signed DeMille to a four-year contract on June 9, 1939.

Meanwhile, DeMille was extremely busy preparing with Jeanie and Jesse Lasky's son, Jesse Lasky, Jr., a special film for the New York World's Fair: *Land of Liberty*, a compendium of one hundred twenty-four motion pictures illustrating the beauty of the homeland, and concluding with speeches by Roosevelt and Chief Justice Charles Evans Hughes.

The first picture under the new Paramount arrangement was to be *The Royal Canadian Mounted*, shot in Technicolor; the title was soon changed to *Scarlet Riders* and then to *North-West Mounted Police*. Joel McCrea was to be the star, but at the last minute he was unavailable. He was replaced by Gary Cooper.

DeMille's associate producer, Bill Pine, traveled to Ottawa, Calgary, Regina, Banff, and Lake Louise looking for locations, and securing the cooperation of the Canadian authorities. In July 1939, Frank Calvin was in Winnipeg and other cities digging up material for a possible script. Alan LeMay, Commodore Frank Wead, Jesse Lasky, Jr., and Jeanie Macpherson all worked on the script, but by mid-August they had come up with nothing except a straggly series of disconnected incidents, and DeMille was in despair. He took off on the *Seaward* on August 28, telling them he gave them one more week to solve the basic problems. They could not. With him on board were Bill Pine, Gladys Rosson, and Frederick Othman, United Press correspondent in Hollywood. During the cruise, a Catalina Island tourist excursion boat came by. "And that, ladies and gentlemen, is the palatial yacht of the film movie mogul, Cecil B. DeMille!" the tour guide announced through a DeMillean megaphone. DeMille picked up his own and yelled back, "I've owned this boat since 1922 and there hasn't been an orgy on it yet!"

In November, the script problems were still tremendous. With war broken out in Europe, the studio was a little nervous about making so large a production—until DeMille pointed out that a stirring picture of life in the British Commonwealth was exactly what was needed at the time. He shrewdly cast the British actress Madeleine Carroll in a leading role.

The real problem was to find an actress to play Loupette, the sexy half-breed in the picture. One day Gladys Rosson came in and said, "Here is Loupette." He told her to collect her wits. Suddenly Paulette Goddard emerged, perfectly made up for the role. She put one *foot* on his desk and the part was hers. She had evidently been doing her homework.

On December 15, DeMille felt a swell of pride when he was called into active service from his reserve post as a major in the Army Signal Corps, and was informed he was on minute call. He also spent several days at army headquarters in the Federal Building in Los Angeles on an examining board for the Signal Corps. The War Department asked him to compile a list of sound technicians, cameramen, and still photographers for recruiting to the corps staff. He had to apply for special leave to fly to Ottawa to help prepare the groundwork for the film, which was now firmly set in the time of the Riel rebellion of

1885. He also had to place the still not quite perfect script before the Canadian government, in order to obtain its unqualified approval.

By the end of the year, DeMille still did not have a male star, Cary Grant and Fredric March having proved unavailable. Finally, in February 1940, he settled on Gary Cooper for the role, and chose, with the aid of Arthur Rosson, a new location at Pendleton, Oregon. At Paramount, construction began on an exact replica of the frontier village, Fort Carlton, as it appeared in 1885. On his desk DeMille had a scale model of the fort, peopled with lead soldiers he bought in a toy store. Then, on March 9, 1940, with a script that more or less satisfied him, he at last was ready to start work. He put in his buttonhole a red carnation, a gift from Barbara Stanwyck, tightened his puttees, and at eight A.M. started work on Take One, Scene One, in which he showed Texas Ranger Cooper invading the stronghold of the Mounties in pursuit of an escaped murderer.

Making *North-West Mounted Police* was a complete delight for DeMille: his stars worked together harmoniously, shooting went on without a hitch, and the picture was completed in record time. The only disappointment was that at the last moment before production started, the studio forbade him to spend the money to go to Canada and all arrangements to film there had to be scrapped.

After *North-West Mounted Police* was successfully launched, following its premiere in Regina, Saskatchewan, on August 15, DeMille began work on a companion piece to *The King of Kings*, *The Queen of Queens*, the story of the Virgin Mary. Faced with an unusual number of script problems, he turned instead to a *Saturday Evening Post* serial by Thelma Strabel, *Reap the Wild Wind*, a story of shipwreck and deep-sea diving off the Florida coast in the early 1840s. He also piled up a drawer full of research on *Rurales*, a Mexican-American story which, in common with *The Queen of Queens*, was never filmed. The *Seaward* was prepared in June 1940 for sailing to Key West where much of the action of *Reap the Wild Wind* was set. Once more, Bill Pine, Allen LeMay, and Jesse Lasky, Jr. set off with DeMille on the location-hunting expedition which took them to areas not far removed from the scene of *The Buccaneer*. A second unit under Dewey Wrigley was assigned to direct the underwater scenes. The English writer Charles Bennett wrote the script.

Robert Preston, John Wayne, Ray Milland, Susan Hayward, and Paulette Goddard were cast in the leading roles. Hedda Hopper played Aunt Harriett. DeMille began work on the picture by informing his production team ironically that he expected Ray Milland to be attacked by a real octopus and that he firmly intended having a real whale in one scene. The team applauded him tremendously.

John Wayne was extremely ill-at-ease about acting in a DeMille picture; he did not relish being shouted at on the set. He had applied for the role of Wild Bill Hickok in *The Plainsman* and had been turned down (DeMille's only remark had been, "You were in *The Big Trail* weren't you? A lot of water has gone under the bridge since then.") When he was offered the role played by Preston Foster in *North-West Mounted Police* he had told DeMille's emissary: "Just tell Mr. DeMille too much water has flowed under the bridge for me to want that role." DeMille was provoked, and when *Reap the Wild Wind* came along, firmly offered him the part. "The only reason you called me here is to make Ray Milland look like a man," Wayne said. "That's right," DeMille replied. After some wrangling, Wayne accepted the role, and they became good friends.

In a ballroom scene DeMille found place for a number of former associates as extras: Maurice (father of Dolores and Helen) Costello, Mildred Harris (who had once been his neighbor), Elmo Lincoln, Monte Blue, Dorothy Sebastian, and George Melford, a director who had given him trouble at Famous Players in the old days.

The scenes of a shipwreck were photographed on the Paramount lot. DeMille wanted a process screen created, showing a boiling ocean and a ragged fringe of cloud. He solved the problem by using three projectors with fused quartz lenses, which could sustain more heat from the arc lights than glass. Three moving images were thrown in superimposition on the backing. Synchronized, they provided a total of twenty thousand candlepower, which created a bright enough background.

One marvelous effect was inspired by an old fascination: the swaying of vividly colored kelp underwater. DeMille wanted to have an effect in which bolts of rich, iridescent cloth from a sunken ship would weave about in the brilliant green depths of the ocean. He didn't find out until too late that the color of silk changes in salt water, so the sequences took a month to photograph. He and his team, led by the cameraman Victor Milner, had to use fresh silk every day, dry out the old silk, and then send it down to be dyed to the exact shade. A waterproof dye had to be used, because the water could not be sullied.

The film's greatest marvel was the giant mechanical squid made of bright red sponge rubber which attacked Ray Milland and John Wayne in the picture. Its insides operated by electric motors, it could lash out and encircle a full-size man with tentacles thirty feet long. The biggest problem was to make these tentacles move convincingly, but it was a problem triumphantly overcome. A twenty-four-button electrical keyboard operated the creature, and a complex forest of hydraulic pistons activated cables extending into the thirty-foot tentacles, so they could be curled in any direction. The squid's large and evil eyes were operated from the switchboard. DeMille's voice was brought to a loudspeaker above the water level of the eight-hundred-thousand-gallon tank so that he could direct the movements of the squid. He directed Wayne and Milland underwater by means of telephone wires which connected his helmet to theirs.

Reap the Wild Wind had magnificent reviews in New York, following its opening at the Radio City Music Hall on March 19, 1942. Bosley Crowther's review in the *New York Times* read like a press release: "Onto a gorgeous panorama representing the southern coast around 1840, Mr. DeMille has crowded a story filled with sea storms, shipwrecks, and gang fights, and peopled with picturesque characters, dashing gentlemen and ladies in crinoline. He has worked a chattering monkey into it, and a squid. He has sent two men, desperate rivals, into the bowels of a sunken ship in diving suits, and there, in the greenish opalescence, has let them manifest the stuff of which they are made."

It was a marvelous adventure and audiences flocked to see it, a perfect escapist romance in the difficult days of 1942.

13

The War Effort

On March 7, 1942, one year ahead of time, Paramount flung a magnificent luncheon party in the old Lasky barn (which had been moved from Selma and Vine to the studio at Marathon Avenue) to mark the director's thirtieth year in pictures. The intention was to invite every single person who had worked with him in any significant capacity. Alas, Dustin Farnum, Thomas Meighan, Agnes Ayres, Theodore Roberts, Elliott Dexter, Milton Sills, Robert Edeson, Henry B. Walthall, Rudolph Schildkraut, Ernest Torrence, and Marie Prevost were all dead. But Winifred Kingston, Gloria Swanson, Geraldine Farrar, Anita King, Leatrice Joy, Vera Reynolds, and dozens of others were available. (Bebe Daniels and the

267

DeMille directing The Story of Dr. Wassell.

apparently immortal Fannie Ward were in London, the latter cabling that she had been bounced out of bed by a bomb.) Theodore Kosloff was unable to come from Mexico City. William, who was tied up at USC, as a professor, sent a congratulatory cable. It read: YOU SEEM TO HAVE WON YOUR THIRTY YEAR WAR / AND DON'T LET SUCCESS GO TO YOUR HEAD / YOU MUST HAVE BEEN CLEAN ALL YOUR LIFE BECAUSE YOU ARE ALWAYS MENTIONED IN CONNECTION WITH BATHTUBS.

Generally speaking, 1942 was no occasion for rejoicing. The war hit DeMille's personal staff very badly. His valet, butler, maid, and two gardeners were enrolled by the army or by Lockheed. Even his beloved *Seaward* was commandeered by the Navy.* DeMille himself became air raid warden for Laughlin Park, and attended defense school on Tuesday evenings. He became chairman of the Red Cross blood donor drive and was constantly broadcasting and giving luncheon speeches to aid in the war effort.

In those days of early 1942, DeMille often spent his evenings after a hard day's work at the studio listening to Roosevelt's inspiring Fireside Chats broadcasts on the radio. He particularly needed inspiration at the time, not only because of the depressing news from Europe and the Pacific but also because the whole European market had vanished, making it difficult to develop new films which called for a lavish budget. *The Queen of Queens* was revived and shelved again. With his writers, he tried to plan out *Rurales*, virtually a remake of *The Volga Boatman* on a Mexican theme, in which a member of the Rurales, or Mexican vigilantes, falls in love with an aristocratic woman. The work was slow and painful, and it gradually became evident that the Mexican government would not give DeMille the assistance he required.

On the evening of May 26, 1942, tired out after a day of futile plot construction and futile negotiation with the Mexican Embassy, DeMille heard Roosevelt give a chat on the subject of

* It was returned in 1947, in so poor a condition that DeMille refused to accept it back.

a noble Christian, Dr. Corydon E. Wassell, in Southeast Asia. Wassell, a former medical missionary to China, had been a commissioned lieutenant-commander in the United States Navy, and had won the Navy Cross after evacuating nine wounded men from the interior of Java, running a Japanese blockade, and taking the men to safety in Australia.

The instant the broadcast ended, Ted Bonnet, DeMille's publicity man, telephoned him and asked him if he had heard it. "It would make a great subject for a picture, C. B.," he said. DeMille agreed—the same thought had flashed through his mind—and he called Y. Frank Freeman. Only minutes later, Freeman called the White House and DeMille sent a lengthy cable to the Navy Department in Washington seeking Wassell's whereabouts.

DeMille's staff was fully alerted and assembled at his office first thing the following morning. Flushed with excitement, DeMille registered the idea at once with the Motion Picture Producers' Association. Then he telephoned Frank Knox, Secretary of the Navy, and said, "I want Dr. Wassell and the United States Navy." Knox replied, "You can have Dr. Wassell, but the Navy is rather busy nowadays."

Wassell was located in Australia, and Knox arranged for him to be flown at once to San Francisco by Qantas airlines, and transferred to Hollywood. DeMille took him to Paradise, and liked him at once: the man was a nice, slow-speaking, Arkansas doctor, a grassroots, unpretentious middle American. DeMille rather overpowered him by telling him that he was going to tell the "glorious story of his life." Wassell had never thought of himself as a hero, and in fact had believed, when the order from Knox arrived, that he would be sent for court martial in Washington: he had disobeyed specific orders during his evacuation of the wounded men. He was incredulous at DeMille's interest, and thought him slightly crazy. At first, he said little. But DeMille loosened his tongue by promising that fifty thousand dollars against 10 per cent of the gross receipts would go to the Navy Relief Fund.

Once Wassell was signed, the Navy assumed the task of finding the survivors of the expedition. They were all in naval hospitals; nine were at Mare Island, off the California coast near San Francisco, and others at Carona and at Coronado, where Commander William B. Goggins, USN, executive officer of the light cruiser *Marblehead*, which was sunk and bombed off Java, lay wounded. Lou Harris and Ted Bonnet of DeMille's publicity staff interviewed the men, the material taken down at great speed in dozens of notebooks by the field secretary Berenice Mosk. One of the survivors—Melvin Francis—even played himself in the film. The material was handed over to James Hilton, who prepared a basic dossier from which the basis of the script could be drawn, and later based a book on the script itself.

From the outset, it was obvious that the only man alive to play Dr. Wassell would be Gary Cooper. Laraine Day was his girl friend, Signe Hasso was a Dutch nurse, and Carol Thurston was enchanting as Tremartini, the native girl.

When he interviewed Carol Thurston for the role, DeMille asked, "Can you act?" "Well, I . . ." she began. "All right," he said, "let's hear you scream." "I beg your pardon?" "You heard, scream." The girl rose and let out a cry so piercing it shattered a wine glass. An assistant put his head around the door. "Anything wrong?" he asked. "No, just humdrum routine," DeMille said.

In January 1943 Charles Bennett finished the screenplay, based partly on Hilton's work. Arrangements were made for the shooting of the jungle scenes in Tapachula, Mexico. Preparations were still continuing in February. On February 26, Arthur Rosson was dispatched to Mexico to shoot jungle scenes. A complete mechanized army division was arranged for the shooting of scenes in the State of Chiapas, near the Guatemalan border, which were simulations of British military movements in Java before the evacuation. Mexican army bombers strafed a Javanese village, Mexican guns, tanks, and armored cars lumbered over a mile-long road cut out of the jungle by

Rosson's crew, and the stunt man James Dundee drove a jeep off a cliff.

While Rosson and his unit were shooting there, a farmer in Michoacan State hit a stone with his plow and uncovered a small hole. Steam came out of the hole, the earth shook, and the Indian ran for his life. A few hours later, Parangaricutiro Volcano had been born. Within a fortnight it was two hundred feet high and flames, rocks, and lava were erupting from it. DeMille wrote in his notebook: "It's an ill volcano that never does anybody any good." He added a volcanic eruption to Bennett's already overloaded script and had Rosson working within one thousand meters of the crater, with boulders crashing around the units. He wrote, "This must be the first time anyone has been given 'the hot foot' by a volcano. It is also the first time a volcano has had its portrait taken during birth."

Even while these sequences were being shot by Rosson, DeMille was still not ready to proceed in Hollywood. Yet again, casting was his bugbear: he had thirty-two male speaking parts to fill and the manpower shortage was so extreme he was at a loss to know what to do. Surrounded by the usual paraphernalia—toy Javanese sarongs, miniature vehicles, a fifty-pound bomb casing, a ship's binnacle, a case of torpedo gyros, a microscope, and a pair of rosary beads, he wrestled miserably with the problem of casting at his office. Right behind his desk was a blazing five-foot-by-seven water color of the Javanese temple of Boro Bodur, silhouetted against the sky. A *Chicago Daily News* reporter who came to interview DeMille wrote (June 15, 1943): "At first it's all a bit breathtaking. You are ushered in, and as soon as the door opens you get the impression that someone has hit you in the face with a tropical sunset."

On July 11, 1943, shooting finally began at Paramount, with a little scene in which Cooper was trying to remove a necklace of snails from a Chinese woman's neck. For the first five days, everything went smoothly. But on the sixth day, DeMille was horrified that neither Charles Bennett, James Hilton, nor even Dr. Wassell himself could determine what Dr. Wassell would say in diagnosing an illness in one of the hospital scenes. "What inefficiency!" DeMille yelled over and over again through the megaphone. "My staff has been reading this script for three months and nobody thought to check an important point like this!"

After the Wassell picture was finished, following the brilliant studio-made scenes of the sinking of a Dutch passenger ship, DeMille traveled to Washington for the opening in April 1944 at Constitution Hall. A series of lavish receptions were held at the Hotel Statler, where DeMille was staying, and at various government offices, embassies, and private homes. He and Dr. Wassell were received in private audience at the White House by Roosevelt, who expressed his admiration of their contribution to the war effort. DeMille then gave Roosevelt a four-thousand-year-old clay tablet, a tax receipt. "It's from Drehem," he said, "and it's very solid evidence that the Tax Department was functioning even then." Roosevelt threw back his head and roared with laughter.

The premiere brought thirty thousand dollars for the Naval Red Cross Fund. Even Corydon Wassell seemed appeased by that, though the film embarrassed him acutely. DeMille attended another premiere in Little Rock, then flew back to Hollywood to supervise the showing of the new opening, added for re-release, for *The Sign of the Cross*. It showed a B-17 bomber flying over Rome, and as the crew looks down, the mists of history part and the original film begins.

On August 16, 1944, DeMille received a letter from the American Federation of Radio Artists, informing him that AFRA required from each of its members the sum of one dollar, in order to accumulate a fund to fight Proposition 12, which was to be put to vote before the California State Legislature in November. The proposition (known as "the right to work" proposition in general parlance) would have made it

Cartoon relating to DeMille's fight against levy.

The Story of Dr. Wassell.

Unconquered.

Gary Cooper and Paulette Goddard: Unconquered.

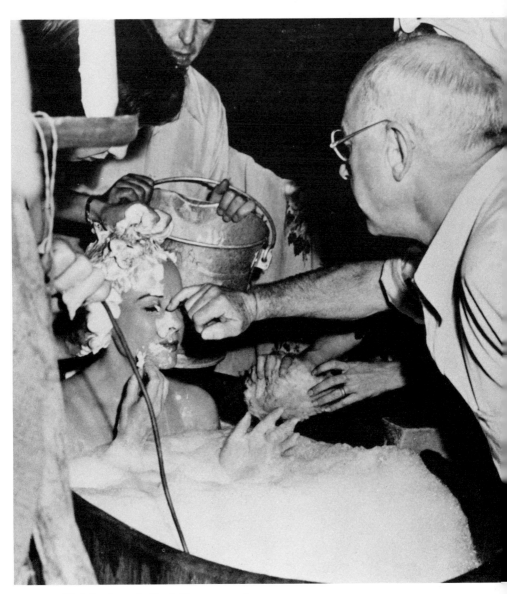

With Paulette Goddard: Unconquered.

possible for any individual resident of the state to work whether or not he belonged to an appropriate craft union. DeMille was given until September 1. He refused to vote against Proposition 12, and in fact voted for it: his old dislike of the power of unions went all the way back to his differences with Alvin Wyckoff over the formation of the cameramen's union in the early 1920s. He knew what his refusal to pay the sum would mean: the conclusion of his part in the Lux Radio Theater, his removal from radio altogether. The date of payment was extended into October, November, and December; but DeMille resolutely refused to meet AFRA's demands. Advised on December 4 that unless he paid by the following Monday, the end of his career on radio would assuredly come, he told the press in a specially prepared statement: "Such grave issues are involved that I consider it a duty to forego, if compelled to, the sum of money which I have been receiving for broadcasting rather than pay one single dollar in a political tribute which acknowledges that I am no longer a free man."

At a loss of five thousand dollars a week, he was firmly retired from the Lux Radio Theater by January 1945. In March, DeMille traveled to Omaha at the invitation of William J. Jeffers, president of the Union Pacific; Jeffers had heard of DeMille's fight for the freedom of speech, and arranged for him to broadcast nationwide from a St. Patrick's Day luncheon attended by leading figures of the city. DeMille recalled the wonderful day six years earlier when he had stepped off the train and seen a lusty frontier town re-created, a sea of beaver hats and sunbonnets. He made it clear that his host was a good union man, that he was a good union man, and that he "did not in any way oppose union thinking." But he insisted on the right of everyone to act freely, citing his own case as an abrogation of that freedom. His closing words were deeply felt: "May I say that I miss, more than I can tell, my visit in ten million homes every Monday night. The friendship of those unseen millions warmed my heart as nothing in life has ever done—but I would rather never visit them again than visit them as a betrayer of the principles that made those homes possible. There is one union that I place above all others—the Union of the United States of America."

Thousands of letters poured in approving DeMille's speech, in many instances with sums of money to enable him to form a DeMille Foundation for Political Freedom, which he established in September 1945, and which he worked for, constantly traveling to give speeches, until the day of his death.

It was later in 1945, with the war at an end in Europe, that DeMille and the DeMille Foundation became involved in the widespread flushing out of communist elements in the United States. A characteristic speech, never released for publication, was given in New Orleans on December 19, 1945, before a selected group of citizens. These phrases were typical of his attitude: "The infiltrating of Communism into the ranks of union labor has created a new force in this land—Red Fascism—something that may be worrying the top labor leaders as much as it worries management, government, and the rest of us." DeMille also named—one of the first to do so—a future member of the Hollywood Ten, the writer John Howard Lawson, as a leader of communist infiltration in California. He added: "Here in America the Communists know they cannot bid for the major elective offices—yet. But they are bidding for the school board elections which control your children's education and which a well-organized minority can swing."

DeMille's urgent pursuit of the anti-communist witch hunts of the immediate post-war period was a natural outcome of his attack on lack of freedom in the unions. He began to associate union impositions with a dangerous subversive Red Front, and the idea grew to an obsession by 1947. His early devotion to all-Americanism, to health, strength, courage, and manly virtue had already begun to topple over into a fanatical patriotism that contained the seeds of the very thing he hated and despised more than anything else: fascism.

Perhaps fortunately, DeMille in 1945 recommended work in

an area in which he was far more competent to act, making motion pictures. He began preparing *Unconquered* in 1945, a film which dealt with indentured servants in the American colonies in 1763. He had been attracted to the subject by reading a novel, *The Judas Tree*, written by Neil H. Swanson, editor of the *Baltimore Sun*. They had met while he was in Pittsburgh for a political speech; Swanson had telephoned him and asked to meet him. Jeanie did some work on the script, followed by a new writer, Fredric M. Frank, recommended by the associate producer Sidney Bedell. It was then given to Swanson who wrote a new version of *The Judas Tree* called *Unconquered*. Finally, Charles Bennett came in and wrote another draft.

To DeMille's acute distress, Jeanie had to withdraw from the work due to cancer.

Neil Swanson's *Unconquered* was published by Doubleday to cash in on the publicity of the film. Meanwhile, DeMille sent Arthur Rosson to Pennsylvania to seek out locations, particularly in Clark Forest, for the second unit to shoot in.

As he started work in Hollywood, the second unit under Rosson arrived in the Cook Forest area on June 7. Farmboys were paid seventy-five cents an hour to clip limbs, replant ferns, spray leaves, and guard the forest's entrances against sightseers. Unfortunately, most of the Cook Forest locations were ruined by rainfall and a plague of stinging insects known as "bunkies," which attacked the crew. Later, additional landscape scenes had to be shot in Oregon.

While the second unit sequences were begun, DeMille completed casting of Paulette Goddard and Gary Cooper in his leading roles, with Boris Karloff made up as a Senecan Indian chief. Karloff's "*s*'s" were very sibilant and all appropriate dialogue had to be eliminated to eliminate the lisp.

DeMille was as meticulous as usual in the preparation of the costumes. His designer, Natalie Visart, brought him a sketch of Karloff's costume and he ruled it out at once. "This won't do," he said. "The Redskin has decorations running up the side of the leggings. This is a Seneca. Senecas never wore frills up the side but always on the front."

By the time Fredric M. Frank and Jesse L. Lasky, Jr. had worked with Bennett on the final draft screenplay, it had virtually become a version of *The Perils of Pauline*; following the casting of Paulette Goddard in the role of Abigail Martha Hale, an English girl transported to slavery in America, it became known jocularly in the industry as "The Perils of Paulette." Miss Goddard was scheduled by the writers to be whipped, sold as a bonded servant on the auction block, tied to a stake by savage Indians, taken on a wild ride over a waterfall, and, in a rare moment of tranquility, compelled to scrub a barroom floor while various barflies tried to seduce her. The obligatory bathroom scene was, for once, not held in a dream of marble and gilt: it took place in a barrel in a blacksmith's shop, and the schedule called for the actress to be immersed in soapy water—for an entire afternoon of shooting.

To DeMille's great delight, Katherine, who was now an accomplished actress, played beautifully the role of Hannah, the gentle Indian wife of the white trader, Garth, played by Howard DaSilva. Victor Varconi and Henry Wilcoxon, among other old friends, appeared in the picture.

As usual, the research was immense and exhaustive and Dan Sayre Groesbeck provided many beautiful drawings of key scenes. DeMille's special team, headed by Walter Tyler, designed the great three-masted merchantman and a reproduction of the Peakstown Fair, including a babble of hawkers, spielers, drummers, soldiers, and all the vivid color of the time.

The most spectacular sequence in the film was the siege of Fort Pitt, which cost three hundred thousand dollars to stage and took several months of careful preparation. The fort, copied as closely as possible from the original designs by Walter Tyler, was peopled with about one thousand players, appearing as trappers, traders, slaves, and members of the Royal American, Pennsylvanian, and Virginian militiamen.

Walter Hoffman, an expert in explosions, used, according to DeMille's publicity man Phil Koury writing in the *New York Times*, fifteen hundred arrows without flames, five hundred with flaming points, three hundred fireballs, and fifty flintlocks. The fireballs were made of dried moss wrapped in birch bark and dipped in kerosene, tossed into the fort by extras or special workers with asbestos gloves. Thirty extras suffered from minor or first-degree burns as a result of what DeMille called "the Hoffman cocktails." In addition, three hundred pounds of dynamite and fifty pounds of flash powder were used.

A particular incident greatly pleased DeMille: the drummer boys were lined up playing a martial tune in the middle of the siege, surrounded by a rain of fireballs. One boy, a fireball burning in his drum, his redcoat smoking, continued—disregarding the danger until DeMille finally yelled "Cut!" DeMille was delighted by the boy's bravery.

DeMille's chief worry in making the picture was not the staging of the siege, to which he brought all the enjoyment, energy, and vigor of a man twenty years younger, but the performance and behavior of Paulette Goddard in the leading role. The cinematographer, Ray Rennahan, had to disguise the late-night rings under her eyes, and she proved recalcitrant in the matter of appearing on the walls of the Fort during the siege, terrified, understandably, of seeing her major stock in trade, her beauty, permanently damaged by a Hoffman cocktail. DeMille flayed her in front of the unit for her lack of bravery, and tried, unsuccessfully, to shame her by hiring a humble extra as the girl who rescues many people on the walls in the teeth of the hail of fire. Miss Goddard was understandably pleased at her own determination when she learned that the extra concerned had suffered minor burns during the sequence.

In order to single out members of the production for their efforts above and beyond the call of duty, DeMille awarded them his special famous half-dollar issued in 1937 to commemorate the two hundred fiftieth anniversary of the founding of

Roanoke Island. He gave one to the property man, Joe Thompson, who solved the problem of Gary Cooper patching Paulette Goddard's torn shoes as they fled through a forest pursued by Indians. The script specified that Cooper cut off part of his coonskin hat and cut it into the shape of a moccasin, but Thompson suggested that Cooper instead patch the hole with a piece of his leather belt. Another went to the brave drummer boy. Boris Karloff received the most deserved medal of all. He learned Seneca dialect—DeMille refused his suggestion he speak gibberish—and played his role in a brace following a spinal operation, the brace covered by a loincloth, feathers, and narrow strips of fur. The great deaf-mute expert in Indian wear, Joe De Yong, dressed him in the role, finally handing a note to DeMille which read: "This man is as patient as a horse."

Despite the relish with which he executed the splendid, richly mounted production, despite his enjoyment of Indian brave against white, of arrow and fireball, siege and succor, DeMille was overshadowed by a deep recurrent sadness during the shooting. Jeanie had worsened, and he knew there was no hope for her. She came to visit the set one day, but was too ill to go to it; pale and unsteady, she sank exhausted on the couch in the office and told him with tears in her eyes, "I won't be able to see the set this time, Chief." He held her hands and tried to force his own strength into her, but it was useless.

Soon afterward, he had word from the Good Samaritan Hospital that she was sinking fast. He and Gladys Rosson went to see her, and, smiling faintly, she tried to reach out to them. They said a tender goodbye. Then, as they left, she turned her face to the wall.

Jeanie's funeral was held on August 15 at the Hollywood Cemetery Chapel. Aside from the personal staff, only the Victor Varconis and Theodore Kosloffs were there. Her death reminded DeMille of how close he was coming to a summing up of his achievements, a final reckoning. On the rare occasions when he ran into Julia, looking at her now wrinkled face, he could see the passage of time inexorably recorded. He turned more and more to his old consolation of religion, frequently reading the Bible to Constance in late hours at Laughlin Park, or leafing through the well-worn book of Doré illustrations to the Bible which he had loved at his father's knee.

In mid-production, a studio strike threatened to bring the immense undertaking of *Unconquered* to a complete halt. DeMille arranged to sleep at the studio, and had his staff bedded down in various rooms, arriving at the studio ahead of the picket line in the mornings, and on rare visits home, leaving behind the line's departure late at night.

Reviews of *Unconquered* following its opening in Pittsburgh were not warm, and indeed the picture was somewhat overweight and overlong. It was severely damaged by the absurdly unconvincing posturings of Miss Goddard, which DeMille had so firmly deplored during the course of shooting. But every cent of the five million dollars the picture cost was visible on the screen, and Ray Rennahan's color photography represented the peak of perfection. Few critics, however niggardly, could deny these facts. *Time* magazine, noting the picture's appearance, noted that DeMille's personal habits had not changed since 1913; "Wherever he goes on the set, one man follows to whip a chair under him, another to shove a megaphone in front of him, while a secretary devotedly notes down every word he says."

14

New Extravaganzas

As early as 1935, DeMille had planned to make the story of Samson and Delilah, with Henry Wilcoxon and (perhaps) Miriam Hopkins, but he had abandoned it. In 1948, he began planning a new version of it, feeling that it was unfortunate it had preceded *Rurales* into oblivion.

At first, DeMille had some doubts about constructing the story, because the tale of Samson and Delilah seemed to lack a connecting thread of narrative. Fortunately, he came across a book, *Judge and Fool*, by Vladimir Jabotinsky, which clarified some aspects of the narrative. It showed him how to overcome the difficult problem of Samson meeting Delilah: in Jabotinsky's version, Delilah was the younger sister of the girl who

In the office, 1949, a posed shot for a "trailer."

rejected Samson's hand in marriage. He arranged for the studio to buy the rights to the work, and he and Fredric M. Frank worked solidly for months constructing a dramatic story.

Unfortunately, the Paramount executives, including Adolph Zukor, who was now seventy-six years old, had grave doubts about public interest in a biblical subject during the disillusioned days of the Cold War. Shrewdly, DeMille realized that only a specifically sexual reference would lighten their executive hearts and equally shrewdly he did not resort to words to prove his point about the film's commercial potential. He simply arranged for Dan Sayre Groesbeck to symbolize the fundamental excitement of the story in a portrait of a massive, primitive brute in a hairy loincloth and a slim, seductive girl in a revealing garment. The Paramount executive staff looked at the picture and immediately decided to give their obstreperous employee his head.

Contrary to critics of the film, it was in no way a distortion of the Bible, creating in bold if vulgar strokes the crude, harsh reality of the world of the Old Testament. Its very primitive rawness was entirely appropriate. But it was severely handicapped by the miscasting of the two central roles, which were the result of DeMille's being unable to find absolutely ideal choices.

He had ruled out Burt Lancaster as Samson on the ground that he was too inexperienced and suffered from a bad back. Unfortunately, he chose in his stead Victor Mature, whom he had admired in a weekend screening at Laughlin Park in a thriller entitled *Kiss of Death.* He had noted Mature's sincere acting style and sinewy physique in gray suitings, but when he first saw Mature at a costume test he was horrified. The man was obviously badly out of condition, with large bones but fatty, flabby muscles. Still tight and bronzed from nude walks and plunges in an icy pool at Paradise, DeMille had a cold contempt for Mature's lack of physical condition, and demanded that he at once repair to the Paramount gym (which used to be the Lasky barn) with the magnificently athletic

Henry Wilcoxon for weeks of severe training, until he lost thirty pounds of fat.

Once shooting began that fall of 1948, Mature turned out to be still more problematical. He was a victim of numerous phobias, fear of water, fear of lions, fear of swords, and of practically everything else as well. His genial, charming personality was far too weak for DeMille's severe and stoical taste. When Mature appeared in the battle of the jawbone in which a great wind swept through the studio, he suddenly took fright at a particularly violent, machine-made gust, and fled, hiding in terror in his dressing room. DeMille had him brought back like a naughty schoolboy who had run away from school. He picked up his megaphone, and in a voice icy with disgust shouted in full hearing of the immense cast and crew: "I have met a few men in my time. Some have been afraid of heights, some have been afraid of water, some have been afraid of fire, some have been afraid of closed spaces. Some have even been afraid of open spaces—or themselves. But in all my thirty-five years of picture-making experience, Mr. Mature, I have not until now met a man who was 100 per cent yellow."

He had different problems with Hedy Lamarr. He discovered to his dismay that although she had been in Hollywood for some eleven years, she had no real command of English and still thought in German. She also had a tendency to pose as though for a portrait photograph at the end of each scene, and despite her beauty, her face never seemed to register fully the depth of emotion. The only consolation in her choice was that she was convincingly alluring, and that she could be relied upon to remember her lines.

The torture of directing the two players was so extreme that it largely destroyed DeMille's pleasure in making the picture, though he relished some sequences: Samson being tormented by a dwarf in the arena, and the destruction of the temple. The temple's destruction was simply helped by narrowing down the columns to their foot; he told Thomas M. Pryor of the *New York Times* that the really specialized work on the picture lay in assembling nineteen hundred molting peacocks around his ranch over a long period in order to clothe Hedy Lamarr as Delilah. Actually, he was pulling Pryor's leg: the costumes, including the peacock feathers, had been collected as early as 1935, and some were adopted from Claire West's work on the first *Ten Commandments.*

The most spectacular sequence in the film was Samson's destruction of the temple, which occupied DeMille and the special effects department of Paramount for many weeks. Two hundred electricians manned three hundred fifty arcs, one hundred fifty Du Arcs, and one hundred pans, providing a total of fifty-one thousand amperes pouring their force on the scene. The cameraman, George Barnes, shot the set in three sections. DeMille worked with an extraordinary model in order to time exactly the movements of the actors and the moment at which he would need to pull the switch which would cause the collapse.

Henry Noerdlinger, the research consultant, discovered the convenient fact that the bases of the pillars of a Minoan temple narrowed at the foot, and that the weight of the entire temple rested upon these. The pillars were made of light plaster; when Victor Mature thrust them apart, the entire scaled-down model began to fall. Together with it, the great idol Dagon crashed: some thirty feet high, with a fire burning in its belly, it was a formidable creation, and fortunately no extras were caught and pinned under its weight. Henry Wilcoxon was unfortunately struck by a falling column, and had great difficulty rising from it afterward. He approached DeMille with blood streaming down his face. "Good God, Harry, you look terrible; you're going to hold up production," was DeMille's only comment. "Well," Wilcoxon replied ruefully, "I won't be the first actor to be destroyed by a column."

After the picture was finished, Wilcoxon left on an extended promotion tour masterminded by the press agent Richard Condon, who accompanied him. Wilcoxon lectured extensively to women's clubs, churches, and various religious groups.

DeMille sent to many areas a special sixteen-millimeter film containing scenes from a number of his productions. Samsonized cornflakes, with photographs of Victor Mature on the packets, were mass marketed by Kellogg, Parisian designers created Minoan period gowns, which were sold by the thousands off Seventh Avenue. Condon made a classic remark at the end of the extensive campaign: "At this stage, we've gotten more on Minoan culture than Arnold Toynbee."

On October 13, 1949, DeMille attended a thirty-fifth anniversary party at the barn at which many of the people who had worked with him in the early days appeared: Winifred Kingston, Blanche Sweet, Jesse, and Pauline Garon among them. In November he enjoyed another social occasion: a Society of Motion Picture Art Directors banquet at which he and Jesse received honorary memberships. His speech of acceptance included references to Wilfred Buckland, Paul Iribe, Roland Anderson, and Walter Tyler, with all of the happy times accentuated and all of the old bitternesses removed.*

That year and the following year, DeMille was often at Paradise, now restored to its former glamor following the flood, as always walking naked to his pool after being wakened at an early hour, conducting colloquies with this or that animal denizen of the rocks, and defying a black widow or carpet snake to sting his bare feet. He was in better health than he had ever been, and when he was not involved working on his new picture with Frank he was involved in passionate new denunciations of the "red menace" in Hollywood, delivered with all of his old asperity.

After the film was released in May 1950, to DeMille's intense delight a major controversy blew up. When a number of people wrote criticizing his facts, he managed to turn up numerous scholarly sources to prove that everything in the film was absolutely authentic. A number of resistant critics pointed out that he had simply quoted the sources most favorable to his

* Like Buckland and Iribe, Anderson had left DeMille following basic disagreements in the matter of design some years earlier.

argument, and that at least he might admit that, say, the idol of Dagon did not contain a fire in its belly. He refused to admit anything of the kind.

He embarked on an extensive cross-country tour lecturing about the picture when Henry Wilcoxon, who had begun the tour, became ill. Henry S. Noerdlinger, DeMille's research consultant, helped along by publishing scholarly articles in magazines on his work on the picture. Richard Condon intelligently organized the publicity but the campaign did not prevent more than one critic infuriating DeMille by referring to "the most expensive haircut in history."

Early in 1949, DeMille was glancing through the *Hollywood Reporter* when he noticed an item that fascinated him. It was to the effect that John Ringling North, of Ringling Brothers, Barnum and Bailey, planned to arrange for a Hollywood company to make a film of life in the circus and that David O. Selznick had relinquished his rights to the material. Enormously enthused by the idea, he began at once to make preparations with Fredric M. Frank for the script.

Negotiations, he read, were proceeding with Barney Balaban and Henry Ginsberg at Paramount. On June 20, 1949, Paramount paid two hundred fifty thousand dollars for the rights to make the picture, which included shooting certain footage at the circus' headquarters in Sarasota, Florida. John Ringling North came to Paradise for a series of preliminary discussions, then left for Europe to arrange for some spectacular acts to be hired. In July, DeMille, with Fredric M. Frank, and his publicity man Phil Koury, and accompanied by his granddaughter Cecilia, age thirteen, left to join the circus on an extended tour, saturating himself in every aspect of circus life. They traveled in John Ringling North's sumptuous private car, consisting of three bedrooms, lounge, kitchen, dining room, baths, and a deep-freeze unit. They were served by a Swiss butler, a French chef, a maid, and a valet.

DeMille spent weeks observing the circus from every angle, with the aid of a viewfinder and his sketch artist John Jensen.

*C. B., Berenice Mosk, Hedy Lamarr,
Georges Anders:* Samson and Delilah.

On location at Sarasota: The Greatest Show on Earth.

He noted how a baby was bathed by her mother in a large iron pail, how a juggler silently practiced for hours behind the big tent, how a girl patiently ironed the ballet frock she would wear for her bareback ride. He told the *Milwaukee Journal* (August 9, 1949): "One of the girl aerialists has a little boy, about four. She fell once and was seriously hurt. I've noticed that every time she goes on the little boy goes with her to the entrance of the tent. She hugs him and gives him a kiss just before she goes on. The boy goes away—he doesn't watch his mother—but he listens to the music and when he hears the music that signals the end of the act, he comes running to the entrance and leaps into his mother's arms as she leaves the tent."

Everywhere he went, DeMille was lifted in a bosun's chair to the top of the tent to observe the aerialists at close quarters. In one of these precarious trips hundreds of feet up, he determined that the canvas top of the tent would make lighting impossible, and that he would have to provide a lighter, translucent fabric before he started filming. He also realized that it would be a formidable task to manage the particular shadows and textures of light inside the Big Top.

DeMille came back with notebooks crammed with data. By now, the film obsessed him completely. Since no adequate book existed on the subject, and he knew of no novels which could adequately convey the specialized atmosphere of the circus world, he decided to develop a story with Frank which was from the outset an "original." It was centered on the character of the head of the circus himself, a driving, forceful personality which was a cross between DeMille's own and that of John Ringling North. As was DeMille's custom, he arranged for Frank to condense the story to two pages, which he told to his grandson, Jody Harper (Cecilia's boy), with great relish. The boy responded warmly to the idea, and the "Jody version" was used. With Frank, DeMille gradually developed a narrative treatment, ensuring that the "plumbing"—the basic story—was sound and properly constructed at the outset, with the exterior decoration to be added later. On this occasion, though, the "plumbing" proved extremely difficult to install, and his meetings with Frank were often fraught with tension.

DeMille was aided considerably by the brilliant work of Johnny Jensen, who sketched scene after scene of circus life with immense vividness and panache. Jensen showed the lines of exhaustion in the face of a clown, the power in the arms of men raising the big tent, the tough women covering animal cages with tarpaulin in a sudden shower of rain. He also worked out all the complex process of setting up a circus: every rope knot was perfectly observed, every minute particular of the clothing, makeup, and performance of the circus stars.

With Frank and Jensen, and Henry Wilcoxon, who helped him enormously with the preparations, and the constant aid of John Ringling North, DeMille gradually began to see the film unfold in his mind. He discovered ways of working the various tasks of the circus people into the warp and woof of the action: a man wraps the bar of his trapeze while he has an intense discussion with his girl friend, a man and woman quarrel while the woman is attending to the special resin which allows her shoes to cling steadily to a high wire.

The experience of following the circus was of the greatest value. In one Minnesota town a violent storm broke out, the rain and wind lashing the tent. During this crisis, DeMille was deeply impressed by the courage and resilience of the circus people, who were totally unaffected by it. Running out of the rain to the damp-smelling canvas cover, he remembered that he had first planned a circus picture back in 1922. He opened a somewhat soaked copy of a book he had carried around, on and off, for years, containing a quotation from Courtney Riley Cooper: "The circus is only the veneer. The circus is a fighting machine waging a constant battle for survival—against adversity, accident, flood and storm—a driving, dogged force which succeeded through the sheer grit and determination of men and women who can live in the face of fatigue, bodily discomfort and sometimes in the very grasp of death itself."

After the marvelous tour of the wheat towns, DeMille

happily settled into several months of work with Fredric M. Frank, and then spent a period at the winter headquarters in Sarasota, followed by a visit to the circus at Madison Square Garden. Another writer, Frank Cavett, did not fit into De-Mille's ideas of a writer, and left after only a few weeks' work.

He began considering cast: Burt Lancaster, Kirk Douglas, Marlene Dietrich, and Hedy Lamarr were all weighed and found wanting for a variety of reasons. Betty Hutton went to the extreme of sending an enormous, thousand-dollar floral piece with a tiny replica of herself swinging on a trapeze on top of it. DeMille was taken with this, and asked to see some bathing beauty poses. He felt she was too heavy in the hips; and told her so when she went to see him. She promised to slim down, and told him she was absolutely fearless.

He sent her a telegram: TOURNAMENT OF ROSES WAS NEVER LIKE THIS / DEFINITELY FAVOR YOUR DIRECTING AS WELL AS PLAYING IN THE PICTURE / YOU ARE MARVELOUS / MY HEART BELONGS TO ANNIE WITH OR WITHOUT A GUN.* C. B. James Stewart was signed as the clown, and—after rejecting Paulette Goddard, whom he had never forgiven for her fear of the fireballs in *Unconquered*—he chose Gloria Grahame to play the elephant girl. When Paulette sent him a telegram reading HOPE ALL THOSE RUMORS ABOUT MY GOING INTO THE GREATEST SHOW ON EARTH ARE TRUE / AM RETURNING MONDAY TO SIGN THE CONTRACT, he threw it in the wastebasket. He cast Cornel Wilde as the high-wire walker, The Great Sebastian, and Charlton Heston as Brad, the circus manager. He had admired Heston in a film version of *Julius Caesar* directed by David Bradley.

In his office at Paramount, DeMille created a replica of the big tent, with tiny animals and people. A battery of lights stood at the edge of the table with a complete set of switches. One battery lit up the center ring, others lit up various parts of the tent. He used this model of the circus for six months to try and solve the problem of lighting the tent. Finally, he devised a

* Miss Hutton had starred in *Annie Get Your Gun* in 1950.

technique whereby the lights were manipulated by remote control, hung on clusters on the tent poles, and moved up and down so as to be concealed by the time the camera was ready to focus on a performer.

Coaching the cast was only one of the problems connected with the picture. Betty Hutton rapidly became DeMille's favorite: trained by Antoinette Concello of the circus, she took to the trapeze with amazing courage and brilliance. Cornel Wilde, however, discovered to his horror something that he had never known: he had stationary acrophobia—a terror of heights. DeMille despised him for this. One day, when Wilde was trying out some clogs, he said, "Better not wear those, Mr. Wilde. You're afraid of heights."

Watched by her nervous husband, the director Nicholas Ray, Gloria Grahame performed the elephant act in the center ring. She rode the elephant, and then lay down in the sawdust and the elephant put its forefoot on the bridge of her nose. Finally she put her right leg in the elephant's mouth as she lay down. She avoided being struck by the elephant's foot as she rolled clear, and almost fell from its back as it sat up and she clasped the saddle.

Dorothy Lamour actually hung by her teeth in one shot. A casting was made of her mouth and the teeth fitted into it. The bit was on a swivel. Gripping the bit, she was pulled up forty feet in the air. The scene was shot at Sarasota.

Betty Hutton went home each night with her hands bleeding and covered with callouses. Lyle Bettger, playing an elephant trainer, narrowly avoided being crushed by an irritated beast. When the unit moved to Sarasota for filming in February 1951, the cast actually performed for the crowds who had come to see the circus and joined the circus stars for an immense parade through the Sarasota streets.

The shooting at Sarasota very nearly failed to take place. As soon as the unit arrived, DeMille found that the Ringling tent was deserted. He was horrified to discover that no entertainers were available for a particular sequence. Then he discovered that a particular individual whose word was law required a bribe. Only when this was settled could the shooting proceed.

The DeMille unit, with George Barnes and W. Wallace Kelley chief among the team of cinematographers, left for a long journey with the circus, shooting as they went. During a location in Philadelphia, Betty Hutton played a scene which brought a cheer from the crowd. After DeMille announced through a megaphone that "special thrills were in store," Betty Hutton gave a few solo flourishes on the trapeze, and was caught by a male partner, Bill Snyder, who pulled her up to his bar. They kissed for a moment and Betty yelled "Let me go!" As he did so she missed her footing deliberately and fell one hundred feet into a net. The crowd cheered ecstatically. "You were supposed to scream with terror!" DeMille shouted. "Betty, do it again!"

At Washington, D.C., the stars appeared in a splendid parade around the ring, Dorothy Lamour in silver spangles, with a new moon in her head, riding a float called "Moonlight Melodies." Betty Hutton wore a costume made up of real roses and thin, rose-colored silk, on a float smothered in roses. Gloria Grahame, who played the elephant girl, was seen riding a ring slung from the jaw of an elephant, and Cornel Wilde rode a superb white stallion, dressed in a white cowboy suit and a ten-gallon hat.

Returning to Hollywood again, DeMille prepared the most elaborate sequence in the film: the wreck of the circus train. Eleven extras and technicians were injured in the scene. Wild animals and reptiles were loose over the set, and the floor was strewn with carefully made up "corpses." Charlton Heston lay pinned under bars ripped from an animal cage, turnbuckles used to screw the wreckage tight against his body and cause his agony to be real.

The animal cages were turned over on the set, and the animals roamed about among the crew. Unfortunately, an immense cage of monkeys proved a real hazard: the monkeys were so terrified of the lions and tigers that they fled from Stage

16 into the adjoining Hollywood Cemetery and it proved almost impossible to retrieve them.

Released at the outset of 1952, the production became an immediate and overpowering success, and even succeeded in earning some tolerable reviews. The public adored the picture, and many people returned to see it a second and third time. At the Academy Awards in March, the director, glowing with pride, received the coveted Irving Thalberg award, honoring him as a producer if not as a director. When he returned to Laughlin Park after the ceremony, his family sat about him, his children and grandchildren, and for a rare hour in his life he was utterly and completely happy.

15

The Last Commandments

After the completion of *The Greatest Show on Earth*, Gladys Rosson, like Jeanie, died of cancer. It was a severe blow to DeMille. He visited her frequently at the Good Samaritan Hospital, trying to give her what comfort he could. She had been his good and true friend—and more than that—for thirty-nine years.

It was time for DeMille to take stock, to weigh everything he had achieved, and to plan a tremendous new production which would crown everything he had done before. It is certain that at this time he was more secure in his own being than he had ever been; we may make an educated guess and say that he probably had not a qualm about the destruction of the vivid

The DeMilles at Laughlin Park, 1957.

young artist who set up shop in a barn in 1913. The terrible
battles, first with Zukor, then with Elek Ludvigh and J. J.
Murdock, and later with the rival factions at M-G-M and
Paramount, had finally stripped him of all hope of sustaining a
career as a personal artist, and the depressing record of so
many films in which he had attempted visual and aural
experiments spelled out its clear message. The public dictated
the quality of the cinema: he knew it now, and he had long
since ceased to impose his will upon the masses. Instead, he
had, since his last fling at a career when he humbly and
desperately returned to Lasky in 1932, been its obedient
servant.

As such, of course, he had every reason to be pleased with
himself. At last he was talking, boldly and clearly, in the only
language men like Zukor and Murdock and Mayer and Lasky
understood or ever would understand: the language of profit.
Exciting though the adventure of film making still was to him,
he knew that he was in effect supplying products. Perhaps, with
his superb record at the box office for more than a decade, he
could crown it all with the most tremendous box office product
of all.

In the mellowness of his wisdom, he would fulfill a dream: he
would remake *The Ten Commandments* with all the tremendous
resources now at his command, and in the very places where
the story was set. And Zukor, who had once forbidden him to
go to Egypt to make the earlier version, should now be made to
bend the knee, and permit him to go anywhere he liked to make
the new one.

As it happened, Zukor, very old now, and serene, made no
demur when the studio which had been his provenance for
almost forty years decided to go ahead with the production.
Barney Balaban in the East and Y. Frank Freeman in the West
were jointly enthused about the project, and despite much
opposition from within the ranks, gave DeMille absolute carte
blanche, asking only that he make the picture in VistaVision,
the new Paramount process.

At Paramount and at Laughlin Park, DeMille dredged up Jeanie's treatments and successive screenplays, and the great files of research of Claire West and Paul Iribe for the earlier version. Thirty years on, he felt it would be impossible to improve on Iribe's designs for the great entrance gate of the city of Per-Ramses originally built at Guadalupe, or for the throne room of the Pharaoh. But he knew that on this occasion, with the immeasurably increased budgets since 1923, some of the rich materials used in building the original structure would have to be sacrified.

In other ways, though, the new version was radically different from the old. Edith Head began doing sketches for the costumes which were in every particular more functional than those designed by Claire West. The research, based on many new discoveries, was more exhaustive than the rush job Miss West had done with Iribe. Henry Noerdlinger and a team spent years, in fact, delving into every aspect of Egyptian history, and came up with some different interpretations from their forbears.

At first, DeMille, working on the outline with Fredric M. Frank, pondered adapting Jeanie's idea of a modern story following the old, but he changed his mind quickly. This time, the story of Ramses II, of Moses and the Exodus, would be the entire subject of the film. With a budget of unlimited millions, no expense need be spared. It was a dream come true.

The casting was easily done. Charlton Heston would make a perfect Moses; Yul Brynner, with his slanting eyes, high cheekbones, and imposing physique could be as impressive a king of Egypt as he had been a king of Siam. Anne Baxter was a plumply attractive Nefretiri, and Yvonne DeCarlo, Edward G. Robinson (just released from a blacklist), and Ian Keith, who had been Saladin in *The Crusades*, were added, with a now frail and elderly Julia Faye, and a ghost from the old days at the Lasky Studios, the former director George Melford, in small roles.

As chief cameraman, DeMille selected Loyal Griggs, who had shown a degree of distinguished craftsmanship in the film

Shane, for which he received an Oscar. Griggs flew to Egypt with the first party in the fall of 1953, and made an exhaustive survey of the terrain both east and west of the Nile. Under the combined guidance of the art directors Hal Pereira and Walter Tyler, working on the basis of Henry Noerdlinger's remarkable job of research, but chiefly upon the previous sets built by Paul Iribe for the earlier version, the team prepared the gates of the city of Per-Ramses with an army of slaves two thousand strong.

After two years of solidly detailed preparation, with rich oil paintings of major scenes as his inspiration, and the brilliant advance work of Loyal Griggs and his team fully studied and made use of, DeMille set out for his great destination in October 1954. His only distress as he looked forward to his great undertaking was that Theodore Kosloff, whom he had wanted to create the dances for the film, had become too ill to proceed. Instead, DeMille engaged LeRoy Prinz, who had worked with him on *Madame Satan* and *Cleopatra.*

In late September 1954, DeMille, with Cecilia and Joseph Harper and their children Cecilia and Jody, Berenice Mosk, Joan Catterlin, and the publicist Donald Hayne, left from New York aboard the *S.S. Constitution.* The Atlantic was as smooth as a billiard board, and DeMille, who badly needed the rest, and was suffering from a bad case of dysentery, gradually gained strength in the sunlight and stiff breeze of the ocean crossing. The vessel docked at Cannes and Henry Michaud, the Paris representative of Paramount, and Luigi Zaccardi, who represented the company in Rome, came aboard for the rest of the journey to Naples. They made another stop at Genoa, and DeMille enjoyed a comfortable day of sightseeing with his family and staff, including a trip to the Cathedral and to the birthplace of Columbus. They returned for the last leg of the journey to Naples in the highest spirits.

Tanned and recovered from the dysentery, DeMille held the journalists in Naples captivated by his stories, and his plans for the new production. He transferred with the entourage to the Italian ship *Enotria* for a largely smooth and uneventful voyage to Alexandria, marred only by Donald Hayne's seasickness. At Alexandria, an immense fleet of cars arranged by the unit managers who had gone ahead picked up the party and drove them into Cairo. All except his family and Joan Catterlin went to the Mena House Hotel; he was installed in a splendid penthouse which had been placed at his disposal.

That same afternoon, the group departed for Beni Youssef, south of Cairo, to oversee the splendid finished gates of Per-Ramses. DeMille must have experienced an extraordinary sense of total recall, as the gates were precisely those which had greeted him on arrival at Guadalupe thirty-one years before. But in one particular they fell short of Paul Iribe's original concept: they were too brightly painted. DeMille ordered the garishness reduced, and Walter Tyler at once set to work to repaint them and sandpaper some of the gold surfaces.

Next day, in a fleet of Chrysler Plymouths, the team left for Mount Sinai. A guide known as "the fox of the desert" had marked every inch of the way with white-painted stones and boulders. They stopped at the Monastery of St. Catherine's after a brief stay at an oil installation in the desert.

Shooting began on the side of Mount Sinai, as close as possible to the sites on which Moses was presumed to have undergone his divine experiences. The heavy equipment was carried part of the way up the mountain by camel and mule train, then unloaded and shouldered or dragged on ropes by the Arab crews, while the company rested at St. Catherine's Monastery. All of the scenes on the mountain were, according to a survey made by the *American Cinematographer* (November 1956), shot by Loyal Griggs and his team without satisfactory booster or arc lights, since it proved impossible to shift the generator up the rocky side of the mountain. DeMille was forced to use reflectors only, creating a remarkably hard and vivid visual effect.

The major work of shooting was at Per-Ramses itself. Here, Griggs had the use of four fine VistaVision cameras, and a Chapman Studio Equipment Company crane, eighteen feet long, seven and a half feet wide, with an elevatable height of twenty-eight feet, and an ability to rotate three hundred sixty degrees at a time. Arthur Rowan recorded in the *Cinematographer*: "Both a gasoline engine and an electric motor drive are included, and are designed to operate either singly or together. The gas motor is intended for use in propelling the crane on land or on highways, while the electric drive serves for moving the crane on the sound stage or where the gas motor cannot be used because of its exhaust."

DeMille assembled some twelve thousand people and fifteen thousand animals for the Exodus sequence. Climbing onto the great crane, he directed the entire sequence through a massive public address system, much as he had directed the first version some thirty years before. Griggs told Rowan that he was equipped with an inventory of six lenses, all specially recalibrated: 28 millimeter, 35 millimeter, 40 millimeter, 75 millimeter and a four-inch telephoto lens. The result was extraordinary precision and clarity, with unusually wide sightlines—three miles of continuous human action were covered in one shot.

Working at a special studio in Cairo, John P. Fulton, in charge of the film's remarkable special effects, arranged for the later scenes of the Exodus to be overshadowed by artificial clouds, a device in which he used a special neutral density filter, graduated very slowly so that some areas of the image were bright and others were dark. Red filters, and superimposed photographs of flames, were used in the sequence of the pillar of fire. A special refrigeration truck was constructed with intricate controls which could increase or decrease the extent of cold in the truck. When the precious film was finished and processed, it was shipped by Trans-World Airlines in packs of dry ice, seen by the executives in New York, and transferred to Hollywood. The cameras themselves were equally protected. Rowan recorded: "When dust storms prevailed or whenever scenes action caused an excessive dust problem, large cellophane envelopes with a narrow slit cut for the lens were slipped over the cameras and tied to the bottom as a means of keeping

Yul Brynner as Ramses II
in The Ten Commandments (*1956*).

Outside the gates of Per-Ramses: The Ten Commandments.

dust from reaching the delicate film movement and the polished steel film gates."

Unlike the first Exodus, the new one went off without a hitch. Then, one day, DeMille had a horrifying experience. In order to check a faulty camera, he climbed with Henry Wilcoxon to the very top of one of the one-hundred-three-foot gates, up an almost perpendicular ladder—an extraordinary feat for a man of his years. As he reached the top and looked down through the brilliant sunlight on the immense multitude he felt an almost overwhelming sense of pride. But a terrible pain suddenly shot through the very center of his heart. He staggered and his face turned green. He began to bend over; the pain was more intense than anything he had felt in his life. For a moment, he was unable to breathe. The intense light shimmered over the thousands of people below, blotting out his vision. Henry Wilcoxon came to his aid, but he impatiently brushed his aside. When Wilcoxon told him on no account must he attempt to descend the ladder he snapped, "How am I going to get down? Fly?" Mustering his extraordinary will power, praying deeply and from the essence of his being to God, he made the descent, then sank miserably to a sitting position. He rallied again, and with Cecilia and Berenice Mosk made his way, ashen-faced, to a chair. Fortunately, his doctor, Max Jacobson, was present, and, under protest, he was taken in the car to his penthouse for a rest. Jacobson told him bluntly he must abandon the direction of the picture, but he, supported by Cecilia, absolutely refused to do anthing of the kind.

That night, DeMille went into his bedroom and prayed as he had never prayed before in his life. We will never know what he asked God to provide, but it may be imagined that he called upon all the strength that lay within his being, that he sought to draw up power from the very wellsprings of life itself. As dawn broke—the acrid, flatly-lit dawn of Egypt—he stood up in his room and cried out. When he took Cecilia's hands in his own later that morning, he knew that he had been spared: his will, just as it had triumphed over rheumatic fever and exhaustion in 1921, had triumphed again.

The great scenes of the raising of a giant obelisk and the pursuit by Pharaoh's chariots were shot without a single technical hitch. DeMille had learned the lesson of 1923: instead of a motley collection of poorly trained extras drawn from every part of the world, this time he had the extremely fit Egyptian Army playing its forebears and perfectly in command of their chariots after just four months of training. No shows of fear this time, no need for the equivalent of Cecilia DeMille to show them how to careen over a dune, and no fear of crashing into anyone—least of all a Ritz-Carlton orchestra. It was a perfectly, mathematically worked-out operation from start to finish, and DeMille felt at last that he occupied the role which he would have chosen if he had not been a film director: a magnifico among generals.

The team flew back to Hollywood in November. There, the shooting of the parting of the Red Sea was easily accomplished, with shots of the Red Sea itself matched to the pouring of tanks into a vast adjoining set, then the shots reversed as the water rushed out. The voice of God was a difficult selection; spiteful journalists suggested that DeMille had chosen his own—a grievous insult to so devout a man. Finally, Donald Hayne was plumped for: his rounded, mellifluous vowels and stentorian delivery were ideally apt. The visitation of the angel of death was shown as a thundercloud passing over a valley; the pillar of fire was managed with the use of superimposed streaks of light, flickering like those in an artificial fire. All these problems, and dozens of others, were triumphantly solved by the special effects man, John P. Fulton, and the sound and visual departments of Paramount.

In the midst of this a sad blow came on March 4, 1955, when William deMille died at his home at Playa del Rey at the age of seventy-six. And now came the immense task of editing the picture. The seventy-five-year-old Bauchens' devotion to her task was an astonishment. For seven months, working eighteen hours a day, she somehow managed to dredge up enough energy to proceed. DeMille did not bully, coax, or cajole her along; he trusted her absolutely, knowing the depth of her love and trust in him. He was overcome with admiration for her work, and his joy was increased by the fact that a new electrocardiogram produced an excellent prognosis. He announced at the luncheon table at the Paramount commissary one day that his heart was completely normal.

The film was, in its complete form, not far removed from a "first cut," the first edited version with which Anne Bauchens delighted him. He did feel that the Exodus was overlong, reaching this decision after the film had been scored in its entirety by the brilliant young Elmer Bernstein. In order not to destroy the music, when Anne re-edited it she had to cut the individual sprocket holes so as not to destroy the flow of the music. It was an extraordinary achievement—with only one assistant and one apprentice.

The Ten Commandments was successfully previewed in Salt Lake City, and DeMille made an extensive promotional tour, meeting with church leaders and civic dignitaries in many American cities.

The opening at the Criterion Theatre in New York on November 8, 1956, was an extraordinary triumph, and even the reviews were quite respectful. Next week, on the fourteenth, the film opened at the Stanley Warner Theatre in Los Angeles, with equal success.

DeMille made a rush trip to Europe and had the pleasure of being received in audience by Pope Pius XII. President Theodor Heuss and Chancellor Konrad Adenauer received him in Germany, as well as the Mayor of Berlin, Willy Brandt. In Paris he was awarded the Légion d'Honneur, and in London an aged and fragile Sir Winston Churchill received him at his home in Hyde Park Gate.

After attending a Royal Command Film Performance, at which he was presented to Queen Elizabeth, DeMille flew back to Hollywood in good spirits on November 8, 1957.

Meanwhile, the picture had achieved impressive financial results, completely quelling all criticism from within the Paramount ranks. DeMille began work on a boy scout story, which would weave the character of Lord Baden-Powell into a complex narrative of the history of the boy scout movement.

Then he changed his mind, with the result that he underwent a severe—and finally crushing—test of his strength. He planned to postpone the boy scout story and instead remake *The Buccaneer* as a musical version of the life of Jean Lafitte, with a Yul Brynner no longer bald in the leading role. A great deal of work was done on the basic script, but Brynner became dissatisfied with the treatment of the material, and was on the point of backing out. One day the DeMille entourage was discussing the matter at the Paramount commissary table, and DeMille was growing bored. Suddenly Katherine's husband, the now very successful Anthony Quinn, stepped by. DeMille asked him if he thought Budd Boetticher might be a good director to assume the project. Quinn said, "Oh, he's not your kind of director. He's quite unsuitable." DeMille said, on a reckless and most uncharacteristic impulse, "Tony, how would you like to direct it?" There was a pause while Quinn's brain began working. He said suddenly, "I'll do it!" They shook hands on it, and Quinn said, "You won't be sorry." That, if ever there was one, was a disastrously false prophecy.

With DeMille as executive and supervising producer and Quinn as director, the picture began shooting in 1958. Quinn tried from the outset to modernize the concept, quicken its pace, and redecorate it—but quite without DeMille's flair. Officially, another actor, Henry Wilcoxon, was supposed to be the producer. He was equally unsuitable to his task. Caught between Quinn and Brynner—who had reluctantly agreed to proceed—Wilcoxon proved unable to handle the situation. From the very outset, *The Buccaneer* was a catastrophe.

Every scene, as it came to DeMille's private cutting room, was desolating in its badness. After the triumph of *The Ten Commandments* and his reprieve from death, he felt that some terrible punishment was being visited upon him. Matters were so bad that Loyal Griggs, the cameraman, told Quinn point-blank he would not help him to get any of the effects he wanted; according to Berenice Mosk, Quinn exasperated the actors by acting out all the parts and refusing to let them improvise—a direct contradiction of DeMille's precept, maintained after the very earliest days, that actors must be given freedom to interpret a role as they chose.

Every day he would look at the cut footage of the film and scream with rage. Each night he would return home and tell anyone who would listen that he was going to dismiss Quinn as director immediately. When the dreadful movie was finished, because of his deep affection for Katherine, and very much against doctor's orders, he agreed to do everything possible to promote the picture, including touring to its premieres. Just before leaving he suffered another heart attack which left him feeling desperately ill, but he proceeded with the trip anyway.

He left by plane for New Orleans on December 9 to attend the world premiere sponsored by the Louisiana Historical Landmarks Society at the Saenger Theatre on the eleventh. Then he proceeded to New York for the opening at the Capitol Theatre on December 22. He dreaded the journey, and still further detested the film, complaining bitterly to Florence Cole, who accompanied him, about the sound and projection in New Orleans. Returning to Los Angeles, he was in pain, felt death very close, and spoke in a strangled voice, seeking for breath, to Florence and to Dr. Max Jacobson, who were with him on the plane. Back in Los Angeles, he could barely see the tarmac through the mist that clouded his eyes, and Berenice Mosk was horrified at his gray, ghastly pallor.

On Christmas Eve—though feeling very infirm—he came to the office, distributed bonus checks to all of those who had worked with him on *The Ten Commandments*, and offered various people who dropped by a glass of wine. Others, special friends at the studio, received gifts from underneath the great Christmas tree in his office. It was getting toward six o'clock and everyone had gone home to their families except the devoted Florence Cole and Berenice Mosk. DeMille buzzed Berenice on the intercom and said, "Sweetie, come in." He handed her the check envelope and a gift, and she firmly expected the usual chaste peck that accompanied these annual presentations. She put her hands on his arms, and almost started back from him; the marvelous power, like the strength in the limbs of an old oak, had gone, and the arms were pitifully, heartbreakingly thin. They looked each other in the eyes, and each knew that the other knew. She flung her arms around him and fled from the scene. As he left the studio and passed her office, he said, "Well, sweetie, we have a lot of work to do in the next three years!" He was, clearly, trying to take the edge off her distress, but it did not really work.

He was uncomfortable, prayed a little, and found difficulty in reading or making notes. On January 8, he dropped in briefly to the studio, but he was insufficiently well to attend properly to any work. On the night of January 20, two miserable bedridden weeks of pain and restlessness later, he was visited, as so often in those last days, by Cecilia and her husband Joseph Harper. He remarked on Cecilia's lovely dress as she began to go to attend a dinner party.

Following her departure, he was alone with a nurse. He began to scribble some notes on a piece of paper. They read: "The Lord giveth and the Lord taketh away. Blessed be the name of the Lord. It can only be a short time . . . until those words, the first in the Episcopal funeral services are spoken over me. . . . After those words are spoken, what am I? I am only what I have accomplished. How much good have I spread? How much evil have I spread? For whatever I am a moment after death—a spirit, a soul, a bodiless mind—I shall have to look back and forward, for I have to take with me both."

At five A.M. the next morning he had a final heart seizure which he did not survive. Constance, who had become somewhat senile and had invariably not recognized him in the previous weeks, was not informed of his death. He was seventy-seven years old.

The funeral was held on January 23 at St. Stephens Episcopal Church, 6126 Yucca Street, the Rev. Harry E. Owens officiating. Adolph Zukor shouldered his former enemy's mortal remains together with Samuel Goldwyn, Neil McCarthy, Russel Treacy, Donald Hayne, Henry Wilcoxon, and Henry Noerdlinger. Then the grand showman was interred alongside his brother William at the Hollywood Cemetery.

The *New York Times* editorial read: "Mr. DeMille combined the flair for showmanship of a Barnum with the cinematic inventiveness of a Griffith. With the driving energy that characterized his entire life, Mr. DeMille imparted his personal stamp of bigness and flamboyance that came to typify American films throughout the world for more than four decades. His mere name symbolized the raw energy, unlimited abundance and florid romance of a make-believe world that multitudes of many tongues thirsted for." It was a summing up which could not possibly have been improved upon.

Just a week before, DeMille had shown that the old, strong spirit was as witty as ever. A visitor to Laughlin Park had asked him casually, what his future plans were. His eyes had twinkled sharply. "Another picture, I imagine," he said. He smiled wryly. "Or, perhaps, another world."

Cecil B. DeMille Pictures*

1. THE SQUAW MAN (1913) Dustin Farnum—Winifred Kingston—Red Wing

2. THE VIRGINIAN (1914) Dustin Farnum—Winifred Kingston

3. THE CALL OF THE NORTH (1914) Robert Edeson—Theodore Roberts—Winifred Kingston

4. WHAT'S HIS NAME (1914) Max Figman—Lolita Robertson

5. THE MAN FROM HOME (1914) Charles Richman—Theodore Roberts—Mabel Van Buren —Anita King

6. THE ROSE OF THE RANCHO (1914) Bessie Barriscale—Jane Darwell—Monroe Salisbury

7. THE GIRL OF THE GOLDEN WEST (1914) Mabel Van Buren—Theodore Roberts—House Peters —Anita King—Raymond Hatton

---

* DeMille also had a number of films researched and partially or wholly scripted which were never actually filmed. Among these were *The Story of Esther* (Mackinlay Kanter), *Samson* (an earlier version of *Samson and Delilah*) (Harold Lamb), *The Hudson's Bay Company* (Jeanie Macpherson, Jesse Lasky, Jr.), *Queen of Queens* (Jeanie Macpherson, William C. DeMille, William Cowan), *For Whom the Bell Tolls* (Jeanie Macpherson), *Rurales* or *The Flame* (Jeanie Macpherson, *Thou Art the Man: The Story of David* (Jeanie Macpherson), *Helen of Troy* (Jack Gariss), and *On My Honor*, based on the life of Lord Baden-Powell, being scripted by Jesse Lasky, Jr., Henry Wilcoxon, and Sidney Box at the time of Mr. DeMille's death.

8. THE WARRENS OF VIRGINIA (1914) — James Neill—Mabel Van Buren—Blanche Sweet—Page Peters—House Peters

9. THE UNAFRAID (1915) — Rita Jolivet—House Peters—Page Peters—Theodore Roberts

10. THE CAPTIVE (1915) — Blanche Sweet—House Peters—Page Peters—Jeanie Macpherson—Theodore Roberts

11. WILD GOOSE CHASE (1915) — Ina Claire—Tom Forman —Lucien Littlefield —Raymond Hatton— Theodore Roberts

12. THE ARAB (1915) — Edgar Selwyn—H. B. Carpenter—Milton Brown —Billy Elmer—Theodore Roberts—Raymond Hatton

13. CHIMMIE FADDEN (1915) — Victor Moore—Raymond Hatton—Anita King

14. KINDLING (1915) — Charlotte Walker—Thomas Meighan—Raymond Hatton

15. MARIA ROSA (1915) — Geraldine Farrar—Wallace Reid—Pedro deCordoba

16. CARMEN (1915) — Geraldine Farrar—Wallace Reid—Pedro deCordoba —Billy Elmer—Jeanie Macpherson—Anita King

17. TEMPTATION (1915) — Geraldine Farrar—Pedro deCordoba—Theodore Roberts—Raymond Hatton

18. CHIMMIE FADDEN OUT WEST (1915) — Victor Moore—Camille Astor—Ernest Joy— Raymond Hatton

19. THE CHEAT (1915) — Fannie Ward—Sessue Hayakawa—Jack Dean —James Neill

20. THE GOLDEN CHANCE (1915) — Edna Goodrich—Cleo Ridgley—Wallace Reid—H. B. Carpenter

21. THE TRAIL OF THE LONESOME PINE (1915) — Theodore Roberts—Charlotte Walker—Earle Fox—Thomas Meighan

22. THE HEART OF NORA FLYNN (1916) — Marie Doro—Elliott Dexter—Ernest Joy

23. THE DREAM GIRL (1916) — Mae Murray—Theodore Roberts—James Neill—Earle Fox

24. JOAN THE WOMAN (1916) — Geraldine Farrar—Wallace Reid—Theodore Roberts—Charles Clary—Raymond Hatton—Hobart Bosworth

25. A ROMANCE OF THE REDWOOD (1917) — Mary Pickford—Elliott Dexter—Charles Ogle—Tully Marshall—Raymond Hatton

26. THE LITTLE AMERICAN (1917) — Mary Pickford—James Neill—Ben Alexander—Guy Oliver—Jack Holt—Edith Chapman—Hobart Bosworth—Raymond Hatton

27. THE WOMAN GOD FORGOT (1917) — Geraldine Farrar—Wallace Reid—Theodore Kosloff—Raymond Hatton—Hobart Bosworth

28. THE DEVIL STONE (1917) — Geraldine Farrar—Wallace Reid—Tully Marshall—Hobart Bosworth—Lillian Leighton

29. THE WHISPERING CHORUS (1917) — Raymond Hatton—Kathlyn Williams—Edythe Chapman—Elliott Dexter—Noah Beery

30. OLD WIVES FOR NEW (1918) — Elliott Dexter—Sylvia Ashton—Wanda Hawley—Florence Vidor—Theodore Roberts—Tully Marshall—Julia Faye

31. WE CAN'T HAVE EVERYTHING (1918) — Kathlyn Williams—Thurston Hall—Elliott Dexter—Sylvia Breamer—Tully Marshall—Theodore Roberts

32. TILL I COME BACK TO YOU (1918) — Bryant Washburn—Florence Vidor

33. THE SQUAW MAN (1918) — Elliott Dexter—Thurston Hall—Katherine McDonald—Helen Dunbar—Theodore Roberts—Monte Blue—Raymond Hatton—Jack Holt

34. DON'T CHANGE YOUR HUSBAND (1918) — Elliott Dexter—Gloria Swanson—Lew Cody—Sylvia Ashton—Theodore Roberts—Julia Faye

35. FOR BETTER FOR WORSE (1919) — Gloria Swanson—Sylvia Ashton—James Neill—Elliott Dexter—Theodore Roberts

36. MALE AND FEMALE (1919) — Lila Lee—Theodore Roberts—Raymond Hatton—Mildred Reardon—Gloria Swanson—Thomas Meighan

37. WHY CHANGE YOUR WIFE? (1919) — Thomas Meighan—Gloria Swanson—Bebe Daniels—Theodore Kosloff

38. SOMETHING TO THINK ABOUT (1920) — Elliott Dexter—Claire McDowell—Theodore Roberts—Gloria Swanson—Monte Blue—Julia Faye

39. FORBIDDEN FRUIT (1920)   King Baggott—Clarence Burton—Ann Forest—Agnes Ayres—Kathlyn Williams—Theodore Roberts

40. THE AFFAIRS OF ANATOL (1920)   Wallace Reid—Elliott Dexter—Gloria Swanson—Wanda Hawley—Raymond Hatton—Bebe Daniels—Theodore Roberts—Monte Blue

41. FOOL'S PARADISE (1921)   Theodore Kosloff—Mildred Harris—Dorothy Dalton—Conrad Nagel—Jacquelin Logan

42. SATURDAY NIGHT (1921)   Edith Roberts—Sylvia Ashton—Jack Mower—Leatrice Joy—Conrad Nagel

43. MANSLAUGHTER (1922)   Leatrice Joy—Thomas Meighan—Jack Mower—Julia Faye—Jack Miltern—Dorothy Cummings—Lois Wilson

44. ADAM'S RIB (1922)   Anna Q. Nilsson—Milton Sills—Pauline Garon—Theodore Kosloff—Elliott Dexter

45. THE TEN COMMANDMENTS (1923)   Theodore Roberts—Charles deRoche—Estelle Taylor—Julia Faye—Terrence Moore—Leatrice Joy—Rod LaRocque—Richard Dix

46. TRIUMPH (1924)   Leatrice Joy—Rod LaRocque—Victor Varconi—Theodore Kosloff—Charles Ogle—Raymond Hatton—Zasu Pitts

47. FEET OF CLAY (1924)   Vera Reynolds—Rod LaRoque—Julia Faye—Ricardo Cortez—Robert Edeson—Victor Varconi

48. THE GOLDEN BED (1924)   Lillian Rich—Henry Walthall—Vera Reynolds—Theodore Kosloff—Robert Cain—Rod LaRocque—Warner Baxter

49. THE ROAD TO YESTERDAY (1925) (DeMille Studio)   William Boyd—Elinor Fair—Victor Varconi—Theodore Kosloff—Julia Faye

50. THE VOLGA BOATMAN (1925) (DeMille Studio)   William Boyd—Elinor Fair—Victor Varconi—Theodore Kosloff—Julia Faye

51. THE KING OF KINGS (1926) (DeMille Studio)   H. B. Warner—Dorothy Cumming—Joseph Schildkraut—Rudolph Schildkraut—Ernest Torrance—Jacqueline Logan

52. THE GODLESS GIRL (1928) (DeMille Studio)   Lina Basquette—George Duryea—Marie Prevost—Noah Beery

SOUND:

53. DYNAMITE (1929) (DeMille's first sound film, Metro-Goldwyn-Mayer)   Kay Johnson—Charles Bickford—Conrad Nagel—Julia Faye—Muriel McCormick

54. MADAME SATAN (1930) (Metro-Goldwyn-Mayer)   Kay Johnson—Reginald Denny—Roland Young—Elsa Peterson—Lillian Roth

55. THE SQUAW MAN (1931) (Metro-Goldwyn-Mayer)   Warner Baxter—Eleanor Boardman—Paul Cavanaugh—Roland Young—Julia Faye—Lupe Velez—Charles Bickford—Raymond Hatton

The following pictures were for Paramount:

56. THE SIGN OF THE CROSS (1932)

Fredric March—Elissa Landi—Claudette Colbert— Charles Laughton—Ian Keith

57. THIS DAY AND AGE (1933)

Charles Bickford—Judith Allen—Richard Cromwell—Harry Green —Eddie Nugent

58. FOUR FRIGHTENED PEOPLE (1933)

Claudette Colbert—Herbert Marshall—Mary Boland— William Gargan—Leo Carrillo

59. CLEOPATRA (1934)

Claudette Colbert—Warren William—Henry Wilcoxon —Gertrude Michael—Joseph Schildkraut—Ian Keith— C. Aubrey Smith

60. THE CRUSADES (1935)

Loretta Young—Henry Wilcoxon—Ian Keith— C. Aubrey Smith—Katherine DeMille—Joseph Schildkraut

61. THE PLAINSMAN (1936)

Gary Cooper—Jean Arthur —James Ellison—Charles Bickford—Helen Burgess

62. THE BUCCANEER (1937)

Fredric March—Franciska Gaal—Akim Tamiroff— Margot Grahame—Walter Brennan—Ian Keith

63. UNION PACIFIC (1938)

Barbara Stanwyck—Joel McCrea—Robert Preston— Lynne Overman—Akim Tamiroff—Brian Donlevy

64. NORTH WEST MOUNTED POLICE (1940)

Gary Cooper—Madeleine Carroll—Paulette Goddard —Preston Foster—Robert Preston

65. REAP THE WILD WIND (1940)

Ray Milland—John Wayne —Paulette Goddard— Raymond Massey—Robert Preston

66. THE STORY OF DR. WASSELL (1943)

Gary Cooper—Loraine Day—Signe Hasso—Dennis O'Keefe—Carol Thurston

67. UNCONQUERED (1946)

Gary Cooper—Paulette Goddard—Howard de Silva—Boris Karloff—Cecil Kellaway—Ward Bond— Henry Wilcoxon—Sir C. Aubrey Smith

68. SAMSON AND DELILAH (1948)

Hedy Lamarr—Victor Mature—George Sanders— Angela Lansbury—Henry Wilcoxon

69. THE GREATEST SHOW ON EARTH (1951)

Betty Hutton—Cornel Wilde—James Stewart— Charlton Heston—Dorothy Lamour—Gloria Grahame —Lyle Bettger

70. THE TEN COMMANDMENTS (1954)

Charlton Heston—Yul Brynner—Anne Baxter —Edward G. Robinson— Yvonne de Carlos—Debra Paget—John Derek— Sir Cedric Hardwicke—Nina Foch—Martha Scott—Judith Anderson—Vincent Price

INDEX